# Treasures of
# Western Washington

By: William Faubion

Part of the Morgan & Chase "Treasures" Series
www.mcpbooks.com

© Copyright 2005 by Morgan & Chase Publishing, Inc.
All rights reserved. No portion of this book may be reproduced or utilized in any form, or by any electronic, mechanical or other means without the prior written permission of the publisher.

Published by:
Morgan & Chase Publishing, Inc.
531 Parsons Drive, Suite 107
Medford, Oregon 97501
888-557-9328
www.mcpbooks.com

Printed by:
C & C Offset Printing Co., Ltd. - China

First edition 2005

ISBN: 0-9754162-2-7

I gratefully acknowledge the contributions of everyone involved in the writing and production of this book. Their tireless dedication to this endeavor is inspirational.

Editors:
    Cindy Tilley Faubion
    Brenda Rosch

Contributing Writers:
    Andrea Adams
    Janice Ariza
    Judy Bailey
    Amanda Bans
    JL Brown
    Vanessa V. Brown
    Craig Callaway
    Diane Dickinson
    Leslie Fazio
    Jonathan Heerema
    Kelly Kenyon
    Joy Kieras
    Amy Laier
    Jan Maddron
    Mickie McCormic
    Yvonne Rains
    Kathy Reynolds
    Ron Turpin
    Ron Van Drongelen
    Susan Vaughn

Graphic Design:
    Jesse Gifford
    Craig Tansley

Story Coordinator:
    Wendy Gay

Website Coordinator:
    Rebecca Woodruff

Special Recognition to:
Devona Brown, Genevieve Hartin, Damon Neal, Janna Sample, and our inspiration - Miss Florence Wilson.

# Dedication

This book is dedicated to people who love adventure and embrace diversity, whether cultural or geographic.

# Table of Contents

**Forward** ................................................................. 6
**How To Use This Book** ............................................. 7
**Western Washington Maps** ...................................... 8
**Accommodations and RV Resorts** ........................... 20
    Olympic Peninsula .................................................. 22
    Washington Coast ................................................... 31
    Kitsap Peninsula ..................................................... 36
    Seattle Metro .......................................................... 38
    Skagit Valley ........................................................... 41
    The Valley ............................................................... 45
    East Side ................................................................. 46
    I-5 Corridor ............................................................. 47
    South Puget Sound .................................................. 49
    Whidbey Island ....................................................... 52

**Attractions** ............................................................. 54
    Olympic Peninsula .................................................. 56
    Washington Coast ................................................... 61
    Kitsap Peninsula ..................................................... 62
    Seattle Metro .......................................................... 67
    Skagit Valley ........................................................... 76

The Valley ................................................... **83**

East Side ................................................... **84**

I-5 Corridor ................................................ **86**

South Puget Sound ..................................... **87**

Whidbey Island ......................................... **88**

## Candy, Ice Cream, Bakeries and Coffee ........ **92**

Olympic Peninsula ..................................... **94**

Kitsap Peninsula ........................................ **95**

Seattle Metro ............................................. **96**

Skagit Valley ............................................ **100**

East Side ................................................. **100**

South Puget Sound ................................... **103**

Whidbey Island ....................................... **104**

## Galleries ........................................................ **106**

Olympic Peninsula ................................... **108**

Washington Coast .................................... **110**

Kitsap Peninsula ...................................... **111**

Seattle Metro ........................................... **114**

Skagit Valley ........................................... **116**

East Side ................................................. **119**

South Puget Sound ................................... **119**

## Gifts ... **120**

    Olympic Peninsula ... **122**

    Washington Coast ... **124**

    Kitsap Peninsula ... **126**

    Seattle Metro ... **131**

    Skagit Valley ... **137**

    The Valley ... **138**

    East Side ... **142**

    I-5 Corridor ... **144**

    South Puget Sound ... **146**

## Health & Beauty ... **148**

    Seattle Metro ... **150**

    I-5 Corridor ... **151**

## Home Décor, Gardens, Flowers and Markets ... **152**

    Olympic Peninsula ... **154**

    Washington Coast ... **157**

    Kitsap Peninsula ... **158**

    Seattle Metro ... **159**

    Skagit Valley ... **163**

    The Valley ... **166**

    East Side ... **167**

    South Puget Sound.................................................**170**

    Whidbey Island..................................................**171**

## Museums.........................................................**172**

    Washington Coast................................................**174**

    Seattle Metro...................................................**175**

    Skagit Valley...................................................**177**

    East Side.......................................................**179**

    I-5 Corridor....................................................**180**

    South Puget Sound.................................................**181**

## Restaurants....................................................**184**

    Olympic Peninsula...............................................**186**

    Washington Coast................................................**196**

    Kitsap Peninsula................................................**199**

    Seattle Metro...................................................**205**

    Skagit Valley...................................................**209**

    East Side.......................................................**215**

    I-5 Corridor....................................................**217**

    South Puget Sound.................................................**218**

    Whidbey Island..................................................**221**

    The Valley.....................................................**221**

## Wineries .................................................................... **222**

    Olympic Peninsula ................................................ **224**

    Kitsap Peninsula .................................................. **225**

    The Valley ........................................................ **226**

    East Side ......................................................... **227**

    I-5 Corridor ...................................................... **228**

## Port Gamble ................................................................ **230**

## Index ...................................................................... **236**

## About the Author ................................................ **Inside Back Dust Cover**

# Forward

Welcome to the *Treasures of Western Washington*, where the Columbia River, the Pacific Ocean and the Cascade Mountain Range surround an oasis of panoramic beauty. Washington is home to advanced technology, the famous landmark Space Needle and a pioneering spirit that is pervasive among its entrepreneurial population. Western Washington is where you'll see amazing waterways, evergreen trees, wild ferns, azaleas and rhododendrons that tower over the tallest of humans.

Western Washington seems to be the perfect business environment. For example, two of the world's most famous and successful enterprises are based in Washington. They are Microsoft and Boeing. There are memorable moments awaiting visitors too. You can dine above the skyline in the Space Needle Restaurant or complete your trip with a Washington State Ferry ride. As you look through this book you will recognize what a special place Western Washington is, and you'll fall in love with its citizens as well.

The *people, places* and *businesses* in this book all work together to entrance their visitors. The personal care and exceptional service you will receive in Western Washington will rival anywhere else in the world. No business can purchase space in the book. Each listing was personally selected by secret shoppers, writers and the publisher's representatives. Only after each business was chosen were they invited to participate in this project.

That's why *Treasures of Western Washington* is so exciting to read and the places listed in this book are such a pleasure to visit. The Publisher is confident that each and every time you step into a "Treasure" you'll be pampered and impressed by a specially selected business that represents the best Western Washington has to offer.

Cindy Tilley Faubion

# How to use this book

This book is divided by geographic areas and type of business. The primary divisions are Whidby Island, the Olympic Peninsula, Seattle Metro, the Valley, the Kitsap Peninsula, Skagit Valley, the Eastside, South Puget Sound, and the I-5 Corridor.

The types of businesses include accommodations, attractions, coffee and sweet shops, galleries, gardens and markets, gifts, health and beauty, museums, restaurants, retirement centers and wineries.

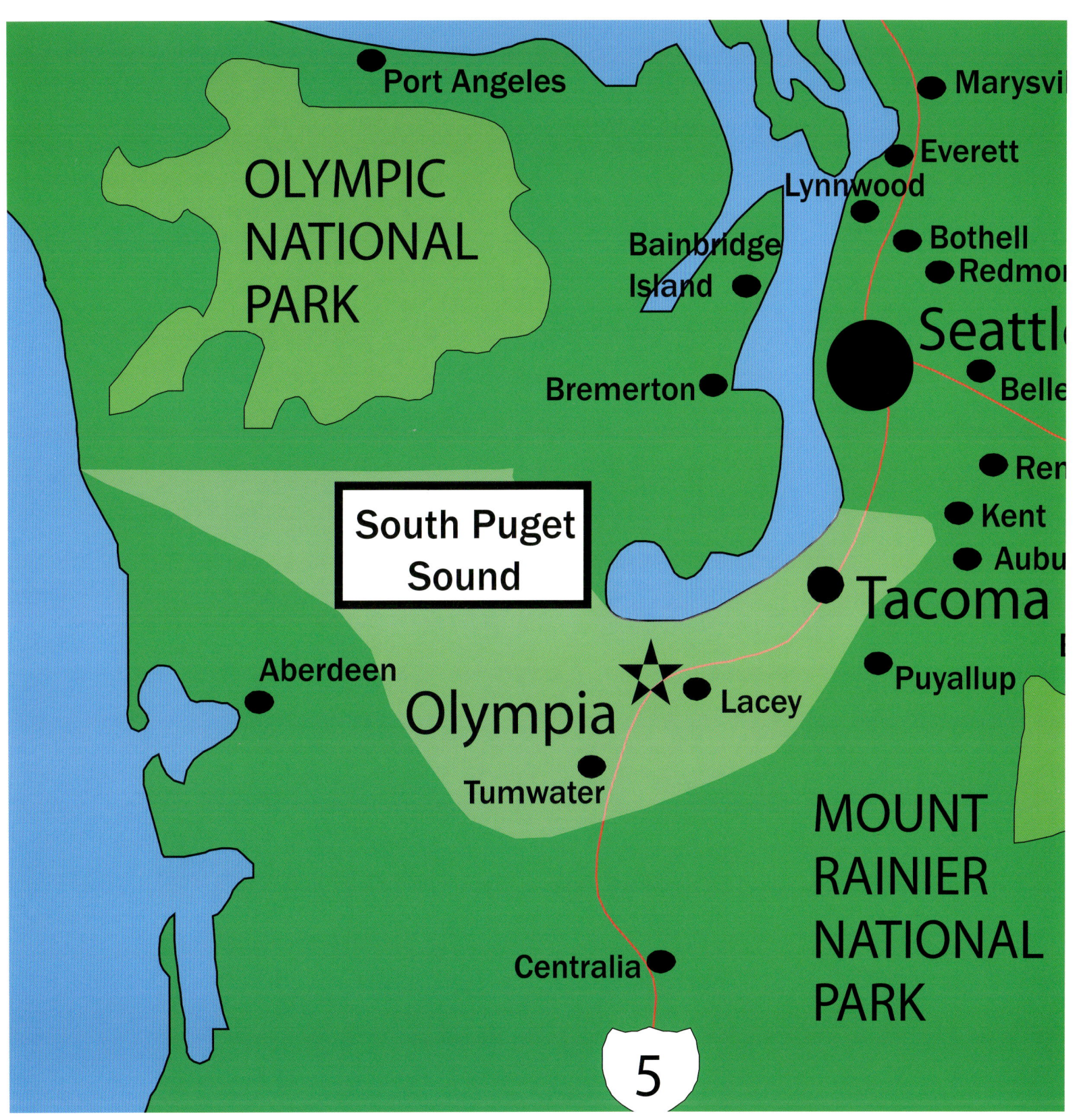

# Accommodations and RV Resorts

## Accommodations / RV Resorts

## Olympic Peninsula

# Groveland Cottage B&B

Simone Nichol's Groveland Cottage B&B is located in the Sequim-Dungeness Valley along the Strait of Juan de Fuca on Washington's beautiful North Olympic Peninsula. Sequim offers convenient access to Olympic National Park, Dungeness Spit National Wildlife Refuge, and the ferry to Victoria BC, Canada. The B&B is open year round and can accommodate special events, retreats, gatherings, and meetings in their large banquet room. A four-course breakfast and Simone's scones are specialties of the B&B. Each of the comfortable rooms offers its own unique décor and all have private baths, cable TV, VCRs and high speed cable Internet connections. Simone can also provide access to information about renting any of over 30 vacation homes in the Sequim-Dungeness Valley. These homes are ideal for families or large groups and range from shorefront houses to mountain view cottages. For further information and photographs of the rooms available at Groveland B&B, call or visit their website.
4861 Sequim-Dungeness Way, Sequim WA
(360) 683 - 3565 or (800) 879-8859
www.sequimvalley.com

# Clark's Chambers B&B

Clark's Chambers Bed & Breakfast offers a unique opportunity to experience the living history of Washington State on a working family farm. The bed & breakfast has four comfortable bedrooms, all featuring beautiful mountain or water views of the Olympic Peninsula's unparalleled scenery. As part of its traditional charm, two of the rooms feature old-fashioned claw-footed bathtubs with hand showers (the others have modern tub/shower combos). Each room is furnished with lovingly restored heirloom furniture, some of it as old as the property itself. As in years past, breakfast is served "family style" in the downstairs dining room. The name commemorates both the Clarks and Glenda's sister Bernita Chambers, who shared Glenda's longtime dream of creating a B&B but sadly passed away before it came to pass. For 154 years, the Clark family has lived and farmed the land where Clark's Chambers Bed & Breakfast now welcomes travelers. The bed & breakfast was originally a farmhouse built in the 1870s, which was moved to its present location and set on a newly-poured basement during the 1940s. It was converted to its current use beginning in 1998, when Bob and Glenda Clark added a covered porch and gazebo. You are sure to enjoy your stay at Clark's Chambers Bed & Breakfast!
322 Clark Road, Sequim WA  (360) 683-4431

# The Inn at Port Hadlock

The Inn at Port Hadlock is nestled on the southern shore of Port Townsend Bay and is just a short trip from Seattle. This 1903 inn is rich in history, has unbelievable views and features an incredible dining experience. The landmark Inn offers 46 rooms, 13 of which are deluxe suites with private patios and beautiful bay views. The rooms include exquisite works of art, unique and colorful furniture with all the amenities of home, microwave, refrigerator, coffeemaker, television and many come with fireplaces. Stop by the lounge in the Inn's award winning restaurant, Nemo's, for a beverage and appetizer, while viewing the beautiful stained glass windows that were designed by local artists. For fine dining, experience the Inn's extensive menu of fine food and exceptional wine collection while enjoying the spectacular harbor views. No matter which season you choose to visit, the Inn offers

many activities from historical walking tours to art and music festivals and several unbelievable hiking trails. The staff welcomes you to their "memorable treasure" in the Northwest. 310 Hadlock Bay Road, Port Hadlock, WA (360) 385-7030
www.innatporthadlock.com

## Accommodations / RV Resorts                    Olympic Peninsula

# Dungeness Panorama Bed & Breakfast

If you are traveling through Washington and are tired of the "motel life," make reservations at the Dungeness Panorama Bed and Breakfast in Sequim, where the term "continental breakfast" is unheard of. Breakfast at the Dungeness is a three-course epicurean feast, which may include their authentic French varieties of handmade crepes and special fillings for a truly unforgettable experience. The Dungeness Bed and Breakfast has two master suites, complete with their own private baths, televisions, kitchenettes and fireplaces. Most of the furniture throughout the house was handmade by Roger Ferrari, with his wife Paulette as decorator, who emigrated from France in 1953. Their daughter and owner/innkeeper, Patricia Merritte, has continued the tradition, displaying a unique variety of family heirlooms and decorations, including a circular table with a raised barbecue pit. The house was designed and built by her husband John. Truly living up to its name, the Dungeness Panorama Bed and Breakfast offers a visual feast with breathtaking views from the strait of Juan De Fuca and Dungeness Bay to the Olympic Mountains. The gorgeous greenhouse and ornamental plants in hanging baskets bring nature's blooms inside. If you are in the mood to explore, tourist attractions are available nearby, contrasting pleasantly with the peaceful lodgings at the Dungeness Panorama Bed and Breakfast.   630 Marine Drive, Sequim WA   (360) 683-4503   www.awaterview.com

# A Hidden Haven

Nestled in the lush forest at the foothills of the Olympics is the secluded 20-acre A Hidden Haven Bed & Breakfast. A luxury destination and a naturalist paradise, this "Piece of Heaven," as stated by numerous guests, provides the ultimate romantic experience. Here you will find an ambience full of enchantment and wonder with waterfalls, ponds, gardens, plants and wildlife. The fairy-tale setting makes this a perfect place to have a small wedding, honeymoon, business retreat, family reunion or just to take some time off to relax. There is an abundance of wildlife to enjoy in this naturalist's paradise (some guests report seeing more birds at A Hidden Haven than in the Olympic National Park). A Hidden Haven's three suites and two cottages offer many luxury amenities including private deck and entrances, whirlpool tubs, fireplaces, in-room massage, satellite TV and much more. In the morning, savor a hot breakfast basket delivered right to your door, or your cottage may be stocked with breakfast goodies. For a truly extraordinary experience, feed the private deer herd, walk the woodland nature trail or feed the koi fish and trout. End your day with a romantic evening stroll in the lighted gardens
1428 Dan Kelly Road, Port Angeles WA  (360) 452-2719 or (877) 418-0938  www.ahiddenhaven.com

# Accommodations / RV Resorts

# Olympic Peninsula

# Domaine Madeleine

Sense the romance at Domaine Madeleine Bed and Breakfast in Port Angeles. A subtle yet unmistakable feeling of love and serenity permeates this quiet paradise

that is snuggled between the stately Olympic Mountains and grand expanse of the Straits of Juan de Fuca. The twinkling lights of Victoria and the starlit sky in the evening, as well as the call of the eagles and whales during the day set the mood for connection to yourself and each other. The gardens are superb with a Monet garden replica, a woodland garden complete with waterfall and meandering stream, cottage garden, rose garden and bamboo garden all vying for attention. The food is as exquisitely presented as it is delicious. A few of the delights awaiting your stay may include: fresh asparagus and mango salsa placed alongside fresh salmon with Crème Brule for dessert; a Dungeness crab omelet with European style vegetables and bananas flambé for dessert; apple crepes covered with fresh berries accompanied by smoked ham with black rice pudding and coconut milk for dessert. Resident chef Victor makes sure everything is done to perfection and any dietary need is met. For a room, pick from the Ming Suite, Monet, Renoir Suite, Rendezvous or Cottage. All have outstanding views of either the mountains or the water. Each one has its own personal entrance so it is very private. The reviews have proven Domaine Madeleine the top in its class as *Sunset* magazine recently named it one of the 20 Best Seaside Getaways along the Pacific Coast. Domaine Madeleine is centrally located to explore the Olympic Peninsula. Hiking, kayaking, rafting, mountain climbing, bikbiking, antiquing and wineries are all close at hand. With only five rooms available, summer bookings fill up fast. 146 Wildflower Lane, Port Angeles WA (360) 457-4174 or (888) 811-8376 www.domainemadeleine.com

# The Bishop Victorian Hotel & Gardens

The award winning Bishop Victorian Hotel and Gardens in Port Townsend lives up to high standards. With sixteen suites, each equipped with a fireplace, living accessories, and kitchenette, this hotel is a place you'll want to mark on your map when you plan your trip through Washington. The Bishop Victorian is nestled next to the picturesque Secret Victorian Garden, which offers a vast stretch of greenery and foliage, as well as a dreamy gazebo and dance arena. After a long, good night's sleep in one of their stunningly furnished suites, you'll wake up to a complementary breakfast delivered to your door. Because the Bishop Victorian is mainly concerned with each guest's stay, if dinner the night before was a bit much, they offer complimentary use of the Port Townsend Athletic Club just a short walk away from their doorstep. 714 Washington Street, Port Townsend WA (360)385-6122 or (800) 824-4738
www.rainshadowproperties.com

# The Swan Hotel

Sleek and sophisticated just like its name, The Swan Hotel is the ideal place for business ventures and vacation retreats alike. Located in the quaint, downtown historic area of Port Townsend, The Swan Hotel offers a magnificent view of the Olympic and Cascade mountain ranges, as well as ocean views of the Juan de Fuca Straits and Admiralty Inlet. Built for flexibility, The Swan Hotel presents several options for your needs. They offer hotel studio units and a penthouse suite with sweeping views, as well as attractive getaway cottages, each with a Jacuzzi and fireplace. Their Penthouse suite doubles as a conference center, which comes complete with a fourteen-foot long Mission oak conference table and absolute privacy. With their impeccably furnished accommodations and dedication to their guests' comfort, The Swan Hotel will provide you with a pleasant stay. 216 Monroe Street, Port Townsend WA (360) 385-6122 or (800) 824-4738
www.rainshadowproperties.com

# Accommodations / RV Resorts — Olympic Peninsula

## The Resort at Port Ludlow

Discover your Northwest here. Just a short ferry ride and scenic drive from Seattle, Port Ludlow is the gateway to the beautiful Olympic Peninsula, on the sunny west side of the Puget Sound. The Resort at Port Ludlow and the Port Ludlow community are tucked into a quiet bay where you'll find the activities and lifestyle that you've dreamed of. Enjoy Port Ludlow's resort facilities: 27-hole championship golf course, 300-slip marina with permanent and guest moorage, waterside Inn with luxurious accommodations (relax with an in-room spa treatment), restaurants, walking trails, gorgeous grounds for parties and get-togethers, and facilities for productive business meetings and retreats. In this lovely setting, you will enjoy a plentiful mix of leisure activities, take part in local festivals and events, explore the Olympic Mountains, or visit the historic towns of Port Townsend and Port Gamble. And you can enjoy everything Port Ludlow has to offer in a drier climate with more sunshine than other Puget Sound areas, thanks to the rain shadow effect of the Olympic Mountain range. As perfect as this is for a romantic getaway, it's also a great place to call home. Because of visionary long-term planning, Port Ludlow's Resort Community has strictly limited future growth, which means this friendly, tight-knit community will be protected from development of its natural open spaces. From the mountains to the Sound, the forests and the beaches, the sun on the sea, at Port Ludlow, you'll discover your Northwest here. 1 Heron Road, Port Ludlow WA (360) 437-7000 or (877) 805-0868 www.portludlowresort.com

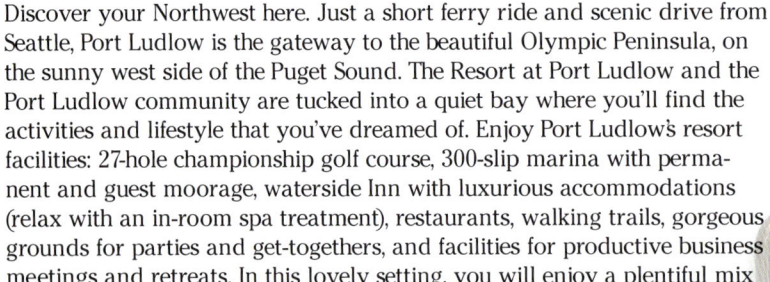

## Holly Hill House

Built in 1872, the Holly Hill House in Port Townsend has been made into a bed and breakfast that brings raves from guests. One couple remarked, "We are amending our wills to read 'Please bury us in the Holly Hill's Colonel Suite bed' – it's the closest we'll come to heaven." Owners Greg and Nina Dortch really hope you'll feel that way after a night or two under their pampering care. They maintain grounds featuring a tree that's on the historical tree register, floral pleasures around every turn, and a peaceful and relaxed atmosphere all about. Inquire about one of the delightful rooms: The Colonel's Suite, Billie's Room, Lizette's Room, the Skyview Room or the Morning Glory Room. Whether you choose a view of Admiralty Inlet and Mount Baker, or wooded privacy with a flower garden and an occasional visit from a deer, you'll relax and rest well. After a great night's sleep, a three-course breakfast awaits you in a formal dinning room on a candlelit table set with linens, china and silver. In the afternoon, tea and home baked pastries are served in the parlor in front of the original Italian fireplace. 611 Polk Street, Port Townsend WA (360) 385 - 5619 or (800) 435-1454 www.hollyhillhouse.com

# Waterstreet Hotel

The Waterstreet Hotel in Port Townsend combines the charm of downtown with a panoramic view of Puget Sound, Mount Baker, the Cascade and Olympic Mountains. Suites with private decks overlooking Port Townsend Bay are available, as are rooms with kitchens. Cable TV is offered, and you can request a non-smoking room. The hotel was built in 1889 and was completely renovated in 1990. It was designed by Seattle architect Elmer Fisher. Fine craftsmanship is displayed in the brickwork and metal craft of the hotel, which was featured recently in Port Townsend's Historic Homes tour. A creative arrangement between The Waterstreet Hotel and the Pacific Traditions Gallery (also featured in this book) allows the presentation of Northwest coastal traditional and contemporary Northwest Indian art in the lobby of the hotel. Located on the first floor is Water Street Brewing & Ale House offering handcrafted brews and casual dining. 635 Water Street, Port Townsend WA (360) 385 - 5467 or (800) 735-9810 www.waterstreethotelporttownsend.com

# Accommodations / RV Resorts

# Olympic Peninsula

## Big Red Barn

If you want a getaway that is indisputably unique, how about a romantic night in a barn? That's right, the Big Red Barn in Port Townsend. This hideout really was formerly occupied by farm animals. Built in the 1890s, the remodeled building features open beams and antique windows. This rustic but chic, private romantic barn for two is grounded near a bluff above the waters of Puget Sound. Outside, a meditation pond and soothing waterfall will lull you and perhaps a bald eagle will give flight to your fancy. Meanwhile, the distant sounds of lapping waves will refresh your mind and spirit. Todd and Carol Eskelin will see to it that your visit is tranquil and rejuvenating. So take the time when planning your travel to check out this romantic hideaway, where you can sink into your jetted tub overlooking the meadow with a peek-a-boo view of the sea. Just think what your friends will say when you tell them about your idyllic stay in a barn. 309 V Street, Port Townsend WA (360) 301-1271  www.bigredbarngetaway.com

## Kalaloch Lodge

Kalaloch Lodge, perched on a bluff overlooking the Pacific, is one of Olympic National Park's most memorable resorts. When Charles W. Becker Sr. acquired roughly 40 acres of land just south of Kalaloch Creek, there were no roads to the property. Milled lumber that washed up on the beach was used to construct the first buildings, erected in the late 1920s. After the Olympic Loop Highway (now Highway 101) provided better access to the area, more cabins were built. The complex, known as "Becker's Ocean Resort," offered simple lodging to auto travelers. In 1942 the U.S. Coast Guard established a beach patrol station there, adapting the buildings to suit its needs. After World War II, the buildings were reverted back to recreational use and the Beckers made a variety of improvements, including adding a new Main Lodge building. In 1978, the National Park Service purchased the property. Soon after, the resort was renamed Kalaloch Lodge. Kalaloch offers the only year-round lodging in Olympic National Park. Visitors can stay in comfortable accommodations in the Main Lodge, secluded Seacrest House, or cozy cabins with Franklin fireplaces. Fresh and artfully prepared coastal cuisine and spectacular views abound in the Kalaloch Lodge Restaurant. Enjoy the grandeur of this glorious coastal land where the wonders of the Pacific are right outside your door. Kalaloch became part of the Olympic Coast National Marine Sanctuary in July of 1994. This Sanctuary is our nation's fourteenth marine sanctuary and covers an area of approximately 3,300 square miles.
157151 Highway 101, Forks WA  (866) 525-2562  www.visitkalaloch.com

# Accommodations / RV Resorts         Washington Coast

## Aberdeen Mansion

Aberdeen Mansion has stood tall and proud for over a century. The present owners, Al and Joan Waters, preside over an acre of beautiful grounds and a building that has maintained its grace, charm and elegance for 100 years. The sweeping verandah and the manicured lawn welcome you on a warm summer day. In 1905, this building was home to the nine-member family of lumberman Edward Hulbert. In 1903, the Hulberts had lost their home to a fire that destroyed downtown Aberdeen. When Hulbert decided to rebuild, he chose the growing Broadway District. The new Queen Anne/Victorian-style home was erected using only materials from the Aberdeen area. Local workers used native woods, setting them on a foundation of stone from a nearby quarry. Hulbert spared no expense on the three-story, 10,000 square foot mansion, with its circular tower, imposing dormers and octagonal reception hall. The house was especially recognized for its "sanitary precautions." Though outhouses were the norm at the time, the Hulbert mansion had four indoor bathrooms. Edward Hulbert died in 1918 and the home has changed ownership only four times since 1939 when his widow Laura died. This spectacular home was converted to a bed and breakfast in1994. The Waters bought it in 1997 and it has become a popular destination for people looking for elegant accommodations and gourmet food. The house is a masterpiece of form and design, a source of pride to the city and a dignified connection to Aberdeen's past. 807 North M Street, Aberdeen WA (360) 533-7079 or (888) 533-7079 www.aberdeenmansionbb.com

## Floating Feather Inn

Bird watchers! Wildlife lovers! Luxury seekers! For a lavish and fulfilling experience, the Floating Feather Inn is it! Innkeepers Nancy and Roger tell us that a "floating feather" is the symbol of travel. "One gathers wisdom and knowledge as the feather floats throughout the world." The Floating Feather Inn was built in 1997 on 120 feet of canal waterfront and is a wildlife and nature lovers' paradise. Fish, canoe, kayak, walk along the jetty or go on over to Damon Point State Park. Water ski at nearby Duck Lake or enjoy the Ocean Shores Interpretive Center. Gold finches, hummingbirds and red-winged black birds are among more than three hundred abundant bird species in the area. Guests experience beauty, serenity and a luxurious experience when they stay in one of the five beautiful Feather Bed Suites. All have private baths, each is decorated with a bird theme and all have canal or ocean views. A full gourmet breakfast is included and served in the Palms dining room. From your canal front dining seat, you can enjoy watching otter and beaver play outside on the shore of the canal. One suite is ADA compliant. Pets are allowed only in the cottage. Give Floating Feather Inn primary consideration when you are making your reservations for a retreat, reunion, wedding, reception, honeymoon or just the perfect weekend getaway. Fine dining and refreshments are also available at Palms and deck side. 982 Point Brown Avenue SE, Ocean Shores WA (360) 289-2490 or (888) 257-0894 www.floatingfeatherinn.com

# Accommodations / RV Resorts — Washington Coast

## Boreas Bed & Breakfast Inn

Silky robes and chocolates await you at this contemporary, oceanfront bed and breakfast, built in the 1920s. Named for the Greek god of the north wind, Boreas Inn is a most picturesque getaway. There are

candy dishes scattered amongst the CDs, videos, games, and other diversions at the guests' disposal, including a baby grand piano belonging to owner Susie Goldsmith's dad. Since purchasing the Inn in 1996, Susie and her co-innkeeper Bill Verner have achieved a reputation for superb service. Their hospitality has won them acclaim and awards as well: the Oregon and Southwest Washington Better Business Bureau named them Business of the Year for customer service in 2002 and 2004. The 2005 Arrington's Book of Lists awarded Boreas the distinction of "Best Breakfast in the Northwest." The setting adds even more charm to Boreas. Separated from the Pacific by an expanse of sand and beach grass, the Inn feels like a private resort, with decks overlooking the sea and a private path leading down to the water's edge. Yet this serenity is just a few minutes away from the shops, galleries and restaurants of Long Beach. No wonder the Inn's five suites are in so much demand! Visit the website for a 360-degree virtual tour of Boreas Bed & Breakfast and to request reservations online. 607 N Ocean Beach Boulevard, Long Beach WA  (888) 642-8069  www.boreasinn.com

## China Beach Retreat

Imagine a respite from the daily grind where you can watch geese and their goslings, plus marsh hawks and herons as they feast in the brush. Most of all imagine simply enjoying the peace and quiet that an expansive view of nature provides from this charming bed and breakfast in Ilwaco. The staff of China Beach Retreat wants you to do just that. The ambiance of this cottage has a spellbinding effect. Floor-to-ceiling plate glass windows in the common room show the dozens of shorebirds careening their way through the tide flats. Here you can watch the coming and going of the local fishing fleet as they transport their harvest across the bar and mouth of the Columbia River. Deer frequently visit, at ease with the peaceful surroundings of the Retreat. Each of the three guest rooms provides similar views, plus elegant, comfortable, antique furniture. All rooms feature queen-size beds and private bath. Hosts David Campiche and Laurie Anderson maintain an atmosphere that causes guests to comment that "One night here is not enough." Coffee and tea is available all day, and a complimentary sumptuous gourmet breakfast is served in the morning at The Shelburne Inn, just a short drive away in Seaview. (The Shelburne Inn, also listed in this book, is a sister property of the China Beach Retreat.)  222 Robert Gray Drive, Ilwaco WA  (360) 642 - 5660  www.chinabeachretreat.com

# Moby Dick Hotel

"Welcome to the Home of the Wild Oyster." Accept the invitation of Moby Dick's owner, Fritzi Cohen, and enjoy the peaceful beauty of Willapa Bay and the North End of the Long Beach Peninsula. Moby Dick Hotel, restored in eclectic spirit, offers a special treat. The buildings and furnishings have been redone in the spirit of the 1930s. Bohemian charm provides a comfortable atmosphere. Eight rooms, each with its own personality, offer variety and price options. A three course breakfast is included in the room rate. Spacious public rooms, landscaped grounds, woodland paths and a serene bayside sauna create plenty of appealing choices. A comfortable yurt with radiant heat bamboo floors and lovely natural light provides an ideal site for relaxation and meditation. The Moby Dick is a great place for all types of gatherings and retreats. Their four star restaurant, with Chef Jeff McMahon, is open for dinner year round, Thursday to Monday. The menus change bi-weekly and reflect the seasonal bounty. Moby Dick oysters are always on the menu. All of the delicious fare may be complemented by a cocktail or a wine from their carefully selected list. Entertainment and recreation abound in the area. Enjoy everything from winter storm watching to kite flying, birdwatching, beachwalking and just plain reveling in the incredible, ever-changing landscape. Moby Dick can be a landing spot for kayaks and canoes of the Washington Water Trails. The grounds are always alive with seasonal color and a memorable experience is assured. 25814 Sandridge Road, Nahcotta WA  Restaurant: (360) 665-4690  Hotel: (360) 665-4543  www.mobydickhotel.com

# Caswell's on the Bay

Celebrating its tenth anniversary in May 2005, Bob and Marilyn Caswell's namesake bed and breakfast is basking in the accolades from far and wide. It is known as the Long Beach Peninsula's premier romantic getaway destination. From Arrington's Book of Lists to the Northwest Best Places guide to the countless satisfied guests, everyone agrees that Caswell's is something special. The 6,700-square foot Queen Anne style building looks like a vision from the past, but it was actually designed by Bob and Marilyn. The five spacious guestrooms combine modern comfort and privacy with the elegance of bygone days. The lush greenery and view over Willapa Bay provide the setting for this jewel that is one minute from the ocean beach and "10 minutes from everything." It was the beauty of the scenery that drew Bob and Marilyn to this location in 1988 and inspired them to create a bed and breakfast so they could share it with others. In addition to comfort, natural beauty, and warm hospitality, Caswell's offers superb breakfasts. Thanks to his distinctive seafood creations, Bob took first place at the OysterFest West Coast cook-off in 2001 and 2004. Marilyn's orange pecan French toast has been singled out for praise by the Oregonian. From gourmet breakfasts to sylvan serenity, at Caswell's you'll cherish the experience. 25204 Sandridge Road, Ocean Park WA (360) 665-6535 or (888) 553-2319  www.caswellsinn.com

# Accommodations / RV Resorts

# Washington Coast

## Ocean Crest Resort

The staff and management at Ocean Crest Resort have made it their mission to have this resort "become your personal oasis on the Olympic Coast." This is a business that is based upon giving you a wonderful resort experience through the little things, the individual touches that set Ocean Crest apart from the others. "The big chains can't do it. It comes down to a family operation to make the personal difference." That's the philosophy of the Curtright family who have been the innkeepers at the Ocean Crest Resort since 1953. Nestled in the trees on a 100-foot bluff overlooking the crashing waves of the Pacific Ocean, Ocean Crest Resort is recognized by Frommer's as having "the most spectacular setting of any lodging on the Washington Coast." A beautiful staircase meanders through a wooded ravine to miles of open sandy beach where boating, clamming, crabbing, horseback riding, kite flying, and beachcombing are among your choices for a delightful afternoon. The resort itself has ac

commodations in all sizes, from studios to two bedroom apartments, many with wood-burning fireplaces and all with full amenities. Enjoy world class dining in their award winning restaurant. The health club provides an indoor pool, hot tub, sauna, tanning, exercise room, and massage therapy. The conference facilities offer an unforgettable business retreat or meeting. Relax, enjoy, and return again and again to the Ocean Crest Resort. 4651 SR 109, Moclips WA (360) 276-4465 or (800) 684-8439  www.oceancrestresort.com

# Quinault Beach Resort & Casino

"Play hard, rest easy." Owned by the Quinault Indian Nation, Quinault Beach Resort & Casino is ready to provide a Native American experience that can transform your visit from the common to the extraordinary. Located directly on the beach at Ocean Shores, Quinault Beach Resort is Washington's premier coastal destination. With broad vistas of the Pacific Ocean and two hundred acres of protected wetlands in every direction, the Resort blends nature, architecture and technology to create an unsurpassed destination for vacationers and business gatherings.

The 150 Northwest décor, oversized guestrooms feature French balconies, fireplaces and sweeping views. Guests may be pampered and renewed in the full service spa, swimming pool and fitness facility. The Activity Center offers educational and recreational opportunities for kids of all ages. The Resort features 16,090 square feet of state-of-the-art function space for meetings, banquets and special events. Emily's Restaurant satisfies the palate as well as the spirit with unsurpassed fresh Northwest cuisine and views of the magnificent Pacific Ocean. There is live entertainment and high energy in the Cabaret and quiet relaxation in the Lobby Lounge. The only thing left to chance is their international style casino that features the latest electronic gaming machines and a complete array of table games. Odds are you will love this place. Quinault Indian tribal members entertain and inform you through traditional music, dance and song. 78 State Route 115, Ocean Shores WA (360) 289-9466 or (888) 461-2214 www.quinaultbchresort.com

# The Shelburne Inn

The Shelburne Inn in Seaview "is to breakfast what the Louvre is to art." So wrote a reviewer from the St. Louis Post Dispatch recently. This is another way of saying that the cuisine and service at this inn are internationally acclaimed. The gourmet breakfast is complimentary, and the Shoalwater Restaurant and Heron & Beaver Pub/Café are right on the premises. The Inn alone is a relaxing retreat for city dwellers and a sanctuary for nature lovers. All rooms are furnished in antiques and have private baths, and most have private decks. Wrote Northwest Palate magazine, "It is the human touch that keeps Shelburne's devoted regulars coming back: a hand-braided rug on the floor by an exquisite four-poster bed...or an antique vase filled with flowers to bring all the fragrance and color of the Shelburne's English side garden indoors." The Shelburne Inn, established in 1896 and listed on the National Historic Register, retains that intimacy and charm of yesteryear rarely found in our modern world. It has offered travelers warm hospitality, wonderful food and comfortable shelter for over a century. Overnight guests delight in breakfast, lunch and dinner here, which feature an abundance of fresh, local ingredients lovingly prepared. 4415 Pacific Way, Seaview WA (360) 642-2442 or (800) INN-1896 www.theshelburneinn.com

## Accommodations / RV Resorts — Washington Coast

# The Polynesian Resort

Professionally managed by Vacation Villages of America, the oceanfront Polynesian Resort Complex strives to meet all of its visitors' needs. Accommodation possibilities are: 1,600 square foot penthouses; 1,100 square foot, two bedroom family suites; condos; single rooms; studios with kitchenettes; and conference or banquet facilities. Generously stocked, full-sized bedrooms tout wood burning fireplaces. Continental breakfast is served every weekday morning in a cozy a room that later provides space for puzzles, reading, board games, and television. If you want special treatment enjoy the luxuriously appointed spa, sauna and indoor pool. Exclusive to the Polynesian Resort is their private park with a sport facility for basketball, volleyball, playground, picnic areas and barbeques. Mariah's is the onsite, award winning rant. There are nightly specials, daily Happy Hours and a fabulous Sunday Brunch. Mariah's is very popular with the locals, a telltale sign of great food and atmosphere. Package deals and discounting programs are available at this family and pet friendly resort. 615 Ocean Shores Boulevard NW, Ocean Shores WA (360) 289-3361 or (800) 562-4836 www.thepolynesian.com

## Accommodations / RV Resorts — Kitsap Peninsula

# The Kingston Inn

The food at the Kingston Inn is so close to home-cooked that they have customers who come for breakfast, lunch, and dinner seven days a week. Some of their regulars drive 45 minutes just for a meal. The menu that brings people in day after day has a treat for every day of the week, from a full turkey dinner every Sunday, to Pot Roast every Monday. Great food every day of the calendar, substantial portions, and reasonable prices: these are what owners Steve Dowen and Michael Prestley promise and deliver. A great view comes along with your meal too. Just footsteps away from the Kingston ferry terminal, you can see Puget Sound and Mount Rainer while you enjoy the excellent service and good food that Steve and Michael and their staff provide with a smile. The Kingston Inn's website promises "delicious food – friendly service." 24886 Washington Boulevard NE, Kingston WA (360) 297 - 3373 www.thekingstoninn.com

# Waterfront Inn

Located at the head of Gig Harbor Bay and just steps from shops and restaurants, the Waterfront Inn offers luxurious suites, each with a rock river fireplace and a private entrance and bath. All the amenities of a first class lodging are also provided. Owners Steve and Janis Denton bought the old fisherman's home and, with the encouragement of friends, renovated it into a beautiful boutique inn. They are known for providing privacy in their peaceful surroundings. Breakfast is brought right to your door. Three of the rooms open up to the waterfront. You may enjoy the incredible view from the privacy of your room or from the huge deck over the water. Watch birds, ducks, seals, otters and the activity of boats on the bay. You may use kayaks for exploring the bay, or walk around town or on the nearby trails. Charters on their sail boat or powerboat are available from their dock. The charter business is also owned by the Dentons (see Westerly Marine in the Attraction Section).   9017 N Harborview Drive, Gig Harbor WA (253) 857-0770   www.waterfront-inn.com

# The Maritime Inn

At the Maritime Inn in Gig Harbor, the area's most distinctive hotel, where personal service and unequaled comfort are combined to create an atmosphere of casual elegance and charm. This European boutique-style hotel is situated in an area of pristine natural beauty that was once the original home and fishing grounds of a small band of Nisqually Indians. Now a bustling village, this postcard perfect area offers many recreational opportunities, including fishing, hiking and world- class golf. The Inn is ideally located within walking distance to the harbor's finest restaurants, art galleries, thriving retail district and beautiful marinas. Graciously appointed rooms await guests with friendly staff, cozy fireplaces, charming Northwest interiors and views of the harbor. The Maritime Inn is truly the "Perfect Small Hotel" and a glorious place to stay.  3212 Harborview Drive, Gig Harbor WA (253) 858-1818 or (888) 506 - 3580  www.maritimeinn.com

# SpringRidge Gardens Bed and Breakfast

At SpringRidge Gardens Bed and Breakfast on Bainbridge Island, the key word is simple: "Romance." Host Wendy Burroughs strives to keep this romantic getaway a place where couples can kindle their relationships. This is the place for married couples to remember why they are married. Nestled in a spectacular garden setting on five peaceful acres, everything here revolves around romance. Even the DVDs and movies for guest use are romantic. Wendy maintains only two rooms here: the Pensione and the Courtyard Suite. The European-inspired Pensione has a full kitchen, queen and full beds, private bath, "Tuscan Summer" lighting and beautiful garden views. You'll feel like you're relaxing in a grown-up playhouse. The Courtyard Suite has a large living room with a fireplace adorned by a handcrafted antique mahogany mantel, baby grand piano, plush down sofa, kitchenette and private hot tub. There's a separate bedroom with a queen bed, antique writing desk and private bath. When you step out of either room, you step into Wendy's gardens, which have been featured in *Better Homes and Gardens, Pacific Magazine,* and *Water Gardening* magazine. It's impossible to stay here and not feel the romance. 7686 Springridge Road NE, Bainbridge Island WA (206) 842 - 7369 www.springridgegardens.com

## Accommodations / RV Resorts — Seattle Metro

# Woodmark Hotel on Lake Washington

For elegance and comfort on the shores of Lake Washington, The Woodmark Hotel is incomparable. At this luxury hotel you can enjoy spectacular views of the lake, the Olympic Mountains and the Seattle skyline from your beautifully appointed room or suite. There's a lakeside bistro, "Waters," and the Spa at the Woodmark, an Aveda concept spa, is world-class. Add to that special touches like an invitation to "Raid the Pantry" for complimentary late-night snacks, a full schedule of seasonal special packages, and a restored vintage Chris-Craft for touring the lake or to be reserved for weddings and other special events, and you have an absolutely wonderful experience. As it says on their website, "Dine, Unwind, and Stay." The Waters bistro has a warm and inviting atmosphere, and features Northwest cuisine with a Mediterranean accent. Just a glimpse of the menu includes delicious dishes like Rosemary Grilled Portabella Mushrooms, and Northwest Paella with shrimp, mussels, clams, halibut and chorizo with saffron rice. The Library Bar lounge offers afternoon teas, espresso, cocktails and hors d'oeuvres. For unwinding, the Spa offers an enormous selection of delightful Aveda services. The packages include highlights with names like Panache, Pure Focus, Radiant Skin Facial, Fusion Stone Massage, Candlelight Soak, and Rosemary Mint Awakening Body Wrap. The Spa experience includes hydrotherapy, manicures, pedicures, massages, skin care, and body treatments – everything for rejuvenation and enjoyment. The Woodmark has a full set of amenities for the business guest as well as the vacationer. The hotel provides high-speed Internet, voice mail and data jacks, desks, in-room safes, a fitness room and concierge services. Just seven miles east of Seattle, this is the perfect place for a business conference. 1200 Carillon Point, Kirkland WA (425) 822 - 3700 or (800) 822 - 3700 www.thewoodmark.com

## Madison House

Nestled in Kirkland, near the eastern shores of Lake Washington with its picturesque parks, specialty shops and art galleries, you will find the best upscale retirement community in the area. For over twenty-six years, Madison House has provided the best of retirement lifestyles with the ambiance of a "residential hotel." An elegant dining room provides a full menu of choices and three meals a day. The fitness center, heated indoor pool and spa, and other amenities assure that the residents feel like pampered guests. At Madison House, residents enjoy an active retirement with a wide variety of outings and scenic drives scheduled weekly. There is plenty of onsite fun including art classes, theater, live music, movies and more. Residents are encouraged to meet their neighbors and participate in social activities including Sherry Hour, High Tea and Happy Hour. Madison House offers luxurious one-bedroom and studio apartments, all featuring a full bath and separate kitchen. Residents who require assistance benefit from trained and attentive staff including a Registered Nurse and Therapeutic Fitness Coordinator. Madison House requires no upfront "buy in" or endowment fee, and offers monthly rentals that include all services and utilities except telephone. Small pets are also welcome. Transportation to shopping, banking, hospital and health care services is provided daily. 12215 N.E 128th Street, Kirkland WA  (425) 821-8210
www.madisonhouseretirement.com

## Villa Heidelberg

For old world charm on Puget Sound, spend a night or more at Judy Burbrink's Villa Heidelberg Bed and Breakfast. The location offers a great view of Puget Sound and the Olympic Mountains, yet is just 10 minutes from downtown Seattle. The Villa is an ideal warm, comfortable and safe place for a single woman traveling alone. In the common area, you'll find beamed ceilings, open staircases and leaded glass windows. You can dine each morning in the dining room or on the old-fashioned wraparound porch. Enjoy seasonal fruit, juice and gourmet coffee with the excellent breakfasts. At night you might rest in the Heidelberg room, with its king-sized brass bed, fireplace, crystal chandelier and view of the rose garden and South Puget Sound. Of the six zimmers (rooms) available, two have private baths. No matter which room you choose, you're sure to enjoy your stay at Villa Heidelberg.  4845 45th Avenue SW,   Seattle WA
(206) 938-3658 or
(800) 671 - 2942
www.villaheidelberg.com

# Accommodations / RV Resorts — Seattle Metro

## McMenamins Olympic Club Hotel & Theater

Opened in 1908, the Olympic Club Hotel and Theater boasts a colorful and thoroughly checkered past. From brawling outlaws and infamous poker games through the scandalous 1920s, this "gentlemen's resort" managed to stay on remarkably good terms with the local constabulary. A classic railroad hotel, the Olympic thrived throughout Prohibition, purportedly spiriting hidden Canadian liquor from the tracks through tunnels leading to the Club's basement. Over time, owners of the establishment have seen fit to respect the impressive 1913 remodel. The splendid mahogany bar, in what is now the Olympic Club Pub, is an extraordinary example of the era as is the massive Round Oak

woodstove, still fired up on chilly days. By the 1930s, the Olympic had earned a reputation for good and plentiful food and people stood three deep waiting for a seat at the counter. The McMenamins contribute to the reputation, but with pristine produce, hormone-free Oregon country beef, and the freshest seafood. The Olympic Club Brewery serves McMenamins' vast array of artisan beers including Hammerhead Ale, Terminator Stout, and the effervescent and raspberry-tinged Ruby Ale. The hotel's 27 guestrooms are fully restored in period style with in-room sinks and private bathrooms down the hall. Each room pays homage to a colorful, historic local character. The classic billiard parlor features some of its original Brunswick pool tables and the sumptuous, vintage 20s movie theater screens new releases. For good food and unique accommodations, revel in a century of local history at McMenamins Olympic Club Hotel & Theater. 112 N Tower Avenue, Centralia WA (360) 736 - 5164  www.mcmenamins.com

# Accommodations / RV Resorts    Skagit Valley

## La Conner Channel Lodge

In LaConner, with its wide variety of cruises, tours, antique shops and magnificent outdoor experiences, there is only one place to stay on the waterfront, at the LaConner Channel Lodge. This romantic getaway, not far from Seattle or the Canadian border, offers a place to relax and unwind with a great view and wonderful shops. Each of the 40 rooms has a balcony, from which you can watch the parade of boats on the Snohomish Channel, gateway to the San Juan Islands. Each room also has a gas fireplace, coffee maker, refrigerator and hair dryer. Twelve of the 40 rooms are King Parlor rooms with Jacuzzi bathtubs. A homemade continental breakfast is served daily in the breakfast room by a fireplace. If you want to host a meeting of up to 20 people, the Channel Lodge has the Dunlap Room and a professional custom catering staff to take care of your group's needs. (Additional meeting rooms off-property can accommodate up to 120 people.) While in LaConner, enjoy services and activities including facials and massages, unique shops and antique stores, restaurants, art galleries, golf courses, a casino, scenic cruises, meal cruises, whale watching, bird watching, nature trails, hiking, biking and boating. 205 N First Street, La Conner WA  (360) 466-1500 or (888) 466-4113  www.laconnerlodging.com

## Skagit River Resort LLC & The Eatery Restaurant

Described as one of the most restful and relaxing places in the North Cascades, Skagit River Resort is on Highway 20 near Marblemount at the western entrance to Washington's breathtakingly beautiful North Cascades mountain range. Situated at the historic village site of Bullerville, the resort is the perfect place to unwind. Established by Tootsie Clark (nee Buller) and her husband Rudy, they used cabins that had originally been built for mill hands working for the Buller Bros. Lumber Company as the basis for the resort. Among the many unique features of the resort are the rabbits. Rudy started raising rabbits in 1961. When the rabbits exceeded his hutch capacity, he let some loose which created the "wild" bunny colony around the cabins that is still enjoyed by the guests today. The Eatery was established in 1982 by Tootsie and her sister Florence McCord. Originally an octagonal 11-foot drive-in, the business became so popular that by 1988 they decided that indoor seating was a must, so the present building was created. The new restaurant also fulfilled Tootsie's wish for a museum to display the history of the Bullers and the other pioneer families on the Upper Skagit, another unique and fascinating attraction at the resort. The Skagit River Resort is open year-round. Milepost 103.5 on Highway 20, near Marblemount WA  Postal address: 58468 Clark Cabin Rd, Rockport WA 98283  (360) 873-2250 or (800) 273-2606  www.northcascades.com

# Accommodations / RV Resorts  Skagit Valley

## Skagit Valley Casino Resort

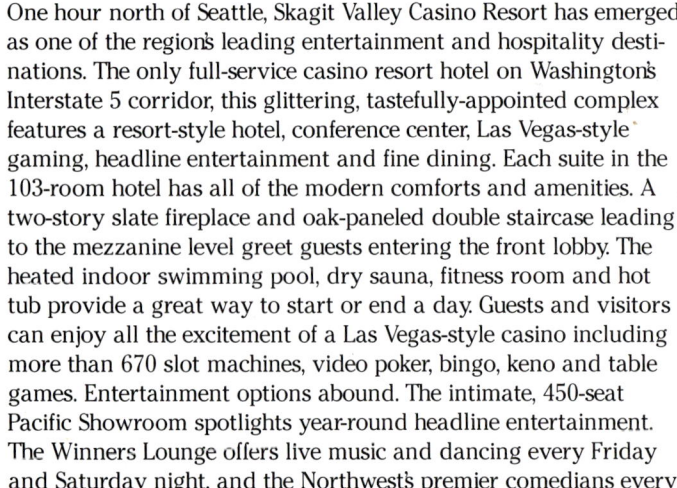

One hour north of Seattle, Skagit Valley Casino Resort has emerged as one of the region's leading entertainment and hospitality destinations. The only full-service casino resort hotel on Washington's Interstate 5 corridor, this glittering, tastefully-appointed complex features a resort-style hotel, conference center, Las Vegas-style gaming, headline entertainment and fine dining. Each suite in the 103-room hotel has all of the modern comforts and amenities. A two-story slate fireplace and oak-paneled double staircase leading to the mezzanine level greet guests entering the front lobby. The heated indoor swimming pool, dry sauna, fitness room and hot tub provide a great way to start or end a day. Guests and visitors can enjoy all the excitement of a Las Vegas-style casino including more than 670 slot machines, video poker, bingo, keno and table games. Entertainment options abound. The intimate, 450-seat Pacific Showroom spotlights year-round headline entertainment. The Winners Lounge offers live music and dancing every Friday and Saturday night, and the Northwest's premier comedians every second and fourth Thursday of the month. Fine dining takes center stage at The Skagit's award-winning Moon Beach Restaurant, featuring choice steaks, seafood and Northwest specialties in an intimate atmosphere. Casual dining alternatives include the Market Buffet and the Northern Lights Deli. Couples looking for a unique venue for their wedding celebration will enjoy The Skagit's combination of luxurious accommodations, delicious dining options and casino fun. The resort also offers more than 14,000 square feet of flexible meeting space. Its enviable location provides an excellent home base for day trips that could include hiking, kayaking, observing bald eagles along the Skagit River or a ferryboat ride on Puget Sound. Skagit Valley Casino Resort is affiliated with the top-rated Semiahmoo Resort, also featured in this book.  5984 North Darrk Lane, Bow WA  (360) 724-7777 or (877) 275-2448  www.theskagit.com

# Semiahmoo Resort – Golf - Spa

Semiahmoo Resort lies just south of the U.S./Canadian border. At Semiahmoo, sea breezes beckon and spectacular sunsets abound. The AAA Four-Diamond, 198-room ocean front resort showcases a full-service European-style spa offering the most extensive menu of skin care services and treatments available in the Northwest. Guests can relish in the latest anti-aging treatments and products from the world-renowned Sothys Institute in Paris. A full-service exercise facility, complete with indoor/outdoor pool, offers an invigorating indoor fitness option. Fine dining is "a must" at Stars. Lunch and light meals are served daily at Packer's Lounge and Oyster Bar. The Blue Heron offers great pub fare with golf course views. Guests and visitors can golf year-round at two of Golf Digest's "Top 100" public play courses: the Arnold Palmer-designed Semiahmoo Golf & Country Club known for its contoured greens and white sand bunkers, and the Graham Cook-designed Loomis Trail Golf Club featuring dramatic bentgrass fairways and greens, and strategically placed water features. For the adventurous, kayaking, hiking, biking, tennis, rollerblading, sailing, horseback riding, salmon fishing and whale watching are all available locally. The Resort is also home to a 300-slip, privately-operated saltwater marina. Wildlife lovers and bird watchers alike will enjoy the rich variety of wildlife that make the Resort home throughout the year. Romantic and picturesque, the Resort offers couples unique settings in which to say, "I do," or to host their reception. It also offers over 35,000 square feet of flexible conference and meeting space. As part of "Washington's Premier Resort Group," Semiahmoo is affiliated with Skagit Valley Casino Resort, also featured in this book. The warm, inviting atmosphere and exceptional service belie the Resort's intriguing history, as the site was once home to the Semiahmoo band of Native Americans and later served as the largest sockeye salmon cannery in the United States. 9565 Semiahmoo Parkway, Blaine WA (360) 318-2000 or (800) 770-7992 www.semiahmoo.com

## The Chrysalis Inn & Spa

At a breathtakingly beautiful location on Bellingham's waterfront, the Chrysalis Inn & Spa is a premiere place to stay when you're visiting northern Washington. With thirty-four deluxe rooms and nine luxury suites, guests can delight in views and amenities that include gas fireplaces, Internet access, down comforters and complimentary breakfast buffets. Be sure to visit The Spa, too! A warm ambience created by natural woods, slate floors and custom lighting will start you on your way to being relaxed and refreshed. Enjoy one of the many treatments available, including massages, facials and hydrotherapy. When you're ready for a meal, Fino Wine Bar at The Chrysalis Inn provides casual dining with classic European-style cuisine and a rich selection of premium vintages. The Chrysalis Inn arose from a personal vision to capture the essence of the Northwest and savor it as a holistic experience. It is a wonderful place for individuals or couples to relax and get away from everyday stress, as well as providing accommodations for groups. With state-of-the-art meeting facilities for up to 50 people and catering from Fino's, you can have a meeting to remember. 804 10th Street, Bellingham WA (360) 756-1005 or (888) 808-0005 www.thechrysalisinn.com  www.finowinebar.com

## Fairhaven Village Inn

In the heart of Bellingham's historic Fairhaven District is one of the true treasures of Washington state and "the most amiable of all Bellingham hotels," the Fairhaven Village Inn. Owner-Managers Gene and Connie Shannon fell in love with the Inn as guests, so it was only fitting that when they had the chance, they became its proprietors. Twenty-two luxuriously appointed rooms welcome travelers, and the Fairhaven is a perfect place for family and group gatherings, with meeting rooms accommodating up to 25 people, broadband Internet access, and more. The Inn is a tremendously popular place for weddings, and the Shannons' extensive knowledge of local artisans, caterers, and florists is a big plus. One look at the elegance and charm of the Inn and you'll see that it's the kind of place that makes memories for a lifetime. Don't miss out on exploring the Fairhaven District while you're staying at the Inn. Known for fine dining, with twenty restaurants and cafés just a short walk, the Fairhaven District also offers unique shops and sightseeing opportunities in a location rich in scenic beauty and historical significance. If you're interested in outdoor activities, Fairhaven is the perfect starting point for boating, biking, mountain climbing trips, and whale watching excursions.

1200 Tenth Street, Bellingham WA    (360) 733-1311 or (877) 733-1100    www.fairhavenvillageinn.com

# The Hogland House

For an incredible view of sailboats, the ferry boat to Whidbey Island and an occasional eagle, you'll need to stay at The Hogland House in Mukilteo. Say the locals, "There is nothing like this place." The turn-of-the-century house displays gingerbread fretwork in the dining area and collectibles throughout. The house was built on the bluff in 1906 by Charles and Isabelle McNab, and purchased by the Hogland family in 1942. It has been in the Hogland family for over 60 years, according to proprietress Beverly Kay Scheller. Previously for 14 years, it was a convent for the Urseline Sisters of Montana. So step back in time and spend some leisurely days in this charming establishment with its vintage furniture, old world finishes and hand painted murals. The Hogland House was the first house to be placed on the newly formed Mukilteo Register of Historic Places in 1992. Each room has unique touches to provide you with comfort and privacy. Walk the trails to the beach or the many wooded paths. Relax on the outdoor porch overlooking Puget Sound, sit in the picturesque gazebo or the outdoor hot tub and watch the ferries pass. 917 Webster Street, Mukilteo WA (425) 742 - 7639 or (888) 681-5101   www.hoglandhouse.com

## Accommodations / RV Resorts

### The Valley

# Larkspur Landing

Larkspur Landing offers first-rate amenities and personalized service in a warm and inviting atmosphere. From custom-designed furniture and signature "FeatherBorne Beds" to exercise and spa facilities, you will find everything you need to rest, relax and stay in shape while you're on the road. Whether you're traveling for business or pleasure, you'll be kept up-to-the minute and in touch with in-room high speed Internet access and wireless Internet access in all public areas of the hotel. Business travelers will appreciate the full size work desks and remote printing that allows you to send a print job from your guest room to a printer in the 24-hour business center. The Larkspur's library loans classic books, movies, CDs and games for quiet recreation. A complimentary Healthy Start breakfast is served seven days a week and complimentary Starbuck's coffee and herbal teas are available in the living room, as are fresh-baked cookies in the evening and fruit in the morning. With truly modern conveniences in a setting with Craftsman-style attention to detail and beauty, Larkspur Landing is sure to please even the most discriminating traveler.

## Accommodations / RV Resorts — East Side

## Sheraton Bellevue Hotel

Whether you are a tired traveler or a high-energy business visitor, the Sheraton Bellevue Hotel has your comfort in mind. They have a health club as well as a heated indoor pool, whirlpool and sauna, and are happy to offer guests complimentary passes to a nearby full-service health club. This convenient, accommodating hotel offers the business traveler a larger working desk and additional amenities including bottled water, complimentary breakfast and access to the Club Level Lounge 24 hours a day for club level bookings. Their state-of-the-art boardrooms are very impressive. They offer built-in projection screens, whiteboards and exquisite mahogany tables surrounded by leather executive chairs. There are rooms for meetings of up to 220 people. The Snoqualmie Ballroom has 2,556 square feet of space for an elegant sit down dinner, grand buffet, wedding reception, holiday party or any other special event. You can choose from an extensive menu, from carving stations tended by their chef to rich Northwest seafood displays. Any event, from a dinner for two to a banquet for 250 people, can be brilliantly accomplished at Sheraton Bellevue Hotel. The Sheraton Bellevue Hotel provides first class accommodations only two blocks from Bellevue's Meydenbauer Convention Center and only six miles from downtown Seattle. A courtesy van provides service to the local shopping venue, Bellevue Square, offering over 250 world-class shops, city parks and fine dining. Complimentary parking is provided. 100 112th Avenue NE, Bellevue WA  (425) 455-3330 or (800) 235-4458  www.sheraton.com/bellevue

## Willows Lodge

For a "Northwest celebration of the senses," try the Willows Lodge in Woodinville. Located on five acres bordering the Sammamish River at the heart of Woodinville Wine Country, the Lodge was recently named one of the best places to stay in the world by *Condé Nast Traveler*, one of only six Washington hotels and resorts to be listed. There are 86 guest rooms and suites. While there, dine in the Barking Frog, a casual bistro featuring country fresh Northwest cuisine with a European flair and extensive Northwest wine collection, or choose the nearby world-renowned Herbfarm Restaurant. A complimentary continental breakfast is served each morning at the Barking Frog and nightly wine tastings are offered in the Fireside Cellars. A different winery is featured each evening. Standard room amenities include a 27-inch stereo TV with DVD/CD player (DVD and CD libraries complimentary), soaking tub designed for two, 300-count Italian linens, stone fireplaces, in-room safes with space for laptop computers, and a selection of robes. Outside the room, there is a 2,000 square foot spa and fitness center, sauna and outdoor Jacuzzi. The Spa offers hydrotherapy, massage,

body treatments and facials. If you or your company are looking for a "Challenge Course" to deliver teambuilding skills, the Lodge offers a 45-foot high ropes course. Looking for romance? How about the Do Not Disturb Package featuring in-tub dining. Said *Travel & Leisure* magazine, while recently naming the Willows Lodge one of the Top 50 Most Romantic Getaways in the World, "Simply put, a weekend here is the height of hedonism." Says the Willows Lodge management, "You'll experience a slower pace, a culinary awakening and a sensory delight."  14580 NE 145th Street, Woodinville WA  (425) 424-3900  www.willowslodge.com

## Accommodations / RV Resorts                          I-5 Corridor

# Skamania Lodge

Skamania Lodge, conference and rustic mountain resort destination, is surrounded by the waterfalls, peaks, forests and canyons of the majestic Columbia River Gorge. The warmth of the Lodge is characterized by the Native American-inspired rugs, original stone rubbings, warm woolen fabrics and Mission-style wood furnishings along with some of the most spectacular scenic views in the world. Guest room types include forest view rooms, river view rooms and one-bedroom parlor suites. The amenities are numerous. The Lodge, member of the International Association of Conference Centers, offers 22,000 square feet of meeting, exhibition and banquet space. Onsite audio/visual equipment and technical support are provided. The Cascade Room at Dolce Skamania Lodge features casual fine dining, serving breakfast, lunch and dinner with an incredible view of the Columbia River and the Cascade Mountain Range. Their menu features hearty, Northwest seasonal cuisine that is centered around their wood-fired oven. Inspired by the great National Park lodges of the Northwest, the dining room has an open, festive feeling with wood and iron decor and a floor that dates back over 200 years. The Skamania Golf Center features a beautiful and challenging 18-hole, par-70 golf course. The indoor Fitness Center includes a 20-yard swimming pool, sun deck and spa. There are also tennis courts, sand volleyball court and over four miles of hiking or biking paths. A distinctive experience provided by Destination Hotels & Resorts.  1131 Skamania Lodge Way, Stevenson WA   (509) 427-7700 or (800) 221-7117   www.skamania.com

# Heathman Lodge

The Heathman Lodge is an Alpine-style lodge filled with the art and charm of the Pacific Northwest. As general manager Brett Wilkerson describes it, it is an unexpected urban retreat that offers travelers and visitors from the Portland/Vancouver area a blend of "heart-felt service, business amenities, and rustic mountain lodge comfort."

The Lodge itself is an impressive work of rustic architecture built by craftsmen out of wood from the Northwest forests. As you walk into the lobby, the first impression is of shining stone floors, gleaming wood wherever you look and, for accents, wonderful handwoven blankets. The Heathman Lodge website has an intriguing feature that allows a virtual visitor to stand in the lobby or several other locations and slowly turn in a full circle, seeing the full scope of the ambiance and furnishings. Hudson's Restaurant features Iron Chef winner Mark Hosack preparing handcrafted American food in the rustic lodge setting. From the hand-carved newel posts in the lobby with their representations of the Raven, a powerful North Coast Indian figure, to the custom-made furniture throughout, you will find many treasures of the region at the Heathman Lodge.  What you will also find is 121 spacious guest rooms, 21 signature suites, a business level, indoor pool, whirlpool, sauna and fitness center, excellent communications amenities including data ports, private dining rooms that can seat up to 300 and service that can't be matched.

7801 NE Greenwood Drive, Vancouver WA
(360) 254-3100 or (888) 475-3100   www.heathmanlodge.com

# Accommodations / RV Resorts  I-5 Corridor

## Holiday Inn Express-Vancouver

While in the greater metro area of Portland and Vancouver, enjoy a rejuvenating stay at the Holiday Inn Express, where you can prepare for the next leg of your travels and relax in style. With easy access from both I - 5 and I - 205, you will be able to see the sights and retire to a home away from home. The Holiday Inn Express provides a great night's sleep as they make sure that you have what you need to be completely fresh for your trip. Each room has a coffee maker, hairdryer, ironing board and iron. You'll enjoy splashing in the large 24-hour swimming pool and working out in the state of the art fitness center. Each morning they offer a complete complimentary continental breakfast. Do not worry if you forgot some grooming items, just ask at the front desk and they'll have it for you. Wanting to get connected? With free high speed Internet access in all rooms and free local calls, you won't be without the information you need. Gabi, Cora and the entire staff are there to help you with any special requests. 13101 NE 27th Avenue, Vancouver WA
(360) 576 - 1040   www.vancouverwahie.com

## Empress Palace

Approaching the Empress Palace in Woodland, Washington, you first see ornamental iron entry gates guarded by two mythical, winged lions on tall masonry gate posts. Upon entering the property you will be amazed by the garden court that features 35 spiraled columns, and then to the enormous Corinthian style columns supporting a massive Italian-style portico with arched and coffered ceilings. A stunning marble entryway with a 40-foot high masonry rotunda (the largest privately owned masonry dome in Washington) awaits. You have found your way into an enchanted place, a 13,000 square foot French-Italian Renaissance edifice called the Empress Palace. This has to be the perfect spot for a wedding – a secluded mountain top retreat on a seven-acre estate overlooking the Columbia and Lewis Rivers. The Neuschwanders, who purchased the property in 2000, have pledged to give the best quality service, making every celebration in this idyllic setting unique and exceptional. Their mission is to "create a sense of place that stirs the imagination to the royal pageantry and splendor of the French-Italian Renaissance period." Their impressive services and facilities include everything you might need to create an unforgettable occasion. The Empress Palace, sometimes called the 'Taj mahal' of the Northwest came to be through the imagination of Dr. Ronald Gerne of Woodland nearly two decades ago. The Neuschwanders have finished the work of art that was more than 15 years in the making, and are delighted to be able to offer this lovely location for unique events. 229 Moonridge Road Woodland, WA   (360) 225-4468 or 800-474-6994   www.empresspalace.com

# Accommodations / RV Resorts — South Puget Sound

## Fertile Ground Guesthouse

Karen Nelson and Gail Sullivan have created a unique bed and breakfast at Fertile Ground Guesthouse in Olympia: "Green lodging for people who care." With a focus on sustainability, all the food served is organic and the bedding comes from organic cotton and wool sources. They also grow a wide variety of fruits, vegetables, herbs and bamboo in the beautiful gardens surrounding the house. Their goal is to provide a demonstration site for sustainable living in an urban community, using resources creatively. Located in an historic Craftsman-style house built in 1908, Fertile Ground has become one of the most popular places to stay in the area. Among the enticing features is the outdoor wood-fired earth oven used to cook pizzas during the summer. It also plays a role in many local fundraisers as they are actively involved in the life of the community. Being located in the downtown district means you can leave your car and walk to the lively restaurants, shops and entertainment nearby. For reservations, call early as they get booked very quickly! 311 9th Avenue SE, Olympia WA (360) 352 - 2428   www.fertileground.org

## Silver Cloud Inn

If you're looking for a service-oriented hotel in Tacoma, travel to the Silver Cloud Inn, where guests rave about the service and hospitality the staff delivers on a daily basis. Located in historic Old Town, the Silver Cloud Inn is the only hotel on the Tacoma waterfront with panoramic water views from every guestroom. Here are some of the features of the Inn and its 90 spacious guestrooms: fireplace and Jacuzzi suites; complimentary Silver Cloud breakfast; in-room high-speed Internet access; in-room coffee, refrigerator, microwave, hair dryer, iron and ironing board; free local calls and voice mail; free laundry facilities; complimentary parking; and a boardroom for small meetings. Adjacent to Old Town and its quaint shopping and wonderful restaurants, the Inn is also within a few miles of the Washington State Historical Museum, the Point Defiance-Tahlequah ferry, Museum of Glass, Point Defiance Park and Zoo, Tacoma Dome, and Tacoma Landmark Convention Center.  2317 N Ruston Way, Tacoma WA (253) 272 - 1300 or (866) 820-8448  www.silvercloud.com

# Alderbrook Resort & Spa

Hood Canal is one of Washington's natural wonders, a glacier-sculpted fjord over sixty miles long, renowned for its sparkling waters and unique ecosystem. Located right on the water in Union, Alderbrook Resort & Spa is the perfect place to stay while enjoying the natural wonders of Hood Canal and the Olympic National Park just a few miles away. Alderbrook offers a PGA golf course and marina with over 1,500 feet of docking space. Having just undergone almost two years' worth of renovations, Alderbrook now offers state-of-the-art lodging and conference facilities. Warm earth tones and windows offering spectacular views highlight not only the beautifully designed guest rooms, but also the Restaurant at Alderbrook. You are invited to enjoy a sumptuous menu featuring the freshest local seafood and a world-class selection of wines. With 7,000 square feet of meeting space and a location just two hours from Seattle, Alderbrook is a perfect place for business conferences and family gatherings alike, and the natural beauty makes an unforgettably beautiful backdrop for open-air wedding ceremonies. The cherry on the sundae is the Alderbrook Spa, offering a full range of soothing and revitalizing body treatments in an incomparable setting.   10 E Alderbrook Drive, Union WA   (360) 898-2200 or (800) 622 - 9370
www.alderbrookresort.com

# Swantown Inn

The Swantown Inn is a beautiful 1893 Queen Anne/Eastlake Victorian mansion built by William G. White. It is situated in a quiet neighborhood in the heart of Olympia, with extensive gardens and views of the Capitol building. Owners and innkeepers Nathan and Casey Allan enjoy the memory of hosting each guest, but hope that each guest leaves with a memory of their own that lasts a lifetime. Whether you're looking for a romantic getaway, a relaxing retreat or a home away from home, the Swantown Inn provides a cozy and inviting atmosphere. The Inn's four rooms are named after Northwest landmarks like the Columbia Room, with its large private Victorian bath featuring a claw foot tub and foot soaking tub, and the Astoria Room, with its four-poster bed and two person Jacuzzi tub. Three-course gourmet breakfasts are provided and the personalized attention will make your stay enjoyable. The Inn is also available for special events, weddings, reunions, corporate meetings, seminars and retreats. With its prime location, the Swantown Inn can be your headquarters for exploring or your escape from it all. 1431 11th Avenue SE, Olympia WA (360) 753-9123 or (877) 753-9123 www.swantowninn.com

# Sheraton Tacoma

Minutes from Seattle, Mt. Rainier and the Olympics, the Sheraton Tacoma Hotel in the heart of Tacoma's business district offers guests an exceptional, full service hotel. As you enter the hotel's three-level lobby, take in works of art by world-renowned local artist Dale Chihully accentuated by the lobby's vaulted ceilings and skylights. With three hundred and nineteen spacious guest rooms featuring all of the amenities of home, guests are sure to be comfortable when staying at the pet-friendly Sheraton. An automated business center provides a fax machine, photocopier and Internet access, and same-day laundry and dry-cleaning service is also available. Choose to dine at either the rooftop Altezzo Ristorante with its fine Italian cuisine or at the Broadway Grill on northwest favorites. If you're anxious to work out after your meal, head to the new on-site fitness room and workout center, where state-of-the art equipment awaits you. Along with the adjacent Bicentennial Pavilion, the Sheraton boasts more than 28,000 square feet of combined meeting space, perfect for weddings or conventions. When you're in Tacoma, look no farther than the Sheraton Tacoma Hotel for a place to stay-this boutique hotel guarantees your stay will be thoroughly enjoyable.
1320 Broadway Plaza,
Tacoma, WA
(253) 572 - 3200 or (800) 325 - 3535
www.sheratontacoma.com

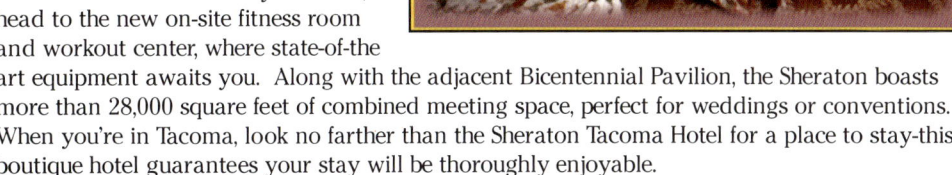

# Accommodations / RV Resorts — South Puget Sound

## Lake Quinault Lodge

On Washington's glorious Olympic Peninsula, Lake Quinault Lodge, listed on the National Register of Historic Places, is the perfect place to leave the cares of the work-a-day world behind. Rejuvenate your spirit under a multistoried canopy of ancient towering trees. Enjoy delicious fresh local cuisine in the panoramic lakeview dining room. Breathe in the fresh air and exercise by hiking, canoeing, kayaking or fishing. Built in 1926, in the tradition of the Old Faithful Inn in Yellowstone and the Sun Valley Lodge in Idaho, the Lake Quinault Lodge reflects the spirit of a bygone era. Period wicker and overstuffed furniture, a massive brick fireplace and ceiling beams decorated with Native American designs all contribute to the ambiance of the Lodge lobby. As far back as the 1880s, Olympic Peninsula travelers gathered near Lake Quinault at the "Log Hotel" for lodging, meals and good times. When improved roads provided easier access, crowds from Grays Harbor often gathered there on weekends to dance and socialize. Then, on August 28, 1924, a fire consumed the entire structure. Turning this tragedy into an opportunity, supporters soon made plans to build a new, better hotel. The area's finest artisans and craftsmen were assembled and work continued nonstop. A mere 53 days later on August 18, 1926, a beautiful new resort hotel was unveiled: Lake Quinault Lodge. And though this grand Lodge is quite different from its humble predecessor, it surely offers the same spirit of gracious hospitality.

345 South Shore Road, Quinault, WA  (360) 288-2900 or (800) 562-6672   www.visitlakequinault.com

# Accommodations / RV Resorts — Whidbey Island

## Fort Casey Inn

Just a short ferry ride across Puget Sound from Seattle, the Fort Casey Inn on Whidbey Island is perfect for a romantic weekend getaway or a family outing. The Inn's charming Georgian Revival cottages have two bedrooms apiece and each comes with a bath, living room and fully-equipped kitchen. They were built nearly a hundred years ago for one of the three U.S. Army forts guarding Admiralty Inlet, and originally served as officers' residences. Large groups can also rent Garrison Hall for special events. The buildings that make up the Inn were sold at public auction in 1956, and opened as public accommodations after being lovingly restored. In 2001, Seattle Pacific University acquired the property and now operates both the Inn and the nearby Camp Casey Conference Center. Guests of the Inn have access to board games, picnic tables, hiking trails and the beach. The former grounds of Fort Casey beyond the officers' quarters are now Fort Casey State Park, a 467-acre public park with a lighthouse, bunkers, 10-inch disappearing guns and other fascinating reminders of Whidbey Island's military history. Other attractions include the bird sanctuary at Crockett Lake and the shops of historic Coupeville, just a few minutes away by car.

1124 S Engle Road, Coupeville WA  (360) 678 - 5050 or (866) 661-6604   www.fortcaseyinn.com

# Attractions

# Attractions                                              Olympic Peninsula

## Port of Port Townsend

Wooden boats on the water – and their crews – find every service they'll need at the Port of Port Townsend. Here, at the place where Puget Sound was discovered by Captain George Vancouver, is one of only four Victorian seaports in the U.S. This town was intended to be what Seattle is today, but railroads were unable to bring their trains this way at the time. Big mansions built back then are used as bed and breakfasts today. Many people who stay in the rooms bring their boats in for repairs and maintenance at the many marine firms who specialize in wooden boats of all eras. Over 200 maritime traders that specialize in wooden boat restoration are here. Whatever your maritime needs, you'll be able to have them met here. Come for the annual Wooden Boat Festival. Or come for the many recreation facilities. Stay at one of the B&Bs, or one of the many RV parks. From the Hudson Bay Marina, it's an easy walk to town. The craftspeople, the festivals and the various recreation opportunities all await you.
333 Benedict Street, Port Townsend WA   (360) 385-0656   www.portofpt.com

## Olympic Game Farm

Just north of Sequim on the Olympic Peninsula is the Olympic Game Farm, a really wonderful place founded by Lloyd and Katherine Beebe. Though you might not recognize the name Lloyd Beebe, he has been a legend in the world of wildlife documentaries, and his legend lives on at Olympic Game Farm. A native of the Pacific Northwest, from an early age Lloyd had a knack for training wild animals. In 1945, he began making movies as a hobby, filming his children and the animals on his ranch: a cougar, a fawn, and a bear cub. Lloyd raised them to play with each other. When he heard that Walt Disney Studios was producing a new series called "True Life Adventures," he wrote to tell them about his footage of wildlife. So began his career for Disney, a career that took him across the world. He visited Antarctica with Admiral Byrd, filmed jaguars in Brazil, and even went to Point Barrow in Alaska to help some polar bears suffering from stage fright. Disney provided additional camera equipment and a soundstage for Lloyd's ranch that became known as the Disney Wild Animal Ranch. In the summer of 1972, while taking a temporary break from his Disney work, Lloyd decided to open the ranch to the public. It was an immediate success and Disney agreed to let him keep it open. The Olympic Game Farm was born! Today people come from all over to see the bison, elk, Kodiak bears, timber wolves, and exotic species such as zebras and llamas. Lloyd's son Ken and his sister-in-law Alice Beebe now run the farm keeping Lloyd's dream alive. They have inherited his knack for communicating with the animals. When the Farm's Bengal tiger sees Alice coming he rolls over on his back so she can give him a belly rub. The Olympic Game Farm is open year round for driving tours and guides give walking tours during the summer.
1423 Ward Road, Sequim WA
(360) 683-4295 or (800) 778-4295   www.olygamefarm.com

# Goodwin Aviation & Spruce Goose Cafe

If you enjoy flying and you love good cooking, Goodwin Aviation and the Spruce Goose Café in Port Townsend are neatly situated to deliver the best of both. Steve Goodwin, who likes to fly and also enjoys spending time close to home, started Goodwin Aviation in 2001. Experienced as a pilot and aircraft mechanic, he founded his business to keep his flying "local." Using either a Cessna 172 or 150, he will fly you to and from the Sea Tac Airport, or he will take you on a personal tour of the Olympic Mountains, surrounding

waters, or the San Juan Islands. These are spectacular flights, showing off some of the best scenery in the world, including glaciers, volcanoes, and ocean beaches. Steve is also available to take aerial photographs, or put you in the air where you can do your own photography. While you're on the ground at the Jefferson County International Airport, before or after a flight with Steve, you can take your appetite to the Spruce Goose Restaurant. Run by Andrea Raymor and Chris Cray, the restaurant serves the best in old-fashioned home-style cooking. Andrea and Chris are known for their homemade pies and breads, pot roast, teriyaki chicken burger, salads, burgers, omelets, and more. The portions are huge. They give "airport food" a good name, so much so that a website that rates such things recently awarded the Spruce Goose's burger five stars. Personal attention in the air, and great food at reasonable prices on the ground: Howard Hughes would have loved it!   310 Airport Road, Port Townsend WA   Spruce Goose Restaurant: (360) 385 - 3185   Goodwin Aviation: (360) 531-1727   www.goodwinaviation.com

# Attractions   Olympic Peninsula

## Manresa Castle

In Port Townsend, you can step back into a time when life was elegant and relaxed, in a real castle. The Manresa Castle has a history dating to 1892, when it was built as a home for Charles and Kate Eisenbeis. Eisenbeis was the town's first mayor and constructed the largest private residence ever built in the town. The Manresa Castle is also a National Historic Site and the fourth permanent building ever built in the state of Washington. In 1928, Jesuit priests bought the home, added a wing and transformed it into a training castle. They named it Manresa Hall, after the town in Spain where Ignatius Loyola founded the order. The Jesuits left in 1963 and the building was converted into a hotel. Much work was done to renovate the building to

modern standards while maintaining its Victorian elegance. Oh, by the way, there are rumors afoot that certain rooms in the castle are haunted, but management cannot honestly say anyone has ever seen a ghost, some guests enjoy ghost hunting though. Most guests, however, enjoy the beauty and elegance of the Manresa Castle and the beauty of the Olympic Peninsula. 651 Cleveland Street, Port Townsend WA
(360) 385 - 5750 or (800) 732-1281  www.manresacastle.com

# Dungeness Golf Course

You're in Western Washington, it's wet, and you'd love a round of golf. What to do? Did you know that Sequim gets a mere 13 inches of annual rainfall, compared to the 35 or so inches most everywhere else in Western Washington? Yes, and Sequim is home to the Dungeness Golf Course as well. It's the "driest" golf course in the western part of the state and, says the management, the most player-friendly and simultaneously challenging. As proof, the course is rated Four Stars by *Golf Digest*. "Our goal," says golf pro Bill Shea, "is to promote golf and player enjoyment in a friendly, relaxational atmosphere." The course is 18 holes, over 6,456 yards. While playing, try to avoid being distracted by the great views of the Olympic Mountains. With four sets of tees to choose from, you'll enjoy yourself whatever your skill level. When you're finished with the game, dine at the Greenside Grill and enjoy panoramic course views with your breakfast, lunch or dinner. The course is walkable. Call to reserve a cart and a tee time up to 30 days ahead. Carts are allowed year-round. The dress code prohibits tank tops or cut-offs (male or female). If you want to stay a while, golf packages are available at *every* hotel, motel, and bed and breakfast in Sequim and Port Angeles. When calling the establishment, let them know whether you want a green-fee-only package, or a Deluxe Package that includes the green fee, cart, range and five percent golf shop merchandise discount. 1965 Woodcock Road, Sequim WA (360) 683-6344 or (800) 447-6826 www.dungenessgolf.com

# Attractions

# Olympic Peninsula

## Seven Cedars Casino

Are you feeling lucky today?

Are you near Sequim, Washington? Then head for the Seven Cedars Casino, where the Jamestown S'Klallam Tribe offers you all the action and excitement of Las Vegas

or Reno in a setting that rivals the finest Northwest resort. This is the life! There are slots, roulette, craps, Let it Ride, bingo, blackjack, keno, live keno, poker, video poker, pull tabs and mega mania, as well as off-track betting. Smoking and nonsmoking slots are available. When you've had your fill of fun at gaming, there is world-class entertainment including live music and comedy. Three restaurants and lounges and an impressive gallery of Native American treasures add to your enjoyment. In the Salish Room Restaurant, try the elegant buffet of International delicacies and regional favorites like salmon, oysters and clams. In the art gallery, you find fine artwork and gift items among the regional treasures of Northwest Native Expressions. Housed in a traditional Indian Longhouse, this unique gallery represents nearly 200 Native American artists including silversmiths, weavers, woodworkers, print makers and jewelers. Prices are reasonable and the quality is exceptional. Seven tall totem poles greet you at the door, serving as staunch sentries for the casino, the premier attraction of Washington's North Olympic Peninsula. 270756 Hwy. 101, Sequim WA (360) 683-7777 or (800) 4-LUCKY-7 www.7cedarscasino.com

# Attractions

# Washington Coast

# World Kite Museum

Long Beach is the favorite destination of kite-flying enthusiasts from all over the Pacific Northwest and even further afield. It has hosted the annual Washington State International Kite Festival for more than twenty years. This is the perfect place for the World Kite Museum. Founded in 1988, it is the only kite museum in North America, but not in the world; it has a sister museum, the Weifang Kite Museum in China. The World Kite Museum has obtained 1,500 kites in its fifteen years, including the David M. Checkley Collection, which is a dazzling array of over 700 kites from Japan, China, Thailand and Malaysia - presented in 1989 in honor of one of the founders of the Washington Kiteflying Association. Among other things, the Checkley Collection is considered to have the most comprehensive selection of Japanese kites anywhere outside Japan. In 2004, the Museum launched a capital campaign to raise money for the purchase of a 10,000-square-foot, two-story building overlooking the beach dunes and the Pacific. The Museum's new home will enable it to offer a wider array of exhibits, workshops and community programs. The World Kite Museum is a true Washington Treasure that should not be missed.  112 - 3rd Street NW, Long Beach WA (360) 642-4020  worldkitemuseum.com

# Attractions
# Kitsap Peninsula

## Exotic Aquatics

Pam Auxier, a medical professional, has a love for the water and all it can offer. Living on Bainbridge Island, she realized there was no dive or kayak shop to fuel her passion. In 1991, she opened Exotic Aquatics as a full-service SCUBA store and added the kayak operation in 1994 to provide everything you need both on and under the water. Pam and her professional staff arrange kayak tours and dives, sell or rent the necessary gear, and provide a comprehensive instruction program. The island is a close-knit community and Exotic Aquatics is well known for its outstanding safety and service, its support of the community and catering to family fun. For example, if you are a diver, you can sample some world-class diving in and around the Bainbridge waters and perhaps see the resident giant Pacific octopus! For kayakers, local destinations include Eagle Harbor, historic Blakely Harbor and a picnic on Blakely Rocks, shooting the Agate Pass currents, or relaxing with a moonlight paddle while watching the distant lights of the Seattle sky-

line. While only a scenic 35-minute ferry ride from Seattle, Bainbridge Island seems like a different part of the world. There are views of Mt. Rainier, bald eagles and osprey, harbor seals, and the migratory birds that frequent the shores and bays. Under water, Puget Sound hosts one of the most diverse marine environments on earth. For anyone who likes the water, Exotic Aquatics can fill your desires. 146 Winslow Way West, Bainbridge Island WA (206) 842-1980 or (866) 842-1980 www.exoticaquaticsscuba.com  www.exoticaquaticskayaking.com

# McCormick Woods Golf Course

Whether you are looking for a better golf course in your area or are vacationing in Washington and want to use your clubs, visit McCormick Woods Golf Course in Port Orchard. Unlike most golf courses, an abundance of natural foliage and wildlife native to the area surrounds McCormick Woods. Also featured is a peaceful, front-row view of Mount Rainier. But what makes McCormick Woods truly unique is their versatility, which is why their course restaurant, Mary Mac's, was voted "Number One" as Best Golf Course Restaurant in *Golf Northwest Magazine* in 2003. Always in the top five, Mary Mac's hosts a chef with a title of "Platinum Dining Chef of the Year." Because McCormick Woods is familiar with single, small and large parties that visit their course every year, the restaurant facilities also cater to small meetings or large dinner parties. In business since 1986 and owned by Shawn Cucciardi and PGA professional Jeff Mehlert, McCormick Woods Golf Course has not only experienced owners, but also a well-trained staff. They are always eager to make your visit memorable and relaxing. Bring your clubs. 5155 McCormick Woods Drive SW Port Orchard WA (360) 895-0130 or (800) 323-0130 www.mccormickwoodsgolf.com

# Karttrak Raceway

Does 49 miles per hour sound fast to you? How about if you're going that fast in a go-kart? Thought so! At Karttrak Raceway in Mt. Vernon, Mike Walker has go-karts with an emphasis on helping you appreciate the sport and art of NASCAR driving. (By the way, if you want your child to try it, kid's cars are limited to 15 MPH.) The facility covers 36,000 square feet of indoor racing and family entertainment. There's an arcade room, snack shop and indoor track featuring Power Wheels, electric cars for younger kids. An upstairs viewing room allows visitors to watch the drivers race around the pretzel-shaped, one-fifth-mile track. There's also a game room with pool tables and big-screen television.

Digital cameras allow racers to take home recordings of their competitions on CDs.

All of this lies under the watchful eye of Mike, a race car fan since he was a child. He aims for a positive, community and family-oriented atmosphere at the track. The idea is to provide a safe, fun place for people of all ages to hang out with friends and enjoy themselves. All sorts of individual, package and corporate specials are offered. If you're really into the sport, you can even rent the entire track by the hour. 3302 Cedardale Road, Mt. Vernon WA (360) 848-1635 www.karttrakraceway.com

# Attractions        Kitsap Peninsula

## Olympic Outdoor Center

Welcome to the exciting sport of kayaking! It is no secret that Olympic Outdoor Center is one of the finest kayak shops with one of the premiere locations for kayaking on the West Coast. Their trip leaders, guides, dock, shop and office personnel are some of the most knowledgeable and customer-oriented in the business. Whether you're a curious beginner or a seasoned paddler, Olympic has something to offer. They have world class paddling in their backyard from the Puget Sound Cascadia Marine Trail and Islands of the San Juans, to the Straights of Juan De Fuca. They cater to youth as well as adults and run one of the largest youth kayak programs in the nation. At Olympic Outdoor Center, kayaking is more than a sport, it is an adventure of the heart, mind and soul. Join them on an adventure and experience the excitement they feel and the wonders they encounter. 18971 Front Street, Poulsbo WA (360) 697-6095 or (800) 592 - 5983 www.olympicoutdoorcenter.com

## Trophy Lake Golf & Casting

The pursuit is the prize at Trophy Lake Golf and Casting in Port Orchard. And the Pacific Northwest has a lot of desirable activities to pursue: golf and fishing, for example. At Trophy Lake, general manager Mark Knowles says the focus and vision is to bring all the great things about the Northwest onto one property. Take the world class-designed golf course, for example. Designed by John Fought, the course offers a daring, risk-reward golf experience with sloping fairways, expansive greens, and more than 80 deep-faced, white sand bunkers placed throughout the course's 7,206 yards. Then there's the clubhouse, emulating a quaint fishing lodge that lends warmth and charm. The Dry Fly Cafe, overlooking the 18th green and a dramatic waterfall that feeds one of Trophy Lake's four stocked fishing lakes, features a home-style menu with generous portions and courteous service. The golf shop offers apparel, merchandise and accessories for the golfer and angler. At the practice facility, PGA professionals provide private or group instruction at natural-grass, state-of-the-art target areas, putting greens and bunkers. So come improve your golf game and fish casting, while enjoying the beautiful setting of Trophy Lake. 3900 SW Lake Flora Road, Port Orchard WA (360) 876-8944 www.trophylakegolf.com

# Bainbridge Garden

A family's 90-year history is rooted in the natural beauty of Bainbridge Gardens on Bainbridge Island. Zenhichi Harui, who came to America from Japan in 1908, created Bainbridge Gardens. By the 1930's, many would travel to see the magnificent sculptured trees and sunken gardens and fountains. Sadly, Zenhichi and his family were forced to leave with thousands of other Japanese Americans during World War II. When they returned, they found the nursery beyond restoration. In 1989, Junkoh Harui, one of Zenhichi's sons who had operated his own nursery business on the island for over 40 years, decided to redevelop Bainbridge Gardens. Today, the 7-acre retail nursery honors the Harui family's living legacy. Japanese red pine trees that the elder Mr. Harui started from seeds brought from Japan grace the grounds and nature trail. The Harui Memorial Garden features an old pear tree that Zenhichi Harui grafted into an exquisite shape. The Serenity Garden showcases Junkoh Harui's blend of Northwest and Japanese garden design. The onsite café serves lunch and espresso. Bainbridge Gardens offers a wide selection of trees and shrubs, perennials, bonsai, garden statuary and gifts for the home and garden. Visit the website for information about special events, classes and guest speakers. 9415 Miller Road NE, Bainbridge Island WA (206) 842 - 5888  www.bainbridgegardens.com

# Gold Mountain Golf Course

Photos by John R. Johnson

At the Gold Mountain golf complex, you can fall in love with the greens and the surroundings. Be assured that the beauty you see will always be preserved the way you found it. That's because the complex is owned by the City of Bremerton. The City has created a full-service golf facility, while preserving important wildlife habitats and a community watershed for future generations to enjoy. Gold Mountain has been named in several publications as the best course in Washington. All that's left is for you to load up your clubs and head to Bremerton to prove it to yourself. After golfing, visit Tucker's Restaurant for casual dinning, good service and pristine views of the Olympic Mountains. The facilities include the Cascade Room, which provides an excellent meeting room for conferences and small corporate retreats, and the Olympic Pavilion, which can accommodate up to 300 people for banquets, weddings and other special events. 7263 W Belfair Valley Road, Bremerton WA. (360) 415 - 5432  www.goldmt.com

# Attractions

## Kitsap Peninsula

## Westerly Marine

Steve and Janis Denton, owners of Gig Harbor's Waterfront Inn, manage two fully crewed luxury charter yachts. The Amazing Grace is a 58-foot Topsail Schooner, which was launched in 1990 to replicate an early 1800s Privateer and looks like it came right off the movie set of "Master and Commander." It has an overall spar length of 83 feet and over 1800 square feet of working sails. When you step below decks, the interior is equally breathtaking with glistening mahogany and old growth fir accented by 14 brass lanterns. The two guest staterooms are stunning and spacious, each with a double berth and their own toilet and sink. Allow the crew to serve you and just sit back and relax or put your hand to the task of learning to sail and navigate. More adventuresome guests or crew may string a hammock between the ratlans and sleep attached to a safety line suspended from the rigging! Week long charters will tour the South Puget Sound, the San Juan Islands and Canadian Gulf Islands or the famous Chatter Box Falls in Princess Louisa Inlet of British Columbia. Amazing Grace was featured in the Tall Ships Festival of Tacoma in July, 2005. The Victory is a fully restored 1974 Daytona 58 classic motor yacht with similar accommodation to the Amazing Grace. Victory also features three double cabins and three heads. Both boats can be chartered together for a dinner cruise or a week long trip. It is fully crewed by staff that will cater to all your needs. Both vessels hail from the Waterfront Inn in Gig Harbor. Call or visit their website for rates and other charter details.  9017 N Harborview Drive, Gig Harbor WA  (253) 278-2438 or (253) 851-0747  www.amazinggracetallship.com

# Attractions

# Seattle Metro

## Blake Island Adventure

Blake Island State Park is a magically beautiful island park just minutes from downtown Seattle by charter boat from Pier 55. With 475 acres of heavily wooded lowland forest, the island's 16 miles of hiking trails and five miles of saltwater beaches provide a natural wonderland on Seattle's doorstep. The cruise on Puget Sound from the Seattle waterfront past the Alki Point lighthouse and Bainbridge Island to Blake Island is a treat all by itself. Visitors to Blake Island can enjoy hiking, mountain biking or tent camping in one of the many campsites provided by Washington State Parks. Black tail deer wander casually through campsites with spectacular views of the Seattle skyline, Mt. Rainier, passing ferries and surrounding islands. Watchable wildlife is a main attraction of the park, with otters, mink, chipmunks, raccoons and a wide variety of birds, including bald eagles, great blue herons, kingfishers and woodpeckers, in addition to the thriving population of black tail deer. With no permanent residents or traffic, the park offers a safe, family-friendly environment with old growth forests, pristine beaches, great picnic and recreational areas and restroom facilities with showers. On the north end of the island, the Tillicum Village Native American Indian Cultural Center offers a gift gallery and a snack bar and features a traditional Indian-style salmon bake, complete with a spectacular stage show of native dances and legends. Getting to the island via passenger tour boat is easy. The trip to Blake Island is a wonderful day tour or a great way to introduce young people to the world of camping. 2992 SW Avalon Way, Seattle WA (206) 933-8600 or (800) 426-1205

## Bill Speidel's Underground Tour

The Underground Tour is a leisurely, guided walking tour beneath Seattle's sidewalks and streets. While you roam the subterranean passages that once were the main roadways and first-floor storefronts of old downtown Seattle, tour guides regale you with humorous stories our pioneers didn't want you to hear. It is fifty years of history with a twist! The tour begins with a seated introduction inside Doc Maynard's, a restored 1890's saloon. Then you walk outside through historic Pioneer Square to three different sections of underground areas, about three blocks in all. Be prepared for the underground landscape to be moderately rugged, where you'll encounter six flights of stairs, uneven terrain and spotty lighting. Dress for the weather and leave your spike heel shoes at home! The tour ends at the Rogues Gallery, where you'll find portraits of Seattle's colorful characters and other displays depicting Seattle's past. Whether you're shopping for shirts, shot glasses, "Sons of the Profits" (the book by Bill Speidel that launched the Underground Tour) or work by local artists, you will be sure to find the perfect memento of your Underground Tour adventure. Doc Maynard's also offers a full menu, with snacks and espresso. It is a great place to unwind after your tour. Upstairs, Doc's game room features pool tables, pinball, darts, vintage video games and sports on TV. Doc Maynard's nightclub is one of Seattle's premiere live music venues, featuring a mix of the Northwest's favorite bands and national touring acts. 608 First Avenue, Seattle WA (206) 682-4646 www.undergroundtour.com

# ACT Theatre

The best contemporary theater in Seattle is otherwise known as ACT. ACT has gone from its original base of 300 subscribers in its 400-seat facility in lower Queen Anne, to its present stature as a nationally-recognized theatre serving nearly 10,000 subscribers, and along the way has received critical acclaim. Just a few of ACT's many awards have been sizable NEA challenge grants, the Washington State Governor's Arts Award and designation as Seattle's Best Theatre by the Seattle Weekly. Forty years ago, ACT Theatre was created by Gregory and Jean Falls to provide a venue for innovative dramaturgy, a goal that still continues long after Gregory's 22 years as artistic director. In recent years ACT has only added to its strengths. In 1994, ACT Theatre and the Housing Resource Group began a new initiative, a collaboration to restore the Eagles Auditorium, a neglected Seattle landmark. The new theatre opened in 1996 to deserved acclaim, reinforcing ACT's national reputation as an outstanding regional theater. Each season ACT presents an exciting mix of American classics and new works by some of the leading contemporary playwrights. Consider a season ticket subscription to enjoy multiple benefits in addition to great theatre.  700 Union Street,  Seattle WA  ( 206 ) 292 - 7676

# Majestic Bay Theatre

In the Ballard neighborhood in Seattle, Kenny and Marleen Alhadeff remember when movie theatres were kept pristine clean, they served real butter on popcorn, and the employees were polite. They have brought back such a place in the renovated Majestic Bay Theatres, but with the addition of modern technology, like the ability to buy tickets online. Built on the site of the oldest continuously operating movie theatre in America, the Majestic Bay combines the names of the original theatre, the Majestic, which opened in 1914, and the Bay, the final incarnation of the original theatre, which closed its doors in 1997 (along the way it was also called the Roxy). The Alhadeffs then opened The Majestic Bay for business in October of 2000. Says a reviewer for the Seattle Times, "It is, in a word, spectacular. Here are theatre owners and designers who truly understand how important it is for movie theatres to have a larger-than-life presence on the street ... [movie goers] are given a feeling of entering a place of elegance and dramas ... The Majestic Bay Theatres are a genuine triumph of architectural and cinematic creativity." Here are a few of the features that rate such praise: Dolby Digital EX sound; stadium seating in all three auditoriums; total compliance with ADA regulations; extensive use of Honduran mahogany and brass; handmade lighting fixtures; and Volga blue marble from Russia on the concession counters and restrooms. The interior décor is so distinctive that a bench from the third floor lobby was used in the movie, Titanic.  2044 NW Market Street, Seattle WA  (206) 781-2229  www.majesticbay.com

# CHAMPS Karting

Experience the thrill of European-style ProKart racing at one of the three CHAMPS Karting locations in the Seattle area: Seattle/Georgetown, Redmond and Mill Creek. CHAMPS features fully enclosed, climate-controlled tracks with innovative zero emissions electric karts that can reach speeds of 35 mph and up to 45 mph for qualifying turbo racers. Strict safety guidelines are standard with the use of helmets, harnesses and safety belts, and the minimum age to race is twelve. CHAMPS offers racing in an upscale sports bar atmosphere with plush leather seating, state-of-the-art surround sound system, wall-to-wall televisions, a game room with pool tables and video arcade style games. The VIP Rooms provide privacy for meetings and  parties, while the concessions stand dishes up pizza, hotdogs, sandwiches, snacks, soft drinks and beer. Wall-to-wall windows allows race viewing from anywhere in the club. Founded by professional racer and software pioneer Mike Conte, CHAMPS features a computerized scoring system that keeps track time to the hundredth of a second. Online ProScores allows racers to maintain their competitive edge while away from the track. From corporate and group events to bachelor parties, racing leagues and walk-in racing enthusiasts, CHAMPS has something for everyone.  5930 Sixth Avenue S, Seattle WA  (206) 768-9800 or (888) 849-9988  www.champskarting.com

# The Driftwood Players

*Photo by Rob Carter*

"A short drive...A quiet stroll down Main Street...Savor the sights and sounds of Edmonds, the friendliest town on the sound. Then treat yourself to a little drama." It all began one day in 1957, over a cup of coffee in an Edmonds living room.  A very keen and talented group of people wanted to form a theatre group.  For more than 40 years, the resulting Driftwood Players have been a cultural assent to the City of Edmonds. The mission of the Edmonds Driftwood Players is to enliven the Edmonds community and the Puget Sound region through quality theatrical productions. Through their pursuit of professionalism and education, it is their goal to both entertain and culturally enrich the community while offering artists and hobbyists the opportunity to hone skills in the performing arts in a supportive atmosphere. Each season The Driftwood Players offer five Mainstage productions on the stage of the Wade James Theatre.  Alternative Stages offer something "short and sweet;" unique one-act entertainments are followed by a dessert buffet in their lobby. The Driftwood Players also present a Classic Movies series. A quarterly dinner theatre reading of new plays puts the focus on Puget Sound playwrights.  Enjoy a three-course dinner with three helpings of brand new theatre at the Café on the Terrace in Mountlake Terrace. In addition, The Driftwood Players offer a series of diverse arts and theatre related classes for adults and children.  950 Main Street, Edmonds WA  (425) 774-9600  www.driftwoodplayers.com

# Attractions

# Seattle Metro

## Olde Thyme Aviation, Inc

Olde Thyme Aviation operates scenic biplane rides in authentic restored antique biplanes at the famous Museum of Flight at Boeing Field in Seattle. The ten planes used in these rides have a history ranging from 1927 to 1944 and are from a private collection in Seattle that are kept in constant airworthiness condition. The planes available are two Travel Airs, two Waco UPF-7's, two Stearman Kaydets, and four Cabin Waco biplanes. Olde Thyme Aviation operates seven days a week on a "first come, first served basis." They do take advance reservations and fly by appointment during the off season. At the end of each ride, passengers are given a "certificate" explaining the type of aircraft in which they have flown and its history. Rides are available as gift certificates. 1222 McGilvra Boulevard E., Seattle WA (206) 730-1412 or (206) 730-1064
www.oldethymeaviation.com

*Photos By Michelle Westmorland*

# Ride the Ducks of Seattle

Ride the Ducks of Seattle has been voted "One of the Must-Dos" in Seattle! You will see Seattle in a WWII amphibious landing craft that has been redesigned to carry thirty-six passengers and one crazy Captain. The Coast Guard-certified Captains will take you on a wacky and informative land and water tour of Seattle. You'll see Pike Place Market, Pioneer Square, the Seattle waterfront, Safeco and Qwest Fields, and then splash into Lake Union to see a spectacular view of downtown Seattle and the famous houseboats. This is not your usual tour: in fact, the Captains are all entertainers and passengers are encouraged to participate in the action. There's sound effects, music and comedy for the entire tour. It's a party on wheels that floats! The Ride the Ducks fleet have all seen real wartime service in Sicily and Normandy as well as South Africa, but now the U.S. Coast Guard ensures that each Duck has been tested and certified to be safe for all aboard. Previous visitors say the 90-minute attraction (60 minutes on land, 30 minutes in the water) was the most memorable thing they did in Seattle. Its guaranteed fun for all ages! Reservations are recommended, but walk-ups are welcome. Private parties and group tours are available.  516 Broad Street, Seattle WA   (206) 441-DUCK (3825) or (800) 817 - 1116  www.ridetheducksofseattle.com

# Smith Tower Observation Deck

Since 1914, the place to go for Seattle's original and most accessible view is the Smith Tower Observation Deck. It puts you in the middle of the downtown skyline and close to Seattle's historic waterfront. The Observation Deck, on the 35th floor, wraps around all four sides of the tower, providing panoramic views of Mt. Ranier and the Olympic and Cascade Mountain ranges. It also provides the closest view in town of Safeco Field, Seahawk Stadium, the Colman Ferry Terminal and Pioneer Square. While at the tower, you must see its crown jewel, the Chinese Room, featuring a hand-carved teakwood ceiling inset with 776 semi-precious porcelain disks. There are also 17th century works of art and a Wishing Chair, nearly 300 years old, that portends marriage within a year to single women who sit in it. Many couples rent the Chinese Room for their fairy tale weddings. The tower, envisioned by New York tycoon Lyman Cornelius Smith, was Seattle's first skyscraper. At 522 feet (160 meters) it was, in 1914, the fourth tallest building in the world. For 50 years, it remained "the tallest building west of the Mississippi," according to a local saying. The exterior of the building is clad in Washington granite and white terra cotta. Interior finishes include hallways and bathrooms lined with Alaskan marble, floors of hand-laid mosaic tiles and a grand lobby paneled entirely in Mexican onyx and watched over by 22 larger-than-life Indian heads. After a $27 million restoration in 1995, the tower is one of the most thoroughly wired buildings in Seattle and is home to many corporate offices and Internet companies. The building's 2,314 windows are encased in bronze frames. Most contain their original 1914 safety glass. Unlike modern skyscrapers Smith Tower windows can be opened and closed. If facts and numbers like that don't impress you, come to the Observation Deck -- the view will, guaranteed!  506 Second Avenue, Seattle WA  (206) 622-4004 or (206) 622 - 3131 (facilities rentals)  www.smithtower.com

# St James Cathedral

In Seattle, St. James Cathedral is noted for its beautiful services, impressive Italian Renaissance-style architecture and extensive outreach to the poor. It serves as a gathering place, a crossroads for learning and a center for the arts. It is a place where ideas are explored in the light of the Gospel of Jesus Christ. Built in 1907, the Cathedral is the other church for the Catholic Archdiocese of Seattle and the parish church for a large and vital community. St. Frances Xavier Cabrini, the first American citizen to be canonized, worshipped in the Cathedral during its early years. In 1994, a restoration and renovation project renewed the beauty of this Seattle landmark, transforming it into a dynamic space for the celebration of the Church's liturgy and for ecumenical, cultural and civic events. The Cathedral's Mary Shrine, designed by Susan Jones, has received national and international architectural awards and is definitely something to behold. 804 Ninth Avenue, Seattle WA (206) 622 - 3559
www.stjames-cathedral.org

# Tillicum Village

Few cities have the natural advantages of Seattle. The surrounding mountains, inspiring waterways and islands create not only spectacular views, but also wonderful opportunities for close to home outings and adventures. One of the most exceptional offerings is the cruise from Seattle's downtown waterfront to Blake Island State Park and the Tillicum Village Northwest Coast Native American Cultural Center. Tiny Blake Island, just off the shore from the site of Seattle's founding settlement Alki Point, is home to Tillicum Village and believed to be the birthplace of the city's namesake, Chief Seattle. Tillicum Village opened in 1962 as a center for the preservation of the Northwest Coast First Nations culture and especially the traditional method of preparing fresh Pacific salmon on cedar stakes around alder wood fires. Tillicum Village encompasses the best of the Northwest. The cruise across Puget Sound to Tillicum Village is followed by the tasty treat of steamed clams in a nectar broth upon arrival at Blake Island. Guests watch as their freshly baked salmon are removed from the fires and released from the five-foot cedar cooking stakes. Following a "potlatch style" feast, a spectacular array of Northwest Coast Native dances and legends are displayed on the elaborately decorated stage. Produced by world famous Greg Thompson Productions, "Dance on the Wind" is an emotionally charged journey through the history and traditions of the First Nations that peopled the coastal areas from Washington State to Southeast Alaska. 2992 SW Avalon Way, Seattle WA (206) 933-8600 or (800) 426-1205  www.tillicumvillage.com

# Space Needle

The symbol of Seattle, the Space Needle is one of the most recognizable structures in the world. In 1959, an unlikely artist was sketching his vision of a dominant central structure for the 1962 Seattle World's Fair on a placemat in a coffee house. The artist was Edward E. Carlson, then president of Western International Hotels. His space-age image was to be the focus of the futuristic World's Fair in Seattle; the Fair's theme would be Century 21. Carlson and his supporters soon found moving the symbol from the placemat to the drawing board to the construction phase was not an easy process. The first obstacle was the structure's design. One drawing resembled a tethered balloon and another was a balloon-shaped top house on a central column anchored by cables. Architect John Graham, fresh from his success in designing the world's first shopping mall (Seattle's Northgate), turned the balloon design into a flying saucer. Since the Space Needle was to be privately financed, it had to be situated on land which could be acquired for public use but built within the fairgrounds. Early investigations indicated such a plot of land did not exist. Just before the search was abandoned, a suitable 120-foot-by-120-foot piece of land was found just 13 months before the World's Fair opening.

Construction, managed by the Howard S. Wright Construction Company, progressed quickly. An underground foundation was poured into a hole 30 feet deep and 120 feet across. It took 467 cement trucks an entire day to fill the hole, the largest continuous concrete pour ever attempted in the West. Once completed, the foundation weighed as much as the Space Needle itself, establishing the center of gravity just above ground. The five level top house dome was completed with special attention paid to the revolving restaurant level and Observation Deck. The top house was balanced so perfectly that the restaurant rotated with just a one horsepower electric motor. The 605-foot tall Space Needle was completed in December 1961 and officially opened on the first day of the World's Fair, April 21, 1962. The Space Needle's elevators were the last pieces to arrive before the opening. New, computerized elevators were installed in 1993. The elevators travel 10 mph, 14 feet per second, 800 feet per minute, or as fast as a raindrop falls to earth. In fact, a snowflake falls at 3 mph, so in an elevator during a snowstorm it appears to be snowing up. Storms occasionally force closure of the Space Needle, but it is built to withstand a wind velocity of 200 miles per hour. The Space Needle has withstood several tremors, too, including a 2001 earthquake measuring 6.8 on the Richter scale. The tallest building west of the Mississippi River when it was built, the Space Needle has double the 1962 building code requirements, enabling the structure to withstand even greater jolts. During the World's Fair, nearly 20,000 people a day traveled to the top and the Space Needle hosted over 2.3 million visitors. Nearly 40 years later, it is still Seattle's number one tourist destination. In 2000, a $20 million revitalization of the Space Needle was completed. The year–long project included construction of the Pavilion Level, SpaceBase retail store, SkyCity restaurant, O Deck overhaul, exterior lighting additions, Legacy Light installations, exterior painting and more. The Space Needle is located at Seattle Center. Whatever your interests - theatre, ballet, opera, professional sports, rock 'n' roll history, roller coasters, science, movies, shopping, exploring or just plain walking around -the city unfurls from the Space Needle.
400 Broad Street, Seattle WA  (206) 905-2100
www.spaceneedle.com

# Attractions

## Skagit Valley

## Airial Balloon Company

For a little adventure and a whole lot of fun, Airial Balloon Company in Snohomish is the perfect place for a unique view of the area, whether you want to simply explore the countryside or to spice up a romance. You'll skim over the waters of Snohomish Valley and glide through the surrounding lowlands. View the green or snow covered Cascades, including Mount Baker and Mount Rainier, for a wide, sweeping picture of some of the most beautiful landscape in Washington. Because Airial Balloon Company truly wants you to have a complete, unique and memorable experience, they offer three different packages seven days a week to fit any occasion, all ending with a toast of a sparking beverage and a personalized French Certificate. If you prefer crisp, beautiful mornings, the Traditional Flight leaves just before daybreak and allows you to witness the spectacular colors of sunrise, traveling through the scenery so that you may watch the dew melt along your journey. You'll be greeted back on the ground with a continental breakfast ready to curb your early appetite. The Sunset Flight offers the awe-inspiring imagery of farmlands and mountain ranges cast in the setting sun, as well as a full-course dinner after your flight prepared by their personal chefs. The third flight is called Romance Aloft, and is strictly for individual couples wanting to share a breathtaking view and an unforgettable experience of the sun disappearing below the horizon, followed by a dozen long stemmed roses presented after the flight and a toast for any occasion. To preserve your memorable experience on their hot air balloons, Airial Balloon Company also features a gift shop open seven days a week, where you can purchase everything from t-shirts to jewelry, or even license plate holders. Come and be swept away!
10123 Airport Way, Snohomish WA  (360) 568 - 3025  www.airialballoon.com

# Harvey Airfield

It's not everyday that an airport is considered a place of entertainment. However Harvey Airfield in Snohomish, a beautiful airstrip carved out of the picturesque Snohomish Valley, is the hot spot for exciting events and activities within its near and far communities. Harvey Airfield offers a wide variety of thrill seeking adventures, including flight training, scenic flights, helicopter rides, skydiving, antique airplane rides and much, much more. The great Northwest is known for its unique and gorgeous landscapes, from the beautiful Cascade and Olympic Mountains to the San Juan Islands, and everything in between. Viewing these treasures from the air, whether it's behind the yoke of an airplane or falling from the sky at 120 miles per hour while skydiving, Harvey Airfield offers an experience one will never forget. While the Curtis Pusher remains the first recorded airplane that flew from the airstrip in 1913, the actual construction of Harvey Airfield wasn't completed until 1944. John and Christina Harvey, homesteaders, who immigrated in the mid-1800's, made a tradition of passing down ownership of the family homestead through generations of Harveys. The Harvey Airfield is currently owned and operated by Kandace Harvey and her family. Today, now home to over three-hundred-and-fifty based aircraft and businesses, Harvey Airfield also boasts an amiable steakhouse restaurant that features breakfast, lunch and dinner. When visiting Snohomish, don't miss visiting Harvey Airfield, where you'll find a fun and professional service-oriented family business. 9900 Airport Way, Snohomish WA (360) 568-1541

# Snohomish Golf Course

Beginners and experts alike will enjoy playing a round of golf at the beautiful Snohomish Golf Course. The 18-hole golf course in Snohomish opened in 1967 and is available for play year-round. The course was designed for golfers of all abilities and measures 6,813 yards from the back tees and 5,345 yards from the forward tees. This is an excellent course to have fun and learn the game. Private lessons are available from Director of Golf Fred Jacobson and Head Pro John Brandvold. Players will enjoy the beautiful mountain views and the gently rolling hills.

The greens are large and are considered some of the best in the state. Snohomish Golf Course also boasts a driving range, two putting greens and a chipping green. Competitive golfers will enjoy the many tournaments hosted here. The tournaments are known for being "the Best Value in Northwest Tournament Golf." Owners Bruce, Dave and Gordie Richards also own two other nearby courses, the Battle Creek Golf Course in Marysville and the Wayne Golf Course in Bothell. If Snohomish Golf Course is too busy or a large tournament is scheduled, play can be arranged on one of the other courses. The Snohomish Golf Course's Pro Shop carries a wide variety of golf equipment and clothing. Players will find the course's café a welcome sight after a day of golf. The food is delicious and the service is impeccable. 7805 147th Avenue SE, Snohomish WA (360) 568-2676 or (800) 560-2676

# Attractions

## Skagit Valley

## Alpacas of Misty Ridge

Alpacas are ordinarily found in the misty highlands of the Andes and extraordinarily found here in Misty Ridge. The owners of one of the fastest growing ranches in North America, John and Shannon Ellis embrace the alpaca lifestyle with enthusiasm and joy. They initially moved to the country for the sake of their two young sons. "Ranching seemed the logical thing to do and we were drawn to alpacas because they're basically hypoallergenic," says Shannon. In February of 2001, they purchased two alpacas. For the family it was love at first sight. In no time at all, the Ellises found themselves caught up in the mystique of the enchanting Andean camelids. Visitors agree, there's magic in the air. With the purchase of a second ranch in 2003, they now maintain two locations and have expanded operations to include close to 200 alpacas at Misty Ridge. Alpaca fleece has many qualities, such as coming in 22 natural colors and it's hypoallergenic. Misty Ridge's Country Store features all sorts of luxurious products crafted from the beautiful fleece. Misty Ridge is a popular destination year round, but a special stop during

annual events like Skagit Valley's famous Tulip Festival You can pick your own tulips, have a family portrait taken in the tulip fields or select a special item from the container of European antiques they bring in each year for the Tulip Festival. In June, Misty Ridge hosts the Skagit Valley Shearing Fest, featuring alpaca shearing, spinning and knitting demonstrations, Andean music and more, for a day of shear delight! 19889 Cedardale Road, Mount Vernon WA (360) 424-0501 or (888)-881-PACA (-7222) www.alpacaranch.com

# Skydive Snohomish

The most exciting way to take in the breathtaking views of Western Washington is to skydive in Snohomish! Whether it's your first leap of faith or your thousandth, Skydive Snohomish has a perfect safety record and provides first class skydiving experiences year round. Located at historic Harvey Field only 20 miles north of Seattle, this drop zone has a convenient location and exciting atmosphere perfect for accommodating jumpers and spectators in groups of any size. Beginners can choose to make a tandem or static line jump for their first experience. The most popular is the tandem skydive. After 30 minutes of training and a 20 minute scenic flight, you will experience the exhilaration of 30 to 60 seconds of freefall excitement while securely harnessed to a highly trained instructor. Freefall is followed by a four to five minute parachute descent featuring a gorgeous, 4000-foot high panoramic view. Skydive Snohomish is perfectly located between the Cascade and Olympic Mountain ranges, overlooks the Puget Sound and San Juan Islands, and has a birds-eye view of the Seattle skyline, Mt. Rainier, Mt. St. Helens and Mt. Baker. Skydiving is a unique extreme sport in that a first-time jumper can embark on the same invigorating venture into human flight as an experienced skydiver with hundreds of jumps. Although there is a weight and age limit, most everyone can live life at 120 miles per hour feeling comfortable and confident at Skydive Snohomish.  9912 Airport Way, Snohomish WA  (866) SKY-JUMP   www.SkydiveSnohomish.com

# Attractions — Skagit Valley

## Woolly Prairie Buffalo Habitat

Dana Jones began with a small herd of bison on a private ranch. However the public's curiosity about these shaggy creatures, so famous in Western history and lore, led her to open the ranch for group tours. Since 1990, thousands of tour guests have come to Woolly Prairie Buffalo Habitat to see these amazing animals for themselves. The grassy, sheltered picnic area is nestled in a shady grove and affords an unobstructed view of the herd of majestic bison. Now in her 19th year of Bison ranching, Dana not only has a deep admiration for these massive creatures, but also a wonderful gift for sharing her knowledge and experiences with visitors. Young children, seniors, and everyone in between will learn something fascinating during their 90-minute visit to the farm. Tour season begins each year on the first weekend of the Skagit Valley Tulip Festival (early April) and extends to September 1. New bison calves are usually born in mid-May, so June, July, and

August are the favorite months to visit. Within hours of their birth, the calves have joined up with the adult herd and are frolicking about in the tall grasses, delighting guests with their antics. Reservations for tours are required with a 10 person minimum group size.
4466 Prairie Lane, Sedro-Woolley WA
(360) 856-0310 or (800) 524-7660
www.BuffaloRanchTours.com

# Viking Cruises

For an exciting and informative cruise around the San Juan Islands, from bird and whale watching to overnight excursions, visit Viking Cruises in La Conner. This company offers cruises ranging from one hour to five days and four nights. Cruises include informative nature tours, cracked crab feasts or catered meals, family reunions, corporate functions, weddings and memorials. "We thrive upon the variety of cruises and the opportunity to show-off this incredible part of the world we so love," say Marci and Bob Plank, owners of Viking Cruises. Located in one of the best migratory bird wintering areas in North America, the off-season (November-March) is a favorite time to view migratory bird populations including waterfowl, seabirds, shorebirds and raptors. It is common to see bald eagles, kingfishers, great blue herons, loons, cormorants and many varieties of ducks, seabirds and shorebirds. Nearby is the March Point Heronry, which is one of the largest heronries in the continental United States with close to 600 active nests. People on board can observe from the large foredeck outside, inside the wheelhouse with the skipper or in the warm cabin below. With 32 large windows on the Viking Star, everyone has a great view. So dress warmly, bring your binoculars and camera, and head for Viking Cruises. Remember, there is always hot coffee, tea or chocolate available onboard!  109 N First Street, La Conner WA  (360) 466-2124 or (888) 207-2333  www.vikingcruises.com

# Attractions

# Skagit Valley

## Outback Kangaroo Farm

The Outback Kangaroo Farm in Arlington was originally supposed to be an ostrich farm. But when Joey Strom, wife of would-be ostrich farmer Ray Strom, bought a wallaby (a small relative of the kangaroo) and brought it home to raise, Ray discovered a previously-unsuspected affinity for the amazing marsupials. Now the Farm is home to seventeen wallabies and ten kangaroos, kept company by llamas, emus, potbellied pigs, parrots, sugar gliders and other exotic creatures, including an ostrich. The Farm was originally a Christmas tree farm, and Ray still sells trees. However, people come year-round to see the animals and take the 40-minute guided tour. Ray explains the nature of these wonderful animals, all of whom have been whimsically named (the wallabies are named after fashion designers and models).

The kangaroos and wallabies are acclimated to human presence and can be petted by visitors. Ray and Joey breed them and they are available as pets, though it's less expensive to enjoy them at the Farm, as they can fetch as much as $3500. Other favorites of visitors to the Farm include Jack, a miniature donkey, and Oreo, a miniature black-and-white horse. The Farm also features a gift shop. 10030 State Route 530 East, Arlington WA (360) 403-7474 www.christmas-treesandroos.com

# Attractions

## The Valley

## Washington National Golf Club

Playing golf at the Washington National Golf Club in Auburn, Washington is as close as you're going to get to the PGA. Not only is the course designed to challenge all players, including professionals, it is also equipped with alabaster sand bunkers imported from Idaho and unique bent grass fairways. Home of the University of Washington's golf teams, Washington National Golf Club features themed golf carts to honor legendary UW sports alumni. They even have a cart in the colors and logo of each PAC-10 school. Owned by Heritage Golf Group, the golf club is extremely dedicated to making everyones experience a memorable one. A few years after opening, the golf club hosted the NCAA Women's National Championship in 2002, as well as several NCAA Regional Championships. Nominated as "Best New Public Course for 2001," the club accommodates more corporate and charity golf events than any other course in Washington. Bring your clubs and reserve your favorite golf cart today. 14330 SE Husky Way, Auburn, WA
(253) 333 - 5000   www.washingtonnationalgolfclub.com

## Northwest Seaplanes

You can see the Northwest Seaplanes difference as soon as you enter their offices at the Renton Municipal Airport. There you will find beautiful antiques, provided for the enjoyment of customers waiting for service. The Adirondack furniture on display provides a much more appealing sight than the drab plastic seats usually found in airplane waiting areas. Northwest also provides free shuttle service from Boeing Field and Seattle-Tacoma International Airport. Clyde Carlson, owner of Northwest Seaplanes, has been in the airline business since 1981, though his first round-trip flight didn't seem to forecast future success when he sold a total of one ticket, and it was

a one-way ticket too. But Clyde didn't give up. He knew there was a market for flights from Puget Sound to the San

Juan Islands and British Columbia, and he proved it. Now he operates a fleet of seaplanes, and his customers include businessmen, adventurers, sportsmen, and anyone else who wants to see the beauty of the Pacific Northwest by the best means available. The seaplanes operated by Northwest are DeHavilland Beavers, tough planes originally designed in the 1940s to serve some of the most rugged coastal terrain in the world. Clyde takes great pride in the fact that his planes are among the best maintained aircraft currently in service, operated by pilots whose professionalism is unexcelled. You'll find information about Northwest's regularly-scheduled flights and charters on their website.  860 W Perimeter Road, Renton WA  (800) 690-0086  www.nwseaplanes.com

# Elephant Car Wash

Whether you're looking for an excellent place to have your car washed or just don't have the time to do it yourself, a visit to Elephant Car Wash at any of its nine locations in the Seattle area is the perfect solution. Home of the huge rotating neon "pink elephant" sign on Battery Street, Elephant Car Wash has a long-standing reputation for quality and service. Founded in 1951, the Elephant Car Wash chain was purchased from the original owners in 1982 by father and son, Bob and Steve Haney, and friend, Mike Hakala. Elephant Car Wash features high-tech hybrid-blend cloth and high-pressure water cleaning, and interior vacuuming and carpet shampooing at extremely reasonable prices. Several times they have been voted "Best Car Wash in the Local Community." But their reputation for excellence spreads beyond the Puget Sound, which is why Elephant Car Wash has been the choice of celebrities, sports figures, political candidates and even U.S. presidents, when they were in Seattle. Elephant Car Wash reclaims the water they use to conserve resources and reduce the risk of pollutants filtering into precious streams, rivers and the waters of Puget Sound. They also work extensively with the Charity Car Wash Program, donating car washes to minimize waterway pollution from fund raiser car washes. With fourteen locations nationwide, the Elephant Car Wash formula for success is its state of the art equipment, employee longevity and commitment to service. 1402 Supermall Way, Auburn WA   (253) 804 - 3498   www.elephantcarwash.com

## Attractions 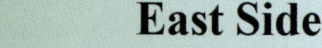  East Side

# Kenmore Air Harbor

When Bob Munro founded Kenmore Air 1946, Seattle was not the bustling metropolis of today.  In fact, folks considered Kenmore to be "out in the sticks." Nearly 60 years later, it's one of Seattle's most desirable neighborhoods and Kenmore Air Harbor, Inc. is a thriving multifaceted business. Bob's gone now but three generations of the Munro family still own and operate the company. Kenmore Air, The Seaplane Airline and its sibling, Kenmore Air Express, fly passengers and cargo throughout the Pacific Northwest. Several times a day, Seaplanes fly from Seattle to Washington's San Juan Islands and Victoria in British Columbia. More than 70,000 passengers choose Kenmore Air annually, with the majority traveling to these two destinations. Kenmore also flies to places throughout Canada's Inside Passage. Kenmore Air Express was launched in 2004 and initially offered wheeled-aircraft service between Seattle and Port Angeles. Service to Portland (Hillsboro), Oregon is the latest addition, and plans are in the works for expansion throughout the Pacific Northwest. It's known as the "center of the seaplane universe" for a reason. Kenmore is famous for taking vintage deHavilland Beaver and Otter aircraft and rebuilding them, seemingly from scratch, into "better than new" state-of-the-art flying machines. Kenmore Air even manufactures their own EDO brand seaplane floats. Today Kenmore Beavers and Otters are in service all around the world. Kenmore Air also offers flight instruction. Both Neil Armstrong (the first man to set foot on the moon) and Harrison Ford are graduates of the program. In fact, Harrison Ford purchased a Kenmore Beaver for his personal use. Kenmore Air is the fast, fun and affordable way to travel. You can even book flights online. Terminals for Kenmore Air, The Seaplane Airlines are located at their original location in Kenmore, in the core of downtown Seattle at the south end of Lake Union, and on the Inner Harbour in Victoria, B.C. Kenmore Air Express maintains terminals at Boeing Field in Seattle, Fairchild International Airport in Port Angeles, and the Hillsboro Airport just west of Portland, Oregon. Kenmore Air is open during daylight hours every day except Thanksgiving and Christmas.   6321 NE  175th Street, Kenmore WA  (425) 486-1257 or (800) 543-9595    www.KenmoreAir.com

# Bubbles Below

If you can survive a wrestling match with an octopus, you can easily wrestle with running a scuba business, right? That is how Bud Gray feels about it. He now puts his efforts into caring for the customers who come through his door at Bubbles Below Dive Center in Woodinville. The incident with the octopus happened in 1970, when Bud was first learning to dive. He and his instructor brought an octopus to the surface and made the mistake of turning their backs on it. The octopus promptly taught Bud a lesson by wrapping up Bud's head, legs and arms. Bud recovered from that mugging and is now one of the Pacific Northwest's most recognized scuba instructors and diving center owners. He became a PADI open water instructor in 1976 and eventually became a master instructor, qualified to teach over 26 specialty courses ranging from Underwater Video to

Marine Biologist. He has certified over 3,000 dive students. Puget Sound is an excellent area to learn to dive as it is rated number three in the world for cold water diving with beautiful blue/green clear waters. Bubbles Below is a place where you can learn the joys of the underwater world. So if you want diving equipment or training, dive into Bubbles Below Dive Center. 17315 140th Avenue NE, Woodinville WA (425) 424 - 3483
www.bubblesbelow.com

# Attractions

# I-5 Corridor

## Chehalis-Centralia Railroad Association

Enjoy the sights, sounds and nostalgia of steam railroading! The Chehalis-Centralia

Railroad Association began with a group of volunteers who ambitiously wanted to restore a 1916 logging locomotive. The locomotive had been in the City of Chehalis Recreation Park for thirty years. After the restoration began, several other railroad cars were acquired. Operations began in the summer of 1989. Trains operate over a nine and a half mile section of tracks that weave through scenic rolling hills and farmland, over several wooden trestles and along the Chehalis River. It is one of the few steam powered standard gauge tourist railroads in the state of Washington. Dinner trains are operated on a seasonal schedule and special charters are available. During late May and early June, special trains are scheduled for school classes. Murder Mystery Dinner Trains are also scheduled on specific dates.
1945 S Market Boulevard, Chehalis WA  (360) 748-9593
www.ccrra.com

## Attractions — I-5 Corridor

# Bonneville Lock and Dam

The Visitor Centers at Bonneville Lock and Dam are located at Bradford Island for the Oregon side and at Washington Shore for the Washington side. Visitors on the Oregon side will find a five-level facility with an observation deck, interior exhibits, a large theater and panoramic views of the Columbia River Gorge, drawing hundreds of thousands of visitors a year to the Dam and Locks. Just a walk away is the viewing area inside the first Powerhouse. Visitors can also watch the navigation lock in operation on the Oregon shore. On the Washington side, visitors will enjoy one of the world's most accessible views of a powerhouse. Inside the powerhouse, visitors will see generators from eighty-five feet above the powerhouse floor, get close-up views of a generator and can examine a rotating turbine shaft through special viewing windows. Visitors can also enjoy fish ladder viewing from this location. Learn about alternative transportation modes, why river transport is an important ecological choice and how power is managed. Learn to identify the local fish types, which are endangered and what is the best time of year to view each type. Educational centers provide films and displays about hydropower, river navigation and the history of this significant area. The Visitors Centers at Bonneville Lock and Dam can be reached by taking Interstate 84 to exit 40 or Washington State Highway 14 to milepost 40. The Bridge of the Gods, located about 2 miles upstream from the Dam, links Oregon and Washington. (541) 374-8820  www.nwp.usace.army.mil/op/b/

## Attractions — South Puget Sound

# Monarch Sculpture Park

Whether you are an art connoisseur or just a curious traveler, make sure to stop by Monarch Sculpture Park in Olympia. With numerous statues and sculptures, the park boasts over eighty local, national and global artists and their creations. Along with several styles and themes of artistic sculptures, the park has a beautiful Japanese Garden and an enormous, rare hedge maze in the shape of a butterfly, one of very few design hedges left in the country. Inspired by European influences including creative affects and layouts from Denmark and Sweden, founders and fellow artists Myrna Orsini and Doris Coonrod opened Monarch Sculpture Park in 1995.

With no entrance fees and eighty acres of displays, Monarch Sculpture Park is a donation-run gathering of professional and emerging artists that come together through Artist-in-Residence Programs or inspiration in celebration of fine art. While the park is available for viewing year-round, special events include painting and recycled art exhibits, workshops and several other events worth viewing. While its purpose is to display, select pieces from the park are available for purchase. Come view the blend of culture and style at the Monarch Sculpture Park. 8431 Waldrick Road SE, Olympia WA  (360) 264-2408

richard taylor

## Attractions — South Puget Sound

# Tumwater Valley Municipal Golf Course

"Firm, fast and friendly" is the motto of the beautiful golf course known as "The Jewel in the Valley." Built by the Olympia Brewery in the late 1960s, Tumwater Valley is an engineering phenomenon. An entire hillside from the brewery's property was used to raise the level of the Deschutes River Valley by some six-plus feet. This made the area into a remarkably good site for a championship 18-hole golf facility. Opening in 1970, Tumwater Valley received rave reviews as one of the driest and most playable year-round golf courses in the Puget Sound Region. *Golf Digest* rated Tumwater Valley in its Top 100 Public Courses nationwide. In 1996, the City of Tumwater purchased the golf course from the owner, Pabst Brewery. During the 2001 and 2002 seasons, Tumwater Valley underwent a dynamic transformation in playing conditions with the installation of a new irrigation system, added drainage and completed golf cart paths throughout all 18 holes. This commitment stepped up maintenance and management of the course ensures that the public will continue to be able to use this fantastic location for recreational and tournament golf.
4611 Tumwater Valley Drive, Tumwater WA
(360) 943-9500 or (888) 943-9500   www.ci.tumwater.wa.us/departments/parks/golf.html

## Attractions — Whidbey Island

# Island Adventure Cruises

If you're a whale watcher or want to be one, and want to hit the water with a company that guarantees you a whale sighting, find it at Island Adventure Cruises in Anacortes. Touring the San Juan Islands, this company prides itself as one of the most experienced and dedicated whale-watching companies in the Pacific Northwest. The crew here has over 100 years of combined experience in the Islands, over 3,300 days with the whales, and has led excursions for over 45,000 satisfied customers. The ships have spacious upper and lower decks and indoor and outdoor seating. The San Juan Islands offer one of the best whale-watching experiences in the world, with calm waters and three pods of resident Orca whales. Thus the company claims a success rate of over 95 percent and guarantees that if you do not see a whale (Orca, Gray, Minke, or Humpback) on the cruise, you will receive a voucher to come again free until you do see one. Says the staff, "What keeps us going is when we hear over and over, 'This was the highlight of our entire vacation.' Every guest is important and deserves our best effort; that's the secret to our success." Tours are available during March through October. Bring warm clothes (layer up), cameras, sunglasses, sunscreen, and comfortable soft-soled shoes.
1801 Commercial Avenue, Anacortes WA   (360) 293-2428 or (800) 465-4604   www.islandadventurecruises.com

# Camaloch Golf Course

Camaloch Golf Course on scenic Camano Island is a wonderful place for golf lovers. Catering to both beginners and seasoned players, this is more than a golf course, it's a golfing community. It's open to the public, but homeowners at Camaloch can enjoy unlimited free golf, as well as swimming pool privileges and bass fishing at the well-stocked lake. Golfers love the smooth, consistent greens and the surprisingly sunny weather. Camaloch is located in Puget Sound's "Sun Belt," protected from the legendary rains of the Washington Coast by the towering Olympic Mountains. The friendly, knowledgeable staff helps to guarantee customer satisfaction at Camaloch, and General Manager Gary Schopf brings knowledge and experience gained as a PGA Professional and puts it to good use. Camaloch offers golfers an exciting challenge, with narrow fairways lined by huge evergreens, heavily-bunkered greens and water hazards. With help always at hand, this par-72 course is a great place to learn the ins and outs of golf. There's a Pro Shop where the staff will help you find the equipment you need, a deli and other amenities at this unique course. 326 NE Camano Drive, Camano Island WA (360) 387 - 3084 or (800) 628-0469
www.camalochnews.org

# Anacortes Kayak Tours

If you want a Pacific Northwest kayak tour that's off the beaten path, visit Anacortes Kayak Tours in Anacortes. It's the only kayak operation that does not require you to take a long ferry ride to get into the San Juan Islands. Says the staff, "Our handpicked sea kayaking trip locations allow you to explore the least-developed shorelines in the San Juan Islands. Off the beaten path, we are free to enjoy some of the most incredible scenery that the Pacific Northwest has to offer without having to worry about crowded beaches, noisy yacht traffic and hordes of other kayak tour groups." You will be comfortable and entertained as their expert staff guides you through the peaceful side the San Juans. Owners Megan and Erik Schorr traveled the world and paddled on five continents and can say with confidence that the best sea kayaking on the planet is "right here in the San Juan Islands." Both born and raised on the shores of this magnificent location, they feel fortunate to be able to share it with visitors from all over the world. Here is their description of just one of the tour locations, Cypress Island: "This is the postcard location for kayaking in the San Juan's. It boasts the longest stretch of undeveloped shoreline in the archipelago. Wildlife abounds here, particularly in the Cone Islands, a cluster of National Wildlife Refuges just offshore. We paddle here for close encounters with seals, porpoise and bald eagles. From Cypress Island we have stunning views of Mt. Baker and the Cascade Mountains. With pocket beaches, hidden bays, island clusters and amazing views around every corner, Cypress Island is the premier destination for kayaking in Washington State." Bring a hat, sunscreen, layered clothing and shoes appropriate for the beach.

1801 Commercial Avenue, Anacortes WA  (360) 588-1117 or (800) 992 - 1801

# Candy, Ice Cream, Bakeries & Coffee

# Candy, Ice Cream, Bakeries & Coffee
## Olympic Peninsula

## The Buzz

You are invited to buzz on in to the best coffee house in Sequim. Founded in 2003 by owner and Queen Bee Deb Ferguson, The Buzz Ice Cream, Coffee & Sweets Café shares space with her other business, BeeDazzled, an Eclectic Mix of Ever-Changing Finds. It recently celebrated a fourth year as the place to go for antiques, gifts and much more. The bee theme came about years ago when Deb discovered that her name, Deborah, means "honey bee" in Hebrew. The Buzz's inviting interior includes one wall that is alive with hand-painted, larger-than-life bees. Two of the highlights of your visit will be the coffee and well-renowned Olympic Mountain Ice Cream. Deb's search for the best ended with Caffé Vita, specialty coffee roaster in Seattle. The Buzz features an antique pastry case stocked with delectable pastries baked fresh daily in the kitchen of the "itty bitty Buzz," a second location. The Buzz is an ever-evolving creative endeavor. Customers enjoy art shows featuring a different artist-in-residence monthly and live music on the weekends. For those who enjoy the game of Scrabble, the Queen Bee invites beginners to experts to bring their Scrabble boards Sunday afternoons. The newest offering is MOVIES! Enjoy foreign, independent and quirky theme weeks.

The Buzz  128 N Sequim Avenue, Sequim WA  (360) 683-2503
BeeDazzled 130 N Sequim Avenue, Sequim WA  (360) 582 - 1936
itty bitty Buzz 110 E First Street, Port Angeles WA
(360) 565-8080
www.thebuzzbeedazzled.com

*Photos by Charlotte Watts*

# Candy, Ice Cream, Bakeries & Coffee             Kitsap Peninsula

## Hot Shots Java

At Hot Shots Java in Poulsbo, David and LeAnne Musgrove feel that life is just too short for bad coffee. So when they brew a pot, they make sure it's good enough to make their store a place where everyone in town loves to hang out. Hot Shots is definitely a community gathering spot. Senior citizens gather here, as do young mothers with babies and kids, and even teenagers. The school kids of coffee-drinking age receive a discount when they bring their books

with them and study. Internet access is provided and there's a lounge with a big-screen TV. There's live music three nights a week and open microphone on Friday.

David and LeAnne are also involved in the community and support local artists. Two of their walls are dedicated to displaying the work of students from the Northwest College of Art. On another wall, other local artists' works are displayed. Visitors and tourists are appreciated here, too. As a visitor, "you are the bonus of our business, the icing on the cake, and you're always welcome," says LeAnne. 18881B Front Street, Poulsbo WA (360) 779-2171

## Island Ice Cream & Coffee

Island Ice Cream & Coffee is locally known for having the best ice cream in town, and the largest selection too. It's so good you'll be surprised the shop isn't constantly mobbed, especially since it's the first thing you see when you debark from the Bainbridge Island ferry. The community calls it one of the best-kept secrets on the island. The comfortable, casual atmosphere and friendly staff

provide the perfect environment for a little ice cream indulgence. The coffee is great too. You'll want to try their frappes, made authentically with crushed ice, ice cream, coffee, milk, and your choice of a variety of flavors. Loral Ann Jorza was an employee of Island Ice Cream & Coffee before she became the owner in 2002. Because she loves young people and

teens, her employees are young locals who need summer or after-school jobs. Many of them go away to college and come back to work for her during the summer break. Loral Ann loves this business because ice cream brings fun along with it; everyone's happy when they're ordering ice cream. You'll see people of all ages there when you stop by. You're welcome to go in and hang out, whether you're buying ice cream or a cup of coffee. Take advantage of the wireless Internet connection to get a little work done on your laptop, or just drop by to say hello to Loral Ann. 584 Winslow Way E, Bainbridge Island WA (206) 842 - 2557

# Candy, Ice Cream, Bakeries & Coffee — Seattle Metro

## Cookies

Photo by Thomas M. Barwick

Photo by C.B. Bell

Photo by Thomas M. Barwick

When you hear the word "cookies," does your mouth water? Are you thinking about eating, savoring, baking, decorating? At Cookies, in the Ballard neighborhood of Seattle, Caryn Truitt and Betsey Toombs will accommodate you. They sell all manner of cookie supplies including plates, jars, cutters, and anything and everything that goes into preparing and serving cookies, right down to the apron you'll want to wear when tending the oven. Cookies is a place where people of all ages can connect with childhood memories. It's a nostalgic business at a time when people want to reconnect with home and family. This is truly a one-stop place for entry to the cookie world. So if you're thinking "Cookies," Caryn, Betsey and staff are waiting for you. They say if they don't have it, they will get it. And if they can get it, you can bake it.  2211 NW Market Street, Seattle WA  (206) 297 - 1015
www.cookiesinseattle.com

## UpperCrust Bakery

Located in the heart of Magnolia Village in Seattle, the Upper Crust Bakery with its delicious pastries is truly a Washington Treasure that shouldn't be missed. The delightful aroma of freshly-baked goodies greets visitors before they even open the door. Mouths will be watering in anticipation when customers first lay eyes on the many varieties of treats in this bakery. The Upper Crust Bakery is known for its incredible Pecan Sticky Buns, Apple Pockets and Danish. One bite of these delicious treats will have customers coming back for more. The bakery's delectable Peach Danish are a favorite, as are the light and flaky croissants and the spicy Jalapeno-Cheese Rolls. The bakery specializes in Scandinavian and other European recipes such as Kringle, Smorkager and various strudels. The bakery is owned by Geoff, Karla and Ken Haigh. Karla creates beautiful cakes and petit fours for any occasion. She also can decorate them to your design and they taste as good as they look! From June through October, the Upper Crust Bakery operates a stall at the Magnolia Farmer's Market on Saturdays.
3204 W McGraw Street, Seattle WA   (206) 283-1003

# Husky Ice Cream & Deli

Husky Ice Cream and Deli has been a community gathering place for more than seventy years. Opened in 1932, it has always been a family business. It is currently owned by Jack Miller and managed by Ian, the eldest of 23 grandchildren of the founders. There is an excellent sandwich counter and a large selection of domestic and imported grocery items. The scores of flavors of justly famous ice cream are made right on the premises, and you can't miss the delectable array of chocolates and candies. Husky's also offers catering for weddings and other events. This well-loved member of the community is a must-visit for longtime loyal clientele and brand new customers. For a day at the beach or for browsing around this historic neighborhood, head on over to West Seattle and treat yourself to a delicious taste of tradition at Husky Ice Cream and Deli.

4721 California Avenue SW, Seattle WA
(206) 937-2810
www.huskyicecream.com

# Candy, Ice Cream, Bakeries & Coffee — Seattle Metro

## Remo Borracchini's Bakery

Whether you're planning a celebration or need to pick up something elegant for a last minute occasion, Remo Borracchini's Bakery has just the thing you're looking for. Located in Seattle, Washington in the heart of the Italian community, Remo Borracchini's Bakery carries everything from their popular cakes to cookies, biscotti, éclairs and doughnuts. Borracchini's also has a large deli that boasts an abundant selection of meats and cheeses, as well as homemade bread straight from their own brick ovens, and olive oil imported all the way from Italy. Founded in 1922 and passed down by parents Mario and Maria Borracchini of Italy, owners Remo and his wife Betty and their family run the bakery themselves to maintain the famous tradition that makes their selections so special. Borracchini's carries only the highest caliber of cakes for weddings, birthdays, anniversaries, and even bar mitzvahs. They never use preservatives or bake anything from store-bought mixes. They have several different sizes, flavors, combinations and styles of cakes to make your occasion memorable. For weddings or larger events, Borracchini's offers several catering options, including delivery services that cover several areas in Washington, as well as packages to make planning easier. If you're still not convinced that Remo Borracchini's Bakery is the perfect place for your event, they also carry a large selection of champagne and wine at unbeatable prices.

2307 Rainier Avenue South, Seattle or call them at (206) 325-1550

## Mad Hatter Party

Glen and Darlene Petersen have introduced a unique tea and dress up trunk concept in Edmonds, a short distance from the ferry dock. Ladies from ages 6 to 96 are delighted as the Mad Hatter greets and serves tea. Alice conjures up Wonderland delectable goodies from her kitchen (Queen of Hearts Cherry Tarts, White Rabbit Carrot Cake, and Eat Me Cookies) for the elegant tea hearkening back to Victorian times. A trip down the rabbit hole allows participation in the Alice Trunk, an entire room filled with hundreds of special occasion dresses, hats, shoes, boas, parasols, pearl strands, jewelry and more. Helping each other select elegant to outrageous ensembles is hilarious fun. In fact, as Alice would say, "It's enough to make a cat bark!" Alice, in her petticoats and pinafore, snaps many photos that are yours to keep for memories. Also, you may select from a boutique of unique handmade items for sale. Be it a birthday party, shower, or just two hours of fun, you will enjoy this one-of-a-kind occasion for your party. There is intimate seating for six to ten ladies. Bring your daughter, granddaughter, niece or friends for a time of sheer fun and supreme delight! 10519 231st Street SW, Edmonds WA (206) 542-8193 AliceTeaAndTrunk@yahoo.com

# Pat's on the Ave.

Are you looking for a friendly place where everybody knows your name? Then introduce yourself to Pat's on the Ave. and you will soon become a regular. At this family business, the soda fountain of yesteryear meets the espresso bar of today. With third-generation roots on Queen Anne Hill, owners Pat and Julie Nolan work alongside daughters Julianna and Isabella and brother Jeff. They dish up good service and a menu that features Trident seafood salmon burgers, fresh sandwiches and ice cream treats. As modern as it is traditional, Pat's on the Ave. provides free Wi-Fi Internet access so you can come on up and plug on in. We know you will enjoy this fun and comfortable place, so join the family for good coffee, good food and good conversation. 1905 Queen Anne Avenue N, Seattle WA (206) 284-0121

# The Tea Cup

How do you like your tea? Strong and black with breakfast? A subtle oolong in the afternoon? A traditional green or herbal blend? If you can say it, you can find it at The Teacup in Seattle. Just let owner Elisabeth Knottingham show you how to slow down, pamper yourself, and enjoy the tea experience. There is every type of tea you can imagine (over 150 teas are on the list), and of course the tea ware to enjoy at home. Educating people about teas is what Elisabeth and her staff do well. And the customers appreciate it to the tune of 200 pounds of loose leaf tea each week. The staff tastes some 2,000 teas each year to select those that make it to The Teacup's list. Whatever your flavor choice in tea, there's a just-right cup waiting for you at The Teacup. 2207 Queen Anne Avenue N, Seattle WA (206) 283 - 5931 www.seattleteacup.com

## Candy, Ice Cream, Bakeries & Coffee — Skagit Valley

## Peggy's Bakery Organica

Peggy, her son Ryan, and their partner Russ believe in bread: bread as the Staff of Life, made by hand in the same environment that produced it when it was considered by the world as the Staff of Life. Their goal is simple: to make the most nutritious and the most delicious bread in the world. When something is needed they take the raw ingredients and process them in-house, right at their bakery. They make their own nut butters for cookies; spreads, many from locally grown nuts; jams and jellies from locally produced fruits; and herbs grown by the bakery itself. There is no wheat in their bakery, no refined sugars and no flour. All of their products are whole grain faro, Triticum dicoccum and Triticum spelta, dating back to ancient Turkey. Emmer is grown here in Mazama, the only field in North America. Spelt is grown in Marlin, produced by Lena Lentz of Lentz Spelt Farms. The rye is grown in Tonasket. All the grains are fresh milled in Peggy's Bakery as they are being used! Recently Peggy, Ryan and Russ have expanded, creating Bombadil's Book & Brew, an eatery featuring Washington State wine and beer. Menu items are made from ingredients produced by local farms, seasonally available, and grown in soils regenerated by conscientious farming practices. The bookstore is an eclectic collection of used first edition hardbacks. Peggy chose the name because Tom Bombadil, of Tolkien's Fellowship of the Ring, is a character that cannot be touched by evil. Bombadil's offers the highest quality food available, grown locally in Washington State, to feed body, mind and spirit. They are open seven days a week. 301 Washington Street, Sedro-Woolley WA (360) 855-1688

## Candy, Ice Cream, Bakeries & Coffee — East Side

## Tiger Mt Tea Co

Imagine feeling transported to exotic places as you are greeted with enchanting fragrances upon entering the door to Tiger Mt Tea Co. Owner Wayne Spence offers a wide variety of whole leaf teas, herbal tisanes and tea accessories from all those places you only dream about. Not only do they carry wonderful teas, they also have unique handcrafted tea gifts, custom tea baskets and books about tea. Their "Tea of the Month Club" would be a welcomed gift for any tea lover in your life. Tiger Mt Tea Co has an organic and earth-friendly atmosphere that is a relaxing respite to the hustle and bustle of the busiest of days. Come in for a wonderful cup of tea and a rich and intellectual conversation with Wayne and his clientele. Tea tasting and sample experts present informational seminars and workshops to enhance your understanding and enjoyment of the many specialty tea varieties. Stop by this beautiful and aromatic shop when you are in the neighborhood. 317 NW Gilman Boulevard # 47, Issaquah WA (425) 391 - 5009 www.tigermtteaco.com

# Boehms Candies Inc

In 1940, an Austrian mountain climber of ethnic Swiss descent immigrated to the United States. Julius Boehm was attracted to the Pacific Northwest by the lure of the Cascades, and he and a partner opened a candy making shop in the north end of Seattle. In 1956, Julius and the business moved to Issaquah, where he built the Edelweiss Chalet above the candy factory. Julius also left his mark on the landscape by building the Luis Trenker Kirch'l, a replica of a 12th Century chapel near St. Moritz in Switzerland. Visitors to Boehms Candies can now tour Julius' house, as well as the candy-making facilities. Julius collected art, music boxes and toys, and filled his house with delightful reminders of his Alpine heritage. In the candy rooms downstairs, you can watch a variety of sweets, from Victorian creams to peanut brittle, being prepared and see the elaborate traditional hand-dipping process for making filled chocolates. The tour ends in the Kirch'l, the chapel that Julius dedicated to mountain climbers who have lost their lives while climbing. (Julius himself scaled Mt. Rainier when he was 81.) After the tour, you are invited to visit the gift shop and enjoy specialties such as Mozart-Kugeln and the chocolate-caramel Mount Rainier. 255 NE Gilman Boulevard, Issaquah WA (425) 392-6652 www.boehmscandies.com

# Theno's Dairy
# Vivian's Pride Ice Cream

If you love ice cream, come to Theno's Dairy in Redmond. Theno's is the kind of place people become attached to – local residents who have had to relocate have been known to have friends ship them emergency rations of Vivian's Pride Ice Cream by air freight. All the ice cream here is homemade, and there are flavors and ingredients you won't find anywhere else. Sandy and LeRoy Bloor were high school sweethearts who married in 1965. LeRoy left his night-shift job for a day job at Theno's Dairy so he could spend more time with his children. He couldn't have picked a better place as family has always come first at Theno's, originally owned by the Theno brothers. (Vivian's Pride is named for their mother.) Sandy later got a job managing the retail store and, in 1991, the Bloors got the chance to own the whole place. Their daughter Kim is now the manager, and son Douglas also works for the family business. Theno's began as a farm with its own herd of dairy cows, but in 1985 the herd was sold off as the suburbs expanded into the farmlands of Redmond. Nowadays, the only cow left

is the big fiberglass one out front – children love to ride on her back, and she's highly photogenic. But even though they can't milk their own cows, the Bloors still use locally-produced milk that's hormone-free. All-natural ingredients are an important part of the Bloors' commitment to quality. As Sandy puts it, "We don't make it if it's not good." There have been a few concessions to modern tastes: Theno's offers non-fat frozen yogurts in addition to old-fashioned ice cream – and it's the best frozen yogurt you'll ever eat. 12248 156th Avenue NE, Redmond WA (425) 885-2339

## Candy, Ice Cream, Bakeries & Coffee — East Side

# The British Pantry

The British Pantry in Redmond is the place to visit when you are in the mood for authentic British food and delicacies. The traditional fare is sure to satisfy, as even the British Royal Family has dined on the delicious cuisine. Owned and operated by the Redman family since 1978, The British Pantry has something for everyone with its British restaurant, bakery, incredible gift shop and imported food specialties. The restaurant, Neville's at The British Pantry, serves lunch, afternoon tea and dinner. Many British favorites are featured including tea cakes and crumpets at afternoon tea and sausage rolls, roast beef with Yorkshire pudding, shepherd's pie and the best fish and chips in the States at heartier meals. The bakery is known for its

savory pies, pastries, tarts and cakes, all handmade on the premises daily. Also famous for its fruitcakes and Christmas puddings, the bakery uses recipes passed down through three generations of bakers in the Redman's family. The gift shop is filled with a wonderful array of collectibles and treats. Visitors can choose from imported teas and gifts, exquisite English bone china, and specialty sweets and chocolates, as well as imported traditional

British foods. President Mavis Redman, along with her son Neville and daughter Alvia, have transformed the business from its humble beginnings with 1,000 square feet to its present day 4,600-square foot enterprise. This popular and unique business has been featured on numerous television programs. The British Pantry can boast of providing British fare on several occasions for members of the British royal family when they visited, a tribute to their authentic taste treats! 8125 161st Avenue NE, Redmond WA (425) 883-7511 www.thebritishpantryltd.com

# Candy, Ice Cream, Bakeries & Coffee

# South Puget Sound

## Wagner's Bakery & Café

Wagner's European Bakery & Café in Olympia is the oldest bakery and café in the Puget Sound area. Since 1939, four generations of the Wagner family have owned, operated or worked at the business, consistent in their commitment to bring their customers the very best. The friendly atmosphere provides an ideal spot for community gathering, and a gracious and attentive staff ensures the customers are well taken care of. Wagner's is also renowned for their distinctive and beautiful wedding cakes. Located one block north of Hands On Children's Museum and two blocks north of the Capitol Building, Wagner's bakery is the perfect place to enjoy breakfast, lunch or dessert when out visiting the city's sites. In addition, the family also owns and operates the Marketplace Bakery, located in the Olympia Farmer's Market and the Lacey Farmer's Market. The Wagner family's dedication to quality food, good service and community involvement is the reason Wagner's is still thriving after 66 years. 1013 Capitol Way S, Olympia WA (360) 357-7268

## Lattin's Country Cider Mill

*Photos By Paul & Shirley Bragg*

The word "farm" is truly defined at Lattin's Country Cider Mill and Farm in Olympia. They boast over twenty-three varieties of pies, including their popular white chocolate mousse with raspberry topping, large apple fritters and warm doughnuts. Lattin's also offers a full assortment of produce fresh from their farm. In fact, owner Carolyn Lattin and her late husband Victor began producing their award-winning cider with just a small apple press thirty years ago. Now with the aid of their two daughters, Carolyn continues to fulfill that just-out-of-the-oven craving for country style food. Becoming nationally renown, Lattin's Country Cider Mill and Farm won two awards from the North American Farmers' Direct Marketing Association in 2004 for making the best cider and strawberry jam in the nation! They also have a petting farm, complete with everything from a pony to peacocks. A horse-drawn carriage provides transportation to their pumpkin patch during the fall. The farm is rich with history, continuing the truly homemade tradition of good, healthy products and a comfortable atmosphere. 9402 Rich Road SE, Olympia WA (360) 491-7328

# Candy, Ice Cream, Bakeries & Coffee — Whidbey Island

## Whidbey Pies

When was the last time you took a bite of loganberry pie? Let's see, loganberry? Yes, you remember, it's that plump, ruby colored berry, a cross between a blackberry and a raspberry. Oh yeah! Well, head for the Greenbank Farm on Whidbey Island and the Whidbey Pies cafe. There, owner Jan Gunn proudly sells buttery crusted loganberry pies, homemade soups including salmon chowder, and sandwiches. Besides loganberry, pies include apple, marionberry, blueberry and cherry. Says Jan in explaining her baking and business philosophy, "Make the best product possible. Make sure it meets your own high standards. Whatever you do, be sure you can be proud of it." She sells pies frozen and ready to bake, so when you get it home you can say, "I baked it myself." Explaining that she considers each pie a work of art, Jan says, "We have devoted ourselves to the lost art of artisan pie making since 1986. Each pie is a unique and intimate experience. With every pie the pastry is tender and rich; the berries dense and not too sweet. When you have perfect fruit you don't need lots of sugar. Whidbey Pies are made with a light touch from the finest ingredients, plump fruit, sweet unsalted butter, cane sugar and unbleached flour." Jan and staff use no preservatives or artificial flavors in their pies.
765 Wonn Road, Greenbank WA   (360) 678-1288
www.greenbankfarm.com

# Galleries

# Galleries

## Olympic Peninsula

## Pacific Traditions Gallery

An eclectic collection featuring local and nationally recognized Native artists of distinction is shown by Pacific Traditions Gallery. The works embody generations of tradition, as well as creative contemporaries' visions of Native art today. Among the tribes represented are the Coast Salish, Cowichan, Nuu-Chah-Nulth, Tlingit and Haida, as well as tribes recognized across the nation. Proprietress Mary Hewitt was "gifted" the gallery from the Jamestown S'Klallam Tribe in 2000. She is honored that the tribes have trust in her insight about Native art and their traditions. Mary strives to maintain a relaxed atmosphere so you feel no pressure in the Gallery, allowing you to enjoy the history, stories and ambiance of Native American art. Recent examples of the art available in the Gallery include a Wolf headdress by Micah McCarty, a member of the Makah Nation; carved cedar plaques by Leonard Sylvester, Penelkut from the Kuper Island Reserve; and traditional reproductions crafted by Gary Buckman of the Oglala Lakota tribe. When you visit this Gallery, you will experience insights into the unique cultural significance and history of Native arts and its artists. 637 Water Street, Port Townsend WA (360) 385-4770 www.pacifictraditions.com

# Williams Gallery

Normally, the term "gallery" might bring to mind a sterile environment filled with encased artifacts and track lighting. At William's Gallery in Port Townsend, strolling through their doors is similar only to what we would imagine walking through a rainbow might be like. Bold colors, sensuous designs and textures are a feast for artistic appreciation. William's Gallery has every nook and cranny filled with gorgeous displays of ceramics, jewelry, wood, textiles, photography, paintings and much more. Balancing a colorful, lively atmosphere with a homey yet pristine structure, owners Bill and Wendi Metzer boast an authentic gallery full of regional and worldwide art. Wendi, a recognized and well-respected jeweler, has been nationally featured in magazines along with her vast and exquisite line of jewelry. While their gallery is fairly new, both Bill and Wendi have extensive experience in business and art. In a shorter time than most, they have created a thriving place in the community of Port Townsend.
914 Water Street, Port Townsend WA
(360) 385 - 3630
www.williams-gallery.com

## Galleries — Olympic Peninsula

# Blue Whole Gallery

Opened in June 1997, the Blue Whole Gallery brings together 37 emerging and well-known artists in a creative celebration of fine art. Works created by our members are as varied as the natural splendor of the Olympic Peninsula. The Gallery hosts a reception for its new monthly show on the First Friday of every month and the public is invited. The 2000+ square foot Gallery is centrally located in downtown Sequim, where you will find the people to be informal and friendly. The name of the Gallery is derived from a term pilots use to describe the "blue hole" in the skies above Sequim, an atmospheric phenomenon which gives Sequim its reputation for sunny weather. The "hole" was changed to "whole" to convey the overall diversity of media styles represented in the Gallery, making the sum greater than the individual parts. When visiting this part of the beautiful state of Washington, plan a visit to the Blue Whole Gallery. You will not be disappointed. 129 West Washington Street, Sequim WA (360) 681-6033 bluewholegallery.tenforward.com

## Galleries — Washington Coast

# Fusions
# The Artist's Gallery

Fusions is a splash of color on the main drag in Ocean Shores that is "absolutely guaranteed to satisfy your art fix." It's a gallery that showcases the talents of local artists. As owner Kelly May designed it, the gallery is a place where artists can meet the community, and a place that is founded on the gifts of the many talented people who live in Ocean Shores and the surrounding area. The art works you will find here are almost all one-of-a-kind; this is an extraordinary, special place. With 70 artists participating, Kelly and Manager Sharon Armstrong have created a happy, exciting home for art. Every Saturday you can meet one of the artists in person. The creations range from jewelry to glass and everything in between. In the gallery, the rooms are set up to show off the different techniques. Kelly and Sharon invite you to come in and find out what Fusions is all about – bringing together the arts for everyone's enjoyment at the town's "newest, boldest art gallery." 834 Point Brown Avenue NE, Ocean Shores WA (360) 289-2811 www.oceanshores.com/fusions_gallery

# Galleries — Kitsap Peninsula

## Image2Art by Winifred

Elegance. Essence. Extraordinary. International award winning photo artist Winifred Whitfield creates fine art and heirloom quality images for her clients. Image2Art specializes in Intimate Portraiture for Women. "Capturing the feminine spirit, whether soft or powerful, sensuous, playful or a little wicked, is what I love to do best," expressed Winifred. In addition to required digital mastery, Winifred establishes trusting relationships so her clients feel comfortable showing their innermost feelings as a key to her beautiful portraiture. "Capturing the image is just the beginning for me," said Winifred. She then transforms the image into an artistically enhanced or a very painterly portrait.

She feels that "I love showing my clients just how beautifully I see them." Lifestyle, wedding, graduate, family, children, and corporate photographic services are provided by Winifred through her affiliate business, Big Valley Photo Art. 27248 Big Valley Road, Poulsbo WA  (360) 779-1375

## The Brick House

There's a wonderful new and inviting space in Puyallup that welcomes collectors, artists and anyone else in the Puyallup area who loves art. After nine months of hard work and preparation, husband and wife team Kim and Shelley Marzolf opened The Brick House Gallery with a catered wine celebra-

tion in November 2004. The Brick House features an eclectic assortment of works by contemporary artists and provides first-rate framing services as well. The Marzolfs bring twelve years of experience in the art world to their new business, which has truly been a labor of love. The gallery's home, a building dating back to 1910, needed extensive renovation. Shelley estimates that cleaning the brickwork required six thousand pounds of sand. But persistence paid off and in the short time since its opening The Brick House has already established itself as a Puyallup fixture, participating in such events as the Downtown Art and Wine Walk. In addition to displaying local artists' works and providing expert framing assistance, the Marzolfs also offer their services as art locators, helping people find works that meet very particular specifications. Plans are underway to install seating and a flat screen display that will allow customers to view works of art at full size instead of relying on catalog pictures.  110 E. Stewart Avenue, Puyallup WA  (253) 435-1800

# Galleries                                                    Kitsap Peninsula

## Raven Blues

Ravens are intelligent birds attracted to bright and shiny objects: just the sort of things you'll find at Raven Blues. Peggy Fiorini and Larry Girardi (pictured) have assembled an eclectic mix of wonderful decorative items from fine art, handmade furniture and art glass to exquisite jewelry and women's "Art to Wear" apparel. Feather your nest with work by some of the most talented craftsmen from Washington and throughout the USA, as well as celebrity artists. Examples include Angela Cartwright's photography (The Sound of Music, Make Room for Daddy and Lost in Space) and whimsical sculpture by Robert Shields (of Shields & Yarnell mime and television fame). "Dare to wear different" with some of the finest women's jewelry and apparel available including the collectible Double D Ranchwear line of clothing and accessories. At Raven Blues they're sure you'll agree that there is definitely a lot to "crow" about. 18827 Front Street NE, Poulsbo WA (360) 779 - 5662

# Roby King Galleries

Photos by Wes King

Wes King and Andrea Roby-King, residents of Bainbridge Island for 27 years, officially opened the Roby King Galleries in 1990. With educations in Fine Art, they spent their years prior to owning the gallery as potters and created a small but nationally recognized line of pottery. The Kings stress their passion for art fills their lives both personally and professionally, and "since our early days as painters and potters, we have sought to promote and give venue to work that inspires us." Roby King Galleries exhibits representational art, from classical realism to Russian impressionism to contemporary. They represent more than two dozen artists, primarily oil painters, although the roster also includes watercolor and pastel painters, as well as textile, sculpture and mixed media artists. Many of the artists are Bainbridge Island residents or from the greater Northwest region. Others such as nationally recognized oil painter Cheri Christensen, now of Santa Fe, were onetime residents of the Island and still maintain their ties with Roby King Galleries. At their website you can also view works by other notable artists such as Diane Ainsworth, Mary Carlton, Hidde Van Duym, Phyllis Ceratto Evans, Pamela Fermanis, Pam Ingalls, Faye Judson, Louise Lamontagne, Patty Rogers, Frank Samuelson, David Turner, Lael Weyenberg, and Tatiana Zaits, but nothing is more enjoyable than going into the gallery to see it all in person. 176 Winslow Way E, Bainbridge Island, WA (206) 842 - 2063 www.robykinggalleries.com

*Going Separate Ways by Cheri Christensen   Oil 24x24*

*Signs of Spring by Raenell Doyle   Oil 18x24*

# Galleries                                          Seattle Metro

# Agate Designs

A family business started in 1965 by Jim and Martha Kullberg has bloomed into a second generation business that is still family owned and operated. Agate Designs believes man can duplicate almost anything on earth, but he cannot match the beauty that Mother Nature has bestowed upon us. At Agate Designs in Seattle, owners Mark Kullberg and Terry Derosier make it their job to find and display nature's beauties for your lasting enjoyment. They stock natural, high quality, collectible crystals, gems, minerals and fossils. All are hand picked for quality and comprise the largest store of its kind in the Seattle area. Many visitors describe the shop as a little museum as they marvel over 500-million-year-old fossils and 250-pound amethyst geodes. While there, you will also see fascinating specimens of rainbow obsidian, petrified wood and agate. They also provide a large assortment of all types of jewelry and handmade stone boxes of lapis, malachite and rhodonite, plus crystal balls, carvings and stunning Baltic amber.
120 First Ave South, Seattle WA  (206) 621 - 3063

# Lakeshore Gallery

Wherever your final destination may be in Washington, as a visitor or a resident, Lakeshore Gallery should be your first stop. Allow plenty of time to visit their location in Kirkland, as you will be wonderfully lost in their abundant collection of everything from handblown glass art, exquisite handcrafted jewelry, metal works, pottery and woodworks, as well as watercolors and other beautiful paintings. Lakeshore Gallery opened in 1983, and is owned by Georgie Kilrain, whose motto is "Love the art you buy." Extremely authentic and carrying one-of-a-kind pieces, Lakeshore's focus is on American-created art and crafts, as they do not import items from outside the States. Also important to this diverse gallery is good customer service, as the majority of their business relies on regular customers. Because of this, Lakeshore Gallery has strong ties to the community. They were one of the very few galleries that began the local Art Walk years ago, and continue to be dedicated participants today. Whether you're looking for a unique wedding gift or just want to expand or start your art collection, Lakeshore Gallery has what you're looking for.  107 Park Lane, Kirkland WA  (425) 827-0606

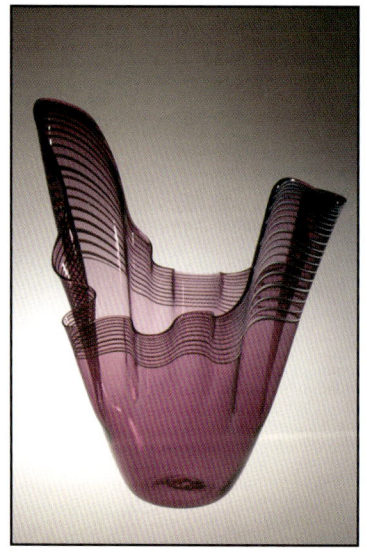

# Flury & Company Ltd.

Lois Flury, owner of Flury & Company Gallery, has been collecting and dealing in photography, specializing in Edward S. Curtis' vintage material since 1972. Curtis was an artist, amateur ethnographer and a man of his time. The North American Indian was his lifelong labor and obsession. Through talent and tenacity, pioneer Curtis chronicled a culture that was rapidly receding into the past. In making a record of what was past, and passing, he hoped to preserve it. He succeeded in publishing his work in a magnificent limited edition of twenty volumes of illustrated text and twenty accompanying portfolios of engravings. Located in historic Pioneer Square, the gallery is a wealth of information for those wanting to learn more about the history of the gallery and its collection of choice photographs and antique Native American art. Their catalogue of new, rare and out-of-print books and a selection of books on Edward S. Curtis and American Indian art and culture are available through the gallery. 322 1st Avenue S, Seattle WA (206) 587-0260  www.fluryco.com

# Galleries

# Seattle Metro

## Seattle Glassblowing Studio

Founded in 1991 by glassblowing artist Cliff Goodman, Seattle Glassblowing Studio is centrally located in downtown Seattle. Offering classes in glassblowing, private lessons and weekend workshops, Seattle Glassblowing has the largest enrollment of any glassblowing school in the United States. Their beautiful gallery showcases numerous local artists, featuring splendid works of art. In addition to

sculptures, vases, bowls and ornaments, Seattle Glassblowing's design team creates custom lighting, installations and commissions. The impressive roster of well-known glass artists who have blown there includes Martin Blank, Fritz Dreisbach, Scott Darlington and Aaron Tate. Attached to Seattle Glassblowing is Hot Glass Color and Supply, a store carrying the largest supply of German-imported Kugler colors in the United States. There is also a restaurant and espresso bar attached serving delicious homemade Italian food, sandwiches, soups and desserts. For a fascinating experience, visit Seattle Glassblowing Studio and watch the magical art of glassblowing. 2227 Fifth Avenue, Seattle WA (206) 448-2181 www.seattleglassblowing.com

## Fancy

The wares of great local artists await you at Fancy in Seattle. Owner Sally Brock has been making jewelry since she was 13, and has created a space for other local artists to sell their work, too. The artwork is handmade and recently featured such names as Trish Grantham, Suzanne Kaufman, Amy Tavern, Shava Lawson, Dotty Speck and Hedy Anderson. Unique rings, bracelets, necklaces and various gifts are abundant at Fancy. You can also special order custom pieces by the owner or one of her Fancy cohorts. The fun of investigating a store like Fancy is the act of discovery. So what are you waiting for? 1932 Second Avenue, Seattle WA (206) 443-4621  www.fancyjewels.com

## Queen Anne's Fountainhead Gallery

Queen Anne's Fountainhead Gallery is housed in an historic brick building built by Anhalt, a famous local builder in the mid twenties. The art gallery, founded by Sue and Ron Peterson nine years ago, brought the space, which initially housed the corner drugstore, back to being the focal point of the neighborhood. The gallery was created to bring original work by Northwest contemporary artists to discriminating buyers. Fountainhead Gallery has become rooted within the community and currently displays artwork from more than thirty regional artists and hold invitationals to showcase the work of others, including nationally-known artists. In addition to the rich and wonderful paintings on display, are beautiful hand-woven contemporary baskets and various sculptures of bronze, ceramics, fiber and wood. Fountainhead Gallery values dialogue and wants to hear from their customers, including the many children who come to view the art. Stop by Queen Anne's Fountainhead Gallery and experience for yourself a wide array of distinctive artwork.  625 W McGraw Street, Seattle WA   (206) 285-4467

Painting by Lyle Silver

# Galleries | Seattle Metro

## Avalon Glassworks

Avalon Glassworks is a neighborhood experience of brightly colored fantasy and fancy. Jon and Shannon Felix, owners and artisans, bring an intense passion for the craft and years of experience to every piece of glasswork they design. Lucky customers have the opportunity to experience that passion coming to life as they watch these glass pieces being made onsite. Since the Felixes took over the 12-year-old company in 2003, they have cultivated a reputation for their unique, modern designs. Evident as you walk in the gallery/studio, you'll be surrounded with fabulous color, whimsy and one-of-a-kind work, including their famous Blossom and Luna Vases. Having both studied glass blowing at Tulane University, this powerful artistic team also benefits from Shannon's background in graphic design and Jon's years as a glass chemist and four years working with Dale Chihuly. Today, they love taking advantage of the real chemistry in colored glass to create new color and pattern combinations, as well as different surface treatments. Through Jon and Shannon's vision, Avalon Glassworks has truly become a must-see destination for glass artists, art lovers and gift givers. From vases to bowls to garden floats, Avalon Glassworks is guaranteed to have the special piece you're looking for at a competitive price.

2914 SW Avalon Way, Seattle WA
(206) 937-6369
www.avalonglassworks.com
Jeff Schmitt Photography

## Galleries — East Side

# Revolution Gallery

Recycling has become a necessity for our environment and this art gallery has taken that ideal to another level. Beautiful and one of a kind artwork can be found at Revolution Gallery. Mary McManus, owner, artist and passionate recycler, has created an art gallery that functions as an artists' co-op and offers a wide range of fine and functional art pieces that you won't find anywhere else. They currently represent over 100 local artists and specialize in recycled and rescued art made from materials that have been ingeniously transformed. Their customers know that they can always find something here for that person who is hard to shop for and there is new work coming in every day. Revolution Gallery believes that beautiful art can be created from recycled glass, old light bulbs, telephone wire, bottle caps and obsolete computer diskettes, and they have the goods to prove it. Revolution Gallery also serves as a resource for artists who need ideas or materials and teaches classes to kids and adults about the importance of recycling and using their ideas to create something new instead of throwing it away. Mary started out as an artist who wanted to turn the ordinary into the extraordinary by recycling obsolete computer components into clocks. Come in and visit this wonderful and eclectic art gallery and gift shop, and don't forget to bring the kids.
317 NW Gilman Boulevard #26 (Gilman Village), Issaquah WA  (425) 392-4982  www.revolutiongallery.com

## Galleries — South Puget Sound

# Childhood's End Gallery

Childhood's End Gallery, located on the waterfront in downtown Olympia, specializes in fine art and crafts of the Pacific Northwest. Owners Bill and Richenda Richardson wanted to create a business where they could work together. Feeling as though the culmination of their college careers was an end to childhood, they celebrated their entry into adulthood by naming and founding Childhood's End Gallery in 1971. A showplace for contemporary works, the Gallery displays a wide variety of original art, including limited edition prints, jewelry, pottery, art glass, woodwork, sculpture and other media. They also mount exhibits featuring Northwest artists. The Richardsons and their staff comb art festivals, artists' studios, trade shows, mail and personal inquiries to find works that meet the Gallery's high standards. On the 3rd Friday of every month, they hold a Gallery Night when they present a new exhibition of fine art. Centrally located downtown on Olympia's waterfront, you will want to visit this jewel of a gallery.  222 West 4th Avenue, Olympia WA  (360) 943 - 3724

# Gifts

# Gifts

## Olympic Peninsula

## Franni's Gift Expressions

For the perfect present for any occasion, have a custom-made gift basket assembled by Franni's Gift Expressions in Port Angeles. With many goodies to choose from, every recipient will be delighted. Owned by Fran and Bill Feeley, Franni's Gift Expressions is a family business. Franni creates the beautiful baskets, while her daughter Andi Feeley manages the store and granddaughter Kayla makes deliveries with Grandpa Bill. Franni has made custom gift baskets for friends and family for years. She then started her business and worked from home until she opened up shop recently in an older home that she and Bill bought and remodeled. Her shop is stocked with an array of distinctive items that can be placed in the gift baskets or purchased separately. The gift baskets are perfect for any occasion such as anniversaries, new babies, birthdays, holidays, graduations, weddings and countless others. Franni's Gift Expressions offers luxurious bath items, delicious gourmet treats, wines, stationary and many other items that customers can select to make their own personalized baskets. Fran supports local vendors and carries many one-of-a-kind items. The gift baskets can be hand delivered within the Port Angeles city limits free of charge or hand delivered outside the Port Angeles city limits for an additional fee. Shipping throughout the United States is also available. 1215 East Front Street, Port Angeles WA (360) 417-0969 or (888) 452 - 2884  www.frannisgifts.com

## The GreenEyeshade

It's not easy to find both the beautiful and practical in the same store, but Marilyn Staples and manager Judy Rich accomplish it at The Green Eyeshade in Port Townsend. Here you will find the best-quality kitchen gadgets and cookware. You will also find a selection of earrings that allows them to claim the title of "Earring Capital of the World." There's a wide range of artisan cookware and table settings. The store is fun, because the merchandise is indeed practical yet beautiful. You can adorn yourself or your home with personality and style. If you want help, the staff is knowledgeable and will gladly do personal shopping for you. Here you will experience an ever-changing selection of fine merchandise from around the globe with old-fashioned personalized service to go with it. Free gift wrapping is provided and UPS shipping is available. 720 Water Street, Port Townsend WA (360) 385 - 3838 or (888) 785 - 3838   www.thegreeneyeshade.com

## The Cottage Company

Susie Tuttle and her daughter, Michelle Lewan, invite you to come visit a little cottage home surrounded by a white picket fence, where a pathway lined with lavender and poppies leads you up to the red front door. Once inside and warmly greeted, you'll see glimmering crystal chandeliers, cozy white furniture, beautiful mirrors, wonderful potpourris, cast iron hardware such as outlet covers, hooks, doorknockers, and much more as you experience the delights of The Cottage Company. Described by the Sequim Gazette as "visionaries," Susie and Michelle rented a forlorn, "underloved" house and spent two months converting it into a welcoming and well-loved shop. In the vintage kitchen with sage walls, marvel at the unique kitchenware in "explosive" red accents: enamelware bowls, platters, colanders, canisters and other cherry-red decor. Gourmet teas, lavender sugar, cookies and other food treats from local producers such as the Chukar Cherry Company are stocked in the hutches. Make your way out to the backyard and covered patio area, where you'll be overwhelmed with trellises, wire baskets of all sizes, cast iron urns, birds and welcome signs. The Cottage Company's best sellers can be seen here, the metal wall stars from two feet to four feet in diameter. People tell Susie and Michelle that their prices are amazing and their store lifts the spirits and just makes them feel good. Why not pay them a visit? 129 S. 2nd Avenue, Sequim WA  (360) 683-7278

# The Gifting Place

At The Gifting Place in Port Angeles, it's obvious that part of the job description for the staff is to pamper customers, play and have fun – and it's contagious! It's their goal that when you leave the store, you feel better than when you came in. Owner Debra Rudolph and her staff greet you with warm smiles and wait on you with hearty hospitality. The store is full of wonderful accessories for you and your home. It's a woman's playground where she can pamper herself and find her fun or crazy side. The store teaches you how to treat yourself well, spoil yourself with lace, boutique ware, jewelry, teas, imports, silks, wools, dresses, practical but elegant linens, organic coffee, truffles, crazy hats and scarves, cosmetics, oils, tea pots, modern art and china. There's a spa line, a wedding section, candles and more. Among the brand names you'll find at The Gifting Place are Chamilia, "Jewelry that defines you," and YiXing Teapots. Even massage therapy is available at The Gifting Place. The focus is on meeting all the needs of women by allowing patrons to blossom into who they want to be. In short, everything in the store is something intended to make you feel good. Try it. On the corner of Peabody Street & 8th: 333 E 8th Street, Port Angeles WA  (360) 565-8090  www.thegiftingplace.com

# Something to Crow About

A great variety of affordable gifts and unique gift packaging are two of the hallmarks of Something to Crow About, one of the finest shops in Port Angeles. Owner Cathy Smith says they'll only sell it if it really is something to crow about! The shop offers wonderful items including well-known collectibles such as Boyds Bears and Big Sky Carvers, Colonial At Home candles, and popular body care lines like Crabtree & Evelyn and Burt's Bees. They also carry gourmet food, cookbooks, nostalgic tin signs and sugar-free candy. Browsers can sip on a free cup of dessert coffee while they make their way through the seemingly endless variety of gifts on display. Whether you're looking for a Ty Beanie Baby, baby clothes or Bulova clocks, you will find something special here. The shop's famous "potted gifts" are packaged inside terra cotta flower pots, wrapped with tissue and cello, and finished with a bow and a flower (though gift boxes are also available if you prefer something more conventional). Something to Crow About also offers personal shopper service for those whose schedules don't allow them time to stop by. Just a phone call gets you expert gift buying assistance and free delivery. Out of town shipping is available as well.   1017 East Front Street, Port Angeles WA   (360) 417-2670

# Forest Gems

Forest Gems Gallery represents only hands-on Northwest artists working with the finest woods from the California redwoods, up through Oregon myrtlewood country to Western Washington. The starting point for all art selected by Harvey and Susan Windle, the gallery owners, is wood which glows with 3-dimensional grain patterns. These special pieces of wood inspire artists to bring forth nature's beauty, adding their own individual style and design. The wood itself influences what emerges in the hands of the artist and many of the resulting treasures are one of a kind. Functional salad bowls, vases, furniture and carved wall pieces are some of the fine woodcrafts offered to Forest Gems' discerning customers. Recent custom work includes beds, fireplace mantels, tables and cabinets in figured and burl wood. Harvey has made his living designing and handcrafting fine woodwork since 1976, where he began at Seattle's Pike Place Market. They opened Forest Gems Gallery in Port Townsend in 1996. Harvey's designs include hand mirrors, pendulum clocks, hair barrettes, various turned items and custom work. The common thread in all of his work is high figure wood grains with smooth flowing lines finished with Danish oil or wax to reveal the natural beauty of the wood. Harvey and Susan, with their long-term employee Charmaine Kennedy, appreciate the work and the artists they show in their Port Townsend gallery, which has become a unique destination for locals and visitors alike.  807 Washington Street, Port Townsend WA  (360) 379-1713  www.forestgemsgallery.com

# Pondicherri

Pami Singh, owner of Pondicherri and its wholesale parent company Handprint, has been offering a beautiful assortment of fabric items created in India for the past 35 years. The Sequim Pondicherri store, currently under the management of Sequim native Jonel Lyons, is a popular destination for shoppers looking for something unique and exciting to liven up their home, perhaps a colorful Chanderi printed table cloth or a Mehrab curtain panel. In addition to housewares, Pondicherri offers scarves, nightwear, clothing and handbags in an eclectic variety of designs and fabrics. You'll find silks and cottons, patchwork and designs inspired by French, Dutch and modern trends. At its production facilities in New Delhi, Handprint uses only natural fibers and ecologically safe techniques in a factory specially designed to allow the craftsmen a comfortable working environment for practicing their centuries-old skills. In addition to the Pondicherri retail stores (there is also one in New York), Handprint provides custom made products for catalog companies such as Neiman Marcus. Retail stores across the country rely on the Sequim sales and customer service team to provide them with these enduringly popular items, which are also featured at showrooms in well-known venues such as Atlanta's Merchandise Mart and trade shows like the famous International Gift Fair held annually at the Javits Center in New York. Pondicherri's products are a true treasure and people in Washington can feel proud to have the original so close at hand. 119 E Washington Street, Sequim WA (360) 681-4431 www.pondicherrionline.

## Gifts — Washington Coast

## The Dusty Trunk

If you've ever experienced the delight of going into an attic and discovering unexpected treasures, you'll understand where The Dusty Trunk gets its name. When you walk in, the first thing you see is the store's oversized dollhouse filled with miniatures and, beyond that, a trunk full of teddy bears in whimsical costumes. The luscious scent of chocolate truffles is in the air; what could be more inviting? The Dusty Trunk is run by Dianne Staats Hansen. Dianne and her husband Bruce were corporate employees for many years before they decided that they needed a change. Visiting Ocean Shores while on vacation, they loved the town so much that they decided to move there. They found the perfect house and the perfect life here in this little community. Now Dianne is delighted to give something back, not just through the store but through her talents as a graphic designer and writer. She produced the colorful Ocean Shores calendar events poster. When you shop at The Dusty Trunk, you'll easily see why Dianne fell in love with Ocean Shores. With the addition of a new pug puppy, Abigail, this store is a true treasure.
849 Point Brown Avenue NW
# 1, Ocean Shores, WA (360) 289-9931

# McCurdy's Celtic Marketplace

Food, teas, hand knit sweaters, hats, woolens, linens, Belleek Parian China Guinness Licensed Products, plus the art of Vettriano and Montague Dawson are just a few of the fine imports you will find in McCurdy's Celtic Marketplace. Owners Jim and Colleen Earp gather the best of Ireland, England, Scotland, Wales, and lesser-known Celtic countries in this charming shop. It was named after Colleen's grandmother, Lulu B. McCurdy (the family immigrated from a fine little whiskey town called Bushmills). Their goal is to bring a bit of Ireland and other Celtic cultures to Ocean Shores. Amongst the beautiful handcrafts, porcelain, art and jewelry you will find many surprises including Beatles memorabilia and a silk Irish chain quilt from the 1700s. The shop is a bit of the old and some contemporary mixed with traditional Celtic wares. The teapot is always on at McCurdy's so you can take pleasure in a cup while you are enjoying the inviting atmosphere. 114 E Chance ala Mer NE Boulevard, #107, Ocean Shores WA (360) 289 - 3955

# First Cabin

"Only the Best" gifts and service in Ocean Shores. First Cabin is not a gallery and they are not "stuffy" even though they are "POSH." "First Cabin" is a nautical term meaning "the best, the front of the ship view of the shore." "POSH" means "Port Out, Starboard Home," the best that can be offered. Owners Brenda Love-Loveland and Al Loveland offer quality at very good prices. The best quality is carried in the merchandise of over 400 vendors. Before making a decision to carry an item, Brenda and Al ask themselves, "Is it First Cabin?" You will find extraordinary accessories for Captain, Crew and Quarters. In addition to nautically-themed gifts, First Cabin carries jewelry, paintings, glassware, nautical textiles, pewter, lamps and weather-related instruments. They have been selling amber for fourteen years and are known for the best pricing of amber jewelry on the West Coast. First Cabin prides itself on above board customer service, which includes free gift wrapping. Special orders are welcome and they will ship anywhere.
698 Ocean Shores Boulevard NW, Ocean Shores WA (360) 289-9070

# Raining Cats & Dogs

When entering Raining Cats & Dogs, you feel like you've stepped into a world of extravagance. You see not only designer clothing and gourmet food for the discriminating dog and cat, but for their discriminating humans too. Cool stuff for dogs and cats and their owners, what could be more fun? Jim and Colleen Earp run the store, but the real owner is Abigale Earp, the seven-pound Maltese who resides in the shop. It's very easy to while away the time in this charming and luxurious atmosphere that has a European flair. They have mood CDs, unusual chess sets, great framed prints, jazzy little martini glasses, and great bath and body products too. And don't forget the home party items and fun entertainment pieces for that special house guest. Raining Cats & Dogs is a twist on everyday accessories and entertainment; go in to enjoy! 698 Ocean Shores Boulevard NW, Ocean Shores WA (360) 289-4100

## Gifts                                Kitsap Peninsula

# Eagle Harbor Book Company

Eagle Harbor Book Company, a locally owned and proudly independent bookstore, has been an integral part of the Bainbridge and Kitsap communities for over 30 years. This mid-sized store of approximately 5,000 square feet presents a warm, intimate atmosphere and is open daily. They stock a diverse selection of over 30,000 new and used titles plus hard-to-find magazines, bargain books, and a large selection of gifts and calendars in season. They are known locally for excellence in customer service provided by a staff of experienced booksellers who love to share their enthusiasm for books and reading. In addition they are proud to have been recognized nationally as winner of the Lucile Panell Award for Excellence in Children's Programming as well as having been nominated for the 2002 Publishers Weekly Bookseller of the Year Award.  157 Winslow Way E, Bainbridge Island WA (206) 842 - 5332

# CARGOHOLD

Whether from local or international venues, people come to Poulsbo to savor its historic, small town ambiance on Liberty Bay. Originally settled by Nordic fishermen who found the locale reminiscent of their homeland, Poulsbo is still affectionately known as Little Norway on the Fjord. This Norwegian heritage is celebrated each May during Viking Fest and again in early December with the Lucia Bride's arrival at the town's waterfront pavilion. Locally owned restaurants and retail stores line Front Street in Poulsbo's historic Old Town district. Favored by people who love nautical treasures is CARGOHOLD, an evolving creation for nearly 15 years by owners Doug and Risa Owen. The two share an interest in local history, weather, and things nautical. Together they bring a rich mix of high quality instruments from clocks, barometers and hygrometers to wind, rain and tide gauges and nautical decor into a blend of merchandise that pleases boaters and land-lubbers alike. If you are looking for model ships or wind vanes, nautical coasters or traditional oil lamps, knot boards or lighthouse collectibles, you'll find it at the one and only CARGOHOLD. 18864 Front Street, Poulsbo WA (360) 697 - 1424 or CARGOHOLD@Earthlink.net

# Esther's Fabrics

What has kept Bainbridge Island sewing since 1959? Esther's Fabrics. Esther's is the oldest fabric store in the State of Washington, and has maintained the charm and selection found in the fabric stores of times past. Esther's has a little bit of everything with enticing new treasures arriving daily. You'll find great fabric for quilting, fashion or home decorating, as well as related resources like crafts, buttons, ribbons and trims. Discover notions for quilting, cross stitch, basic sewing, garment construction and drapery hardware. There are hundreds of bolts of fabric, cottons from Alexander Henry, Freespirit, and Hanamomen in Japan, exquisite silks from India and China, wools from Europe, and ribbons and buttons from France and Italy, including numerous Vintage offerings. If they don't have it, they are happy to special order it for you. They have an extensive library of home decorating sample books for your ordering ease. Whether your project is big or small, generally it is one stop and you have everything you need. The staff of knowledgeable, creative and dedicated seamstresses in all fields of sewing is led by "Esther" #4, Jennifer Rhoads, who began sewing at the age of 4 on her mother's knee, and is a fourth generation seamstress. Jennifer is a fashion designer with a degree from the Fashion Institute of Technology, NYC. She was enthusiastic about trading her job in corporate fashion design for the unlimited creativity she found at Esther's Fabrics. Best of all, everyone is willing to share ideas and projects. Check their website for a current schedule of wonderful classes and events. 285 Winslow Way E, Bainbridge Island WA (206) 842-2261 www.esthersfabrics.com

# Gifts    Kitsap Peninsula

*Photos by Jonathan Hollander, S.G. Photo*

## The Beehive

The Beehive in Gig Harbor is an antique, vintage and home decor store. It is all that and more. Owner Vicki Dyer explains that the store is a place where women can come for conversation, relaxation and renewal while they browse at their leisure. Vicki's goal is to own a beautiful store that people come back to again and again. She carries old things, new things, antiques, books, housewares, furniture, collectibles, linens, chandeliers, home decor, tools, shelves, potpourri, spices, and candles.   3306 Harborview Drive, Gig Harbor WA (253) 853 - 3443

## Heirloom Quilts & Fabric

In business since 1981, owners Carol Swanson, Evelyn Bright, Donna Endreson and Norma Tipton invite you to come share their passion for quilting.  Interestingly, all of the owners come from very different backgrounds, but all have one thing in common and that is their love for fabric and creating beautiful handicraft. In addition, the employees at Heirloom Quilts and Fabrics are knowledgeable and all are avid quiltmakers who are happy to share their talents, skills and ideas.  One of the employees is an experienced long arm quilter, which enables the shop to offer custom quilting as an additional service for their customers.

Heirloom is known for having one of the largest quilting selections in the area.  There are endless supplies for quilt making and the stock is always changing.  The shop keeps tabs on newly available quilting books so that their clientele knows the latest in the quilting world. Heirloom Quilts offers a multitude of quilting classes. If you really want to immerse yourself, try a mini-retreat. For additional quilting fun, ask about "Shop Hop."  18833-B Front Street, Poulsbo WA  (360) 697-2222

# Higuera Imports

When you walk into Higuera Imports, you feel like you've stepped into a colorful Mediterranean marketplace. Their Majolica ceramic items imported from Italy are stunning. The town of Deruta (a small hilltop town in Umbria) has made high-quality Majolica ceramics for centuries and has become known worldwide as the best source for these artistic objects. The Majolica ceramic pieces are world renowned for their brilliant color, designs, glazes and clays. Deruta also is known for its unique tables; Higuera Imports is proud to offer tables that are handmade in the Old World ways with travertine antique terracotta and solid volcanic stone tables. The travertine terracotta tables are made of materials from ancient farmhouses or villas throughout Tuscany and Umbria, these farmhouses and villas are estimated to be between three to six hundred years old on an average. Both types of stone tables are ice proof, heat proof and sun resistant. Higuera Imports decided to dedicate the flooring division solely to high quality bamboo products because of the benefits to the environment. Although the market share of bamboo flooring is currently less then 3.5% of the entire flooring industry, Higuera Imports sees a bright and unlimited future for their A-grade bamboo flooring. It will continue to grow if only due to the conservation and quality aspect

alone. Higuera Imports also strives to bring you the latest innovative designs in teak furniture. The owners of Higuera Imports spent some time living in Europe and traveled all over the world for many years before opening their store. Ruth and Joe's experiences abroad not only educated them on quality but also opened the door for many important personal relationships with their sources abroad. Higuera Imports currently has import divisions in European countries, China and Indonesia. The results are outstanding selections of exceptional quality and affordable imported items.

19006 Front Street, Poulsbo WA
(360) 779-4050 or (888) 300-2059
www.higueraimports.com

# Gifts

## Kitsap Peninsula

## Skookum Clothing Company

Experience an amazing shopping adventure! Owners Jack and Randi Morgan have created a store where the sale is secondary to caring about the customer. They are known for personal service geared toward helping women create a look that is individual, exciting and just right for them. The staff is welcoming, knowledgeable and caring and most have been with the store since its inception in 1994. The owners and staff have created a safe space. No matter what size or background you are, once you walk in the store, you are special and Skookum will serve your personal needs. Randi wanted to make a contribution to the community and felt that too many times people just want to make a sale. At Skookum they want you to have a great experience and leave feeling wonderful about who you are and how you look. The clothes at Skookum are designed to flatter a woman's shape and to move with you. Additionally, the goal is to provide unconditional comfort all day. To complement their clothes, Jack and Randi have chosen special body products and lingerie, in short: all the "stuff" that makes you feel good. They also carry fabulous children's clothes, newborn to size seven. This merchandise is fun and geared toward the celebration of new babies and young children. 126 Winslow Way W, Bainbridge Island WA (206) 842 - 0681 www.skookumcompany.com

## Liberty Bay Books

Bookworm's delight! This is not your conventional bookstore. The ambience generated at Liberty Bay reflects the personality of its owner, Suzanne Droppert. Suzanne has always loved books and people. When this quaint, old fashioned, independent bookstore became available, she jumped at the chance to become the new owner. The store is full of energy; it's a fun place to relax. The lounge area and latte stand open early and close late. Liberty Bay is a general interest bookstore. Of particular interest are titles that are imported from Norway. Most are beautiful coffee table books that are often carried back home by Norwegian visitors. There is a great selection of Native American books, children's books and CDs. Interior design books are especially popular. Fiction and non-fiction selections are plentiful. Nautical books are one of their specialties. All of their staff love to read and enthusiastically share their most recent "favorite picks." Many books are discounted. Shop and compare! Order on their website and they'll send books to your friends and relatives anywhere. Liberty Bay Books may not be the biggest bookstore that you've ever been in, but it just may be the liveliest. 18881 D Front Street, Poulsbo WA (360) 779 - 5909 www.libertybaybooks.

# Gifts
## Seattle Metro

## Coastal Surf Boutique

In Seattle, the only retail shop on Alki Avenue is a surf and skate shop with a twist. It is a boutique, carrying lifestyle clothing and accessories from the surf, skate and snowboard industries for women and girls (and a few things for men). The store has evolved into a resource for West Seattle, allowing women to stay and shop in their own neighborhood. As such, Coastal Surf Boutique has received great support from the community and other business owners. The shop has turned into a fun spot for visitors and residents, hosting barbeques, sponsoring events and supporting community efforts. Among the new activities, owners Sarah Steere and Christy Metzger plan to rent beach cruisers and longboards for beachgoers to enjoy. 2532 Alki Avenue SW, Seattle WA  (206) 933 - 5605  www.coastalseattle.com

## Gift Gallery at Tillicum Village

The Gift Gallery at Tillicum Village is located on Blake Island just a short cruise from Pier 55 on Seattle's central waterfront.  The cruise to Tillicum Village is breathtaking, as is the Gift Gallery, located just inside the Tillicum Village longhouse which houses Native American distinctive art and craft treasures selected for viewing and purchase.  The Gift Gallery is a wonderful addition to the world famous Tillicum Village salmon bake and spellbinding performance, "Dance on the Wind". The Gift Gallery is a visual delight that invites you to stroll leisurely through its offering.  You will find tempting Native American art, prints, designs, one-of-a-kind items, hand-carved masks, plaques, miniature totem poles and beaded jewelry.  The color and texture found here are a treat to the senses.  Wood carvings, glass plates, copper items, engraved boxes, adult and children's clothing, souvenir shirts, afghans, books, dream catchers and art card designs so unique they can be framed. Each item is carefully selected to provide a memorable reminder of your visit. 2992 SW Avalon Way, Seattle WA   (206) 933-8600 or (800) 426-1205

## Eastside Trains

You can purchase a gift certificate anywhere, but if you're looking for something new and different this year, visit Eastside Trains in Kirkland. Greeted by sounds from the past as you enter their domain, you'll be delighted at the world of tradition, class and history provided in their extensive collection of collectible train sets that vary from older models to more contemporary styles. Whether you're collecting train sets for a personal hobby or introducing an imaginative activity to a newer generation, Eastside Trains truly has something for everyone, including state of the art sound systems that are digitized onto electronic chips for authentic sounds. Inspiration for this store began in a small room of the home of Barilyn and Steve Suskin and their daughter Stacy, and evolved into a large store equipped with everything essential for train sets, including creative influence and extensive personal knowledge acquired through years of experience. Far from a hobby thrift store, Eastside Trains not only has experience but strong local ties to the community as well, constantly donating their merchandise to day care centers, school auctions, and other local charities that keep their tradition alive. They also provide tours for nursing homes, scouts and tourists from all over the country. Portrayed in Sunset Magazine twice and gaining more recognition every year, Eastside Trains will be displaying their creativity in the Great American Train Show in Puyallup, as well as being involved in other activities within their community in the future. 217 Central Way, Kirkland WA    (425) 828-4098 or (877) 857 - 7246

# Gifts

# Seattle Metro

## Magic Mouse Toys

Magic Mouse Toys has been serving the wholesome fantasy needs of Puget Sound since 1977. They are Seattle's Downtown toy store. Founder Gilbert H. Gorilla earned his Ph.D. from Stanford the same year, having majored in Fantasy, and graduated "summa cum cuddly." A toy store which does not discriminate against adults, they offer a varied collection of elegant chess sets, backgammon, go and mahjongg sets, juggling equipment and European playing cards, including an extensive selection of tarot cards.

Magic Mouse Toys occupies two floors of the gloriously ornamented Mutual Life Building, built in 1897, which is on the National Registry of Historic Sites. The German toy maker Steiff has designated Magic Mouse Toys as a "Best of America" store as they carry a large selection of Steiff collectible teddy bears and animals. The two floors of quality and hand-chosen toys include an extensive game room downstairs featuring the best of children's American games, as well as the German brand Ravensburger. You can also explore an excellent collection of children's books that covers the classics and the latest award winners. Whether you're looking for jazzy birthday party favors, that special French baby doll or a well-engineered German tricycle, you will find it at Magic Mouse Toys. 603 First Avenue, Seattle WA (206) 682 - 8097 www.MagicMouseToys.

## Ye Olde Curiosity Shop

"Everything in the world sardined into one fantastic shop," claims Ye Olde Curiosity Shop, located on Seattle's waterfront. When you walk in, you may not find "everything," but you will find an amazing collection from the sublime to the sort of silly from around the world. Where else will you find Sylvester, one of the most well-preserved mummies in North America? (It seems that Sylvester was coated in arsenic, thus his preservation. You can learn more in the shop.) You will also find the world's smallest shrunken head, a pig with three tails, Native American artifacts, a ship made from Alaskan ivory and likely something to fascinate everyone in your family. Since the store opened in 1899, Ye Olde Curiosity Shop has been an Indian trading post, where Northwest Coast and Alaskan Native Americans bring their crafts to sell. Says fourth generation owner Andy James, "My great grandfather bought from the great grandfathers of some of the artists we buy from today." The result is an extraordinary collection of Native American art, including C. Alan Johnson figurines. Come see these adorable Eskimo children created by this local artist, but be warned that you're likely to fall in love with them. Each figurine has its own name and a personality. Not forgetting the "sort of silly" items, Ye Olde Curiosity Shop sports rubber chickens, celebrity dollar bills, lucky 3-legged clay pigs and gator backscratchers, side by side with fine imports and jewelry. So come on in. The Lord's Prayer engraved on a grain of rice awaits you. So do the smallest ivory elephants in the world, a 67-pound snail, a six-foot crab and countless other treasures to be discovered from every corner of the world. 1001 Alaskan Way, Pier 54, Seattle WA (206) 682 - 5844 www.yeoldecuriosityshop.com

# Paint the Town

When you need to find the perfect gift for someone on your list or you just want a reason to be creative, visit Paint the Town in Seattle. This contemporary ceramics painting studio allows people to make their own ceramic works of art! Customers can choose from over 200 unpainted ceramic items such as mugs, plates, figurines, vases and other collectibles. Once the pottery (bisque ware) has been chosen, the fun begins as customers decorate their pieces using the paints, brushes and tools provided by the studio. After an item is painted, it is clear-glazed and fired by the Paint the Town staff, and the finished masterpiece is ready to be picked up in just a few days! Owner Mary Anne Stusser opened Paint the Town in 1995. Previously an elementary school teacher and avid craft painting enthusiast, Mary Anne brings a warm, friendly presence to the studio. Her business allows everyone the opportunity to be an artist! The friendly and helpful staff guide customers throughout the selecting and painting process, ensuring every painter feels confident and well taken care of. Paint the Town is the perfect location for children's birthday parties and other special events, including catered bridal showers and family reunions. They can also bring all materials off site for a creative corporate function or classroom project. Located in the University Village, enjoy live concerts during the summer months on Wednesday evenings, along with many other special events such as art walks and an annual Sidewalk Sale. No experience or reservations are necessary to create a work of art at Paint the Town! 4611 Village Court NE, Seattle WA (206) 527-8554 www.ceramic-painting.com

# Enexile

Finding "the right" outfit is hard enough without worrying about seeing someone else in the same dress or shirt you've hand-selected for a specific occasion. At Enexile, a funky, hip clothing and accessory store located in the Fremont district of Seattle, at least one concern can be eliminated. They have created a store filled with a unique mixture of classic and modern clothing and jewelry for both men and women. Enexile sports not only big name fashion brands, but also smaller independent brands, both at affordable prices. Enexile offers a style all its own, bordering on chic with a hint of mischief. Co-owned by sisters Heather and Shannon Koszyk, Enexile also offers a variety of personal and home accessories from belts, glasses and hats, to paintings, candles, locally-made pillows and many other specialty items. They love jewelry and carry a wide-ranging selection of classic, modern and punk styles. 611 N 35th Street, Seattle WA (206) 633 - 5771 www.enexile.com

# Gifts  Seattle Metro

## The Spirit of Christmas

Nestled in Old Downtown Kirkland, there is a wonderful little shop known as The Spirit of Christmas. It celebrates Christmas with a wonderland of dozens of Christmas trees, true masterpieces in the art of tree trimming. Each tree has its own theme, from Nautical to Northwest Lodge, Country French to A Woman's Night Out, and many other enchanting themes. Owner Ruth Ann Young uses her considerable artistic talent to select each ornament that adorns these magical creations. She selects many of these unique ornaments during her travels, and many of her trees have been featured in magazines and on television. Some ornaments are custom designed by her and only available in her shop. The Patriotic Tree, which was dedicated to honor our men and women in uniform both past and present, is still very special. When smoke damage from a nearby fire made it impossible to open for the 2003 holiday season, she used her 2,400 square foot space to organize Operation Iraq – The Spirit of Christmas. Many volunteers lined up to help, the effort snowballed, and almost 6,600 individual packages containing snacks, personal items, music, books and letters from schoolchildren were sent. Operation Iraq – The Spirit of Christmas has become so large and popular (14,000 this year) that it had to find its own separate space. Ruth Ann received the nationally recognized "Raytheon Award" in Washington, D.C. recently for her volunteer efforts. Her store has now reopened and it's well worth a visit just to soak up the magical atmosphere and feel the real tradition of Christmas around you. Yes, The Spirit of Christmas is a true Treasure of Western Washington.  200 Central Way, Kirkland, WA  (425) 739-9627  www.thespiritofchristmasusa.com

## Petticoat Junction

Dancers, if you are near Lynnwood, you are in luck as you're at the home of Petticoat Junction Dance Shop, "the Fun Dance Store!" They specialize in dancewear for all kinds of dancing, from square dancing to swing, ballet to ballroom, tap, jazz, clogging, hip hop and theatrical venues, too. Founded in 1987, owners Bonnie and Dave maintain two floors amply stocked with clothing, shoes and accessories. They carry brand names recognized by dancers everywhere, including Capezio, Danskin, Freed, Coast, Glide and Tic Tac Toe shoes. The store carries over 7,000 pairs of dance shoes including Two Steppers, their own exclusive line. Bonnie and Dave have gained their knowledge of dancewear needs from a lifetime of dancing themselves, as Dave has been a square dance caller for over 40 years! At swing dance or square dance conventions, you will often find Bonnie and Dave with an exhibit helping dancers find dancewear and shoes. They even have a trailer in the style of a railroad caboose usable on location at smaller dance events. On the Internet, their online store is gaining worldwide recognition among all dancers. Stage show costume departments from far and wide including the country-music headquarters, Branson, Missouri, have placed numerous orders for petticoats from Petticoat Junction Dance Shop.  14523 Highway 99, Lynnwood WA  (425) 743-9513 or (800) 344-3262 www.petticoatjct.com

## Tricoter

Beryl Hiatt, Lindy Ward and their staff are passionate about knitting and it shows the moment you walk through the door at Tricoter in Seattle. Says Lindy, "Our goal is to make every knitter and every knitted sweater a success." Catch a session of knitters at work at Tricoter and you might think you've come across a social club; it is that and more. "Tricoter," comes from the French word tré co ta, meaning "to knit." Their aim is to have the most complete selection of luxury fibers and novelty yarns available in this country in an array of gorgeous colors and textures. You start by picking out the yarn then, if you like, have Beryl, Lindy or one of several staff members design your garment for you. Once you get started, you'll receive unlimited assistance and guidance free. At least three staffers are available at all times. The glory is in wearing the garment, feeling great and loving it. Whether you're a novice or expert knitter, you'll find the supplies, encouragement, help and advice that you need at Tricoter. 3121 E. Madison Street, Seattle WA (206) 328 - 6505 or (877) 554 - YARN www.tricoter.com

## Synapse 206

Step into this small contemporary-feeling fun shop in the heart of Seattle's historic Pioneer Square neighborhood and you will almost certainly be amazed at the creativity and diversity of the clothing artists represented here. From the unique work of local and regional clothing artists to the careful selection of offerings from smaller established labels, Synapse 206 presents true alternatives to personal fashion and expression. The shop was established to provide a springboard for local artists to bring their work and creative talent to the public and to help put beautiful clothing and accessories within the reach of a broad audience. Local artists represented include Neodandi, Idora, Cleo Wolfus, Reflect, Joanne, Joy Prescott, Elohe and Makool, along with many others. New designers and their work join the offerings on a regular basis and there is always something new to intrigue and tempt you. Selections and styles span the taste of almost all ages with literally something for everyone. From a simple tank or tee and a great pair of jeans to gowns which would be at home on the red carpet, it is a bit like playing dress-up in your favorite closet. Owner Tina Bueche is focused on finding just the right pieces to allow you to express your own individuality through your apparel choices. Primarily a women's shop, there are a few very special items for men as well. 206 First Avenue, Seattle WA (206) 447-7731 www.synapse206.com

## Pioneer Square Antique Mall

One of the pleasures of exploring a great city is discovering one of its hidden treasures. Down a staircase in the Pioneer Square district of Seattle is just such a gem, the Pioneer Square Antique Mall. Residing beneath the historic Pioneer Building, one of the few remaining Romanesque commercial buildings in the world, the mall is home to over sixty dealers catering to both new and veteran collectors. Featuring vintage jewelry and toys, mid century glass, delicate Chinese and European porcelain and many other collectibles, the mall has been a showcase for local antique dealers since 1985. The staff is friendly and knowledgeable as many of them are antique dealers themselves. There is also an extensive library of collector reference books available for on the spot research. Tiled floors and tin ceilings bring to mind the origins of the space itself, a public bathhouse that predated indoor plumbing. Adjoining the mall is the famed Seattle Underground Tour, a delightful guided tour through Seattle's storied past. Together they lie at the heart of Seattle's oldest district, surrounded by scores of restaurants and shops and mere blocks from Puget Sound. Next time you're in Seattle, don't miss the Pioneer Square Antique Mall. 602 First Avenue, Seattle WA (206) 624-1164 www.pioneersquareantiquemall.com

# Gifts　　　　　　　　　　　　　　Seattle Metro

## Simo Silk

Near Seattle's famed Pike Place Market, John Man has created a shop dedicated to the world's most luxurious and fabulous fiber – silk. Named for his sons Simeon (Si) and Moses (Mo), Simo Silk features a dazzling array of marvelous items for men, women and the home. You will find silk shirts, scarves, kimonos, Chinese blouses and jackets, silk comforter sets in all sizes, pajamas, camisoles, ponchos, chemises, gowns and more. You can even keep warm in the winter in silk long underwear! Softer than angora and more luxurious than cashmere, most of these silks are also washable. John's goal when he created the original Simo Silk ten years ago was to provide top-quality silk fashions from Asia at affordable prices. His success in doing so has enabled him to open a second shop in Pioneer Square. He looks forward to many more years of providing fine silks to Seattleites and visitors alike. Pike Place Market Store  1411 First Avenue, #108, Seattle WA - Pioneer Square Store   118 First Avenue South, Seattle WA  (206) 521-8816 - (800) 700-4393  www.simosilk.com

## Simply Seattle

It's simple, if you want a gift that speaks "Seattle," visit Simply Seattle. That's the name of the store that has all the local flavor you could ask for, from high-end souvenirs to local gourmet foods and mementos of Seattle sports teams. Owned by Michel and Valerie Brotman, for 15 years this store has specialized in items that are "particularly Seattle" by nature. Here is a sample of the wares. If you're looking for salmon, how about Copper River salmon, salmon chowder or a "Got Salmon" gift pack? For a special treat, how about a Seattle Chocolates ferryboat, Sleepless in Seattle coffee, a Chukar Cherry sampler or Space Noodles? Specialty gifts include a Washington blanket, Seattle jigsaw puzzle, Space Needle model, Smile at the Rain shirts, Mariners cribbage board, Space Needle salt and pepper shakers or Mariners Monopoly board game. If you're thinking about Christmas decorations, how about an ornament depicting the Seattle skyline, Mariners baseball or the Space Needle? Whether you're looking for something gourmet to eat or something that simply says "Seattle," find it at Simply Seattle.
1600 First Avenue, Seattle WA   (206) 448-2207   1201 Alaskan Way #102 at Pier 56, Seattle WA   (206) 447-BOAT (2628)  www.simplyseattle.com

## Curious Kidstuff

Wouldn't it be nice to walk into a store and describe the person you're buying for and let the knowledgeable staff pick just the right gift for you? That's exactly what many of the customers at Curious Kidstuff in Seattle do. They tell owners Monica Joyce-Walker or Ann Walker who they're buying for and Monica, Ann or one of the staffers knows exactly what to select for the child. Dedicated employees and customer service win the day at Curious Kidstuff. Many kids will remember this store as part of their child-hood. Says one recent customer, "It's the selection of toys that feeds children's minds" that brings her (and her kids) back. "They have bug houses and nets and gardening tools. Things like that are so wonderful for children and in such short supply." Another customer comments, "They have the most wonderful toys – a good selection of toys that work together to explain to kids how life works." Even the Seattle city govern-ment has commented about the store. Recently a panel of nine judges selected Curious Kidstuff for its nual Small Business Awards honor. The judges commented that Monica and Ann "transformed a neglected retail space into Curious Kidstuff, a highly interactive store made for frolicking, and for customer interaetion with their products." They provide a great selection of high-quality, nonviolent, imaginative toys, arts, supplies, crafts, music, and other playthings for children newborn to 12 years old.   4740 California Avenue SW, Seattle, WA  (206) 937-8788

# Gifts

# Skagit Valley

## Bunnies By The Bay

Bunnies By The Bay has been known for their plush collectible bunnies and friends that have brought delightful glad dreams into homes and hearts since 1986. But it's not just bunnies anymore. Come visit this beautiful new shop to see, feel, touch, taste and smell all the great things they are designing and creating exclusively just for the General Store. Their new Bunnies By The Bay Baby gift line is simply adorable. Soft bunny Cuddle Coats, funny Flipper Slippers, fuzzy Quacker Jackets and froggy Croak Coats are some of the endearing gifts for wee ones with sweet buns. Then take a hop, skip and a jump across the garden path to the old green house next door known as the Hareytale Museum. Gram's cat Miss Mercy Me will greet you as you journey back in time and hear the tale of why bunnies came to live in Gram's old house, The Attaberry Mending Shop. It all started when the family sailed north for the fishing season and Gram's grand girls came to stay. They turned her once peaceful home upside down and inside out. We wish we could tell you that their mischief and mayhem was the only tragedy that took place on Cricket Island. But alas tragic news is delivered to The Attaberry Mending Shop and hearts are broken. You'll hear how a family's tragedy taught them everything can be mended…even broken hearts. It's a true story of an amazing rescue. To see the complete line of Bunnies By The Bay gifts visit their website. Hareytale Museum 617 Morris Street, LaConner WA - General Store 623 Morris Street, La Conner WA (360) 293-8037 ext 221    www.bunniesbythebay.com

## Old Silvana Trading Post

For a small-town trading post with a backwoods character, the place to be when near Silvana is the Old Silvana Trading Post. Check out the locally handcrafted crafts, furniture and whimsical gifts. Enjoy the atmosphere provided by the rustic plank flooring and the country store home interior. The building went up in 1896 and looks like something out of the Wild West, with its covered boardwalk and high false front. There is plenty to buy: gifts, antiques, furniture, fishing supplies and licenses, espresso,

and old-style hot dogs made fresh by Silvana Meats and served from an authentic street cart. Here are a few of the brand names you'll find in the store: Country Barn "barn candles," Homespun grunge candles, Picnic Time picnic baskets and day packs, Wing-Time wing sauce, Kentucky Bourbon-Q hot BBQ sauce, Leanin' Tree cards, Tumbleweed Pottery, Sassafras kitchen accessories, GreenBriar baskets, Bellagio gourmet hot chocolate, Wassail cider, SeaBear smoked salmon, Brookins fly fishing candles, Gooseberry Patch cookbooks, and Over and Back pottery. Owner Dan Schroedl says some of his most popular items include Mr. and Mrs. Wonderful talking dolls and the amazing Airzooka.  1401 Pioneer Highway, Silvana WA  (360) 652 - 0747 or (877)-Silvana  www.OldSilvana.com

## Nasty Jack's Antiques

With a name like Nasty Jack's, you mighty expect ... what? But what you actually find at Nasty Jack's Antiques in La Conner is "the finest American and European antiques in Western Washington." Okay, let's deal with the name first. In 1972, the business was established by "Nasty" Jack Wilkins and his partner, "Diamond" Jim Reynolds. Jim left the business some time later, but Nasty Jack ran the business until he died of a heart attack in 1994. Present owners are Marlo and Gary Frank, daughter and son-in-law of Jack. "Who says antiques can't be fun?" asks Marlo, adding that she gets a warm feeling when she is able to find something that a customer can't find anywhere else. A sample of offerings includes a large selection of early American pieces such as fireplace mantles, church pews, tables and chairs, dressers, hall trees, parlor tables and bookcases. Every month, Nasty Jack's receives 40-foot containers from Liverpool, England, containing draw leaf and drop leaf tables, chairs, dressing tables, buffets, tea carts, occasional tables, stained glass windows, garden gates and more. Nasty Jack's invites you to contact them via phone or their website with your requests. If they do not have what you are looking for in stock, they will keep your request in their "want" file. They deliver from Tacoma to the Canadian border and will make shipping arrangements for out-of-state sales. 103 E Morris Street, La Conner WA (360) 466 - 3209 www.nastyjacksantiques.com

**Gifts**  **The Valley**

## New England Saltbox

The New England Saltbox in Sumner features a collection of country décor and antiques for your home, as well as a variety of giftware. Lodge furniture and décor has recently been added in the shop. Home decorating services are also offered. Marlene Grantham, shop owner, developed a love for the homey New England look after spending 17 years on the East Coast during her husband's naval career. Upon their return to the West Coast, she opened a shop that encourages an appreciation for the New England décor and the New England Saltbox is the result. In 2002, the shop received the Judges Award for the "Best Interior Decorating" for the Boardwalk Home at the Pierce Country Street of dreams in nearby DuPont. Here is a sample of what you'll find during your visit to the shop: upholstered furniture, lodge furniture, Shaker cupboards and furniture area rugs by Country Cat Loom and Weymouth, Old Heritage reproductions, Lt. Moses lighting, framed prints, faux wall finishes, quilts, American folk art, country wallpaper prints, Olde Century paint, wrought iron, pottery, baskets, dolls including Byers Choice dolls, tinware, samplers, vintage fabrics and candles. 1115 Main Street, Sumner WA (253) 826-3506

# Golden Rule Bears

Golden Rule Bears is well-known as a teddy bear lover's dream come true. Featuring thousands of bears and other stuffed animals, this shop has one of the largest inventories of Steiff, Cherished Teddies and Boyds Bears in the world and a vast array of Gund, Ty, R. John Wright, Deb Canham Artist Designs, Bearington, Ganz and Muffy VanderBear. They are honored to be a Boyds "Gold Paw" Dealer, as well as the only Cherished Teddies "Cherished Retailer" in the Pacific Northwest. They are an authorized club store for many of their lines. From miniatures and figurines to puppets and toys, you'll find just what you are looking for snuggled in the heart of downtown Sumner. Tom and Lorraine Young founded the store in 1986 and pride themselves on exceptional customer service, as well as unmatched selection. Their sales associates are all collectors themselves and are knowledgeable about details of their diverse lines. Golden Rule Bears has built a twenty-year international reputation of excellence. They accept all major credit cards, and mail and phone orders are never a problem. 1115-B Main Street, Sumner WA (253) 863-0280 or (800) 932 - 2327   www.goldenrulebears.com

# Nifty's Toy and Novelty Company

In Sumner, Nifty's Toy and Novelty Co. is an old-fashioned toy store. Nifty's offers fun and unique, non-electronic games and toys for children ages 1 to 99. At Nifty's, the idea is to provide the opportunity for kids to have fun and use their imaginations by offering hands-on children's toys and novelties. The store is browser shopper friendly. Original painted murals give it a warm, friendly, and fun atmosphere. Kay Kiser has owned Nifty's (formerly The Button Patch) for a decade. She stocks a wide selection of wooden toys and puzzles, including train sets, ramp racers and pull toys. For infants, there are soft and safe cuddle and teething toys. Little girls enjoy the fairy dresses, ballerina jewelry boxes and dolls. There is also an extensive selection of art supplies and kits. For boys, there are die-cast cars, kites, sport balls and yo-yos. In addition, there are board games for every age. With a gift from Nifty's, the fun has only begun!  1117 Main Street, Sumner WA    (253) 826-2635

# Victoria Sells

For 10,000 square feet of antique and collectible mall, visit Victoria Sells on South Meridian in Puyallup, Washington. Not big enough? Then try the Fircrest location on Regents Boulevard, between Tacoma and University Place. It covers 14,400 square feet. In either shop, what a selection! Shelley, chintz, art pottery, art glass, elegant and depression glass, china and porcelain, jewelry, linens, primitives, sports memorabilia, furniture. And of course, "a whole lot more." At the Fircrest location, that includes a frame shop and a bistro. In either location, you find a very friendly atmosphere with music from the 1920's and 30's in the air. Now and then you'll see people dancing. Customer service is high because the employees are the owners of the products they sell. Mall owners Jack and Judy Doepke have been antique collectors "forever." Opening the malls was a natural extension of their lifelong passion for antiques plus mall leasing and management.
125 S. Meridian, Puyallup WA or 1115 Regents Blvd., University Place WA
(253) 445-8330 or (253) 564-6599

Gifts                                       The Valley

## A Picket Fence

A Picket Fence is an inspired gift shop in the heart of downtown Sumner. For twelve years, owner/shopkeeper Lu Ann Iselin and her staff have been providing customer service that goes above and beyond. They make it a point to get to know their customers, even keeping detailed lists of customers' purchases so they can anticipate future needs and provide better service. When you come to shop at A Picket Fence, you will make a new friend. In addition to extraordinary service, A Picket Fence offers an eclectic array of gifts, focusing on the different and unusual, from old-fashioned candy in jars and specialty pre-packed soups and desserts, to Brighton jewelry and leather goods. Other popular lines offered here include Wee Forest Folk collectibles and the Crabtree & Evelyn line of body care products. Naturally, gift wrapping and delivery are available. A Picket Fence also serves espresso at an old-fashioned counter where you can pull up a stool. Customers love the store and come back again and again, delighting to see the changing assortment of offerings as the seasons progress. Christmas is an especially popular time of year, but absolutely any time is a good time to shop here.   1006 Main Street, Sumner WA  (253) 863-6048

## Simple Tidings

Suzanne Sallander had a wonderful idea and the result is this charming and different store in the heart of downtown Sumner she has been operating since 1984. Simple Tidings is a store full of useful luxuries; there are no dust-catchers here. Everything is useful and you will be charmed by the affordable prices as well as the array of choices. Simple Tidings is a place where you can go to pamper yourself without breaking your budget. Suzanne has built a steady

clientele, who come for both the genuinely helpful and courteous staff and the extensive variety of reasonably priced linens, bulk potpourri, soaps and body care products, candles and other home furnishings. Customers also love the old-fashioned candy, sodas and gift items.
1107 Main Street, Sumner WA  (253) 863-7933

# Joyful Things

Perhaps it was just coincidence, or maybe fate played a hand in putting the lovely old house on the market just as Joyce Compton, who had admired it so often in passing, was thinking about starting her own business. Six years later, Joyce's business and the house are still a perfect fit, as anyone who shops at Joyful Things can attest. Appropriately for a business based in a hundred-year-old home, Joyful Things has been a family affair. Joyce and her husband Jim spent all their free time putting the house back in shape. Their children pitched in as well, financially, artistically, and with plain old elbow grease to get this quaint little shop running. The shop's number one employee is "cosmic daughter" Stephanie. Befitting its family theme, Joyful Things is a store full of beautiful gift items that people can afford. The heart and soul of this store is based on customer service and small town hospitality. Jim suggested the name, and it fits the store's joyful, welcoming atmosphere to a "T." Joyce says, "We are very blessed because through these doors pass the nicest people in the world." Here you'll find soaps, clocks, candles, games, stationery, jewelry, kitchenware, and much more. Customers say that "if you're having trouble finding a gift, you'll find it at Joyful Things." Free gift wrapping is offered as well. Joyful Things really does have everything you need. 315 Second Street NE, Puyallup WA (253) 840-4941

# Baskets & Things

If you're looking for a unique gift shop in Puyallup, Baskets & Things is the place for you. For twenty-five years, Cheryl Metcalf and her loyal staff have provided a wide variety of home accessories. Home décor, antique furniture, candles, jewelry, bath and soaps, Puyallup Valley jam and gourmet foods and candy. Baskets & Things carries a large line of greeting cards, including Northwest photographer Connie Disney's cards. Having a problem picking out a gift? Baskets & Things specializes in customer service and complimentary gift wrap all year round.
121 Meeker Avenue SW, Puyallup WA (253) 841-7981

# Today's Country Store

Visitors in search of unique gifts and antiques should be sure to stop in at Today's Country Store in Sumner. With an amazing array of old and new products, there is truly something for everyone. Owners Amy McCoy and Kris Williamson opened the store six years ago, but they are not new to the world of antiques and collectibles. Between the two of them, they have over 30 years experience buying and selling antiques. Today's Country Store is located in the heart of downtown Sumner. The building once housed the old general store and guests walk across the original old fir floors. The store is well-known for showcasing a seasonal display that is changed throughout the year. New collectibles are always added to the stock, which means every visit is a new experience. The store carries an impressive array of early country furniture, ironstone and glassware, vintage holiday décor, garden antiques, old windows and screen doors, artist and one-of-a-kind jewelry, bath and body products, whimsical paper products and home accents! Williamson and McCoy are always willing to help customers choose the perfect item to add to their décor. The owners specialize in teaching customers how to include antiques with newer items to create a unique personal style.
1008 Main Street, Sumner WA (253) 826-6646

## Gifts — East Side

# Birth and Beyond

Ten years ago, John and Lyndsey Starkey opened this wonderful store that caters to all your new family needs. Birth and Beyond brings together all those must-have items for families with a new baby on the way. Whether you are breastfeeding or bottle feeding, Birth and Beyond can provide you and your baby with all you might need. They are the most complete Breastfeeding Center in the Northwest. The large selection of nursing bras is amazing and their sizes will fit almost all new moms. The Birth and Beyond staff are all experienced moms who are ready and able to assist you to find products and information that have passed the real life test of quality and practicality. Birth and Beyond designs and makes its own brand of slings and manufactures a full line of cotton diapers, swaddling blankets and burp cloths. They carry a variety of lotions, oils, herbs and soaps to spoil and pamper mom and baby. If you're pregnant, have a new baby or are just interested in learning more about childbirth, this store should be a definite stop. Now in two locations.
2610 E Madison Street, Seattle WA  (206) 324-4831   317 NW Gilman Boulevard # 48, Issaquah WA  (425) 392 - 6665   www.birthandbeyond.com

# White Horse Toys

Issaquah's Gilman Village is a one-of-kind open-air shopping center where the shops are all located in historic buildings that have been saved from destruction. One such building is the Wold Barn. It dates from 1908, and is now home to White Horse Toys. The business was created in 1995 by Molly and Bill Handley and daughter Debra Lewis, who moved to Issaquah from California, and is now the shop manager. They started it in smaller quarters, seven years before moving into the 3,000 square foot barn in 2002. The shop offers a dazzling array of toys.

Appropriately for a business that appeals so much to families, White Horse Toys is a multi-generational enterprise. In fact, opening a toy store was something Debra and Molly had wanted to do for many years before it finally became a reality. And for Molly and Bill's ten grandchildren, having a toy store in the family must seem like a dream come true. In addition to carrying European toys, White Horse Toys also stocks high-quality manufactured toys, such as Steiff animals and William Britain soldiers (the same classic figures that were once made with lead, now made with consumer-safe materials). White Horse Toys offers free consultations for customers with special shopping needs and free gift wrapping, too.
317 NW Gilman Boulevard #13, Issaquah WA (425) 391-1498   www.whitehorsetoys.com

# The Picture Show

The Picture Show provides a very meaningful and deeply personal service. The mission of owner Deborah Johnson is to preserve artwork and family memorabilia and to include the stories that accompany them. Deborah frames photos, paintings, medals and other treasures that you may bring to The Picture Show. The service that sets her apart is having the customer write the history of the piece to be framed. She carefully has customers use acid-free paper and a de-acidified ink pen, then places the information on the back of the item being framed. The cherished belonging is preserved for the family's heritage and for generations to come. Deborah has "gold star" customers who framed photos of their wedding, their children, their children's weddings and then their grandchildren. Her heritage preservation links the past to the future. She encourages the framing of children's artwork. It is a very special message to pass on that a child's work of art can be taken care of in a way that would allow it to be shared with their great grandchildren. The Picture Show has a special order art department for open stock and limited edition prints. They also carry cards and gifts. Visit The Picture Show in Issaquah's precious Gilman Village for inspiring ways to preserve the treasures that you hold dear. 317 NW Gilman Boulevard, Bldg. 12, Issaquah WA (425) 392 - 5199

# Rosa Mundi's

With two showrooms in the greater Puget Sound area, you will find beautiful, hard-to-find furniture and accessories in two distinct venues. In the heart of downtown Edmonds, you will find traditional American furniture from early 1800s through the 1930s. The enduring craftsmanship of this collection in woods of mahogany, walnut, cherry and rosewood are showcased in elegant, room-like settings. This 4,000 square foot showroom features a large selection of china, a surprising selection of transferware, as well as service plates, sterling silver, cut glass, Meissen porcelain and more. In the wine country of Woodinville, quality English, French and Italian furniture and hard-to-find decorative accessories make this store a must-see! If the English Manor or the French Chateau lifestyle is for you, you will find special items you have long sought after. Both stores deliver within the greater Puget Sound area and ship nationwide.
318 Main Street, Edmonds WA (425) 771-6598  13109 NE 175th Street, Woodinville WA (425) 806-1732  www.rosamundis.com

# Spoiled by Nana

Spoiled by Nana is a one of a kind find for grandparents who love to spoil their grandchildren. The owners, Lyndsey and John Starkey opened the store two years ago when they became grandparents for the first time. The store carries a wide variety of high quality infant and children's wear from preemie to size 6X. It features fantastic lines like Kissy Kissy, Baby Nay and Biscotti. Along with a great selection of clothing, you can find special gift items like Bunnies by the Bay huggable animals, Little Giraffe chenille blankets and robes, and Kaloo's plush toys. Even your special occasions' needs are covered. Spoiled by Nana has tuxedos for the youngest gentleman, and communion and flower girl dresses for the little princess in your life, with all the accessories to make them special. The staff at Spoiled by Nana are all grandmas or grandmas-to-be and are experienced in helping you find the perfect gift for the best grandchildren in the world – yours. Spoiled by Nana is located in Gillman Village, an Eastside specialty shopping landmark. It doesn't get any better than this! 317 NW Gilman Boulevard # 42, Issaquah WA (425) 392 - 6507  www.spoiledbynana.com

# Doll Palace General Hospital at Country Village

Doll Palace General Hospital has been treating special patients for over 20 years. There Dr. Ken Smith D.D.R. and Dr. Esther Smith D.D.B. have looked after and lovingly healed countless damaged dolls. Carefully bringing beloved dolls back to near perfect health is the best reward for Ken and Esther. As retailers of fine quality dolls such as Madame Alexander, Ginny and many other doll artists, they understand what a treasure these dolls can be. More than mere toys, they are works of art, treasures and priceless memories. The Doll Palace General Hospital receives repair items from all over America and around the world. The Smiths are well known for their artistic abilities in reversing damage. You can trust that the repairs done will be of excellent quality. They will also be completed quickly as the Smiths carry a constant supply of repair products for all types of dolls from porcelain to vinyl and composition. They also keep on hand ample supplies of hair, eyes, bodies and accessories for many different doll types. But the Doll Palace General Hospital is not just a hospital for the sick; it is also where your new addition can be acquired. With a good selection of choice collectable dolls and global shipping options, you will be able to find that special gift for that special someone and have it sent anywhere you choose. 23814 Bothell-Everett Highway, Bothell WA (425) 481-6522

## Gifts — I-5 Corridor

## Duffy's Antique Mall

Dan and Nancy Duffy, fourth-generation Centralians, had a flower shop for 27 years. In 1992, they turned their business sense and eye for beauty toward antiques. They bought a historic building, a car dealership in the 1920s and later a furniture store, and with great help from family and friends, turned it into Duffy's Antique Mall. With Robb Berry, their long-term mall manager, the Duffy's have crafted a fine showcase of beautiful things at reasonable prices for discriminating buyers. Specializing in refinished furniture, glassware, paintings, and Native American basketry, the carefully selected items are displayed in two stories of vignettes and groupings enjoyed by a loyal clientele and first-timers as well. A newer area of the business features decorative items for the home, ranging from the unusual to traditional and classic home décor, and including tasteful, framed prints. Knowledgeable about the State of Washington and steeped in the history of Centralia, the Duffys have been instrumental in the preservation and revitalization of their community. You will find beautiful selections in a one-of-a-kind setting at Duffy's Antique Mall. 310 N Tower, Centralia WA (360) 736-1282 www.duffysantiquemall.com

## Common Folk Company

Inviting, charming, approachable. These are terms customers use to describe the Common Folk Company located in Centralia. Common Folk is anything but common. Imagine walking into a shop that literally takes your breath away with its huge floral arrangements and beautiful treasures. Now imagine the smell of fresh baked pie and steamy espresso drifting towards you from the adjoining Good Lunch Café. Kathryn and Eric Straub, along with their long time employees, sell beautiful gifts and home décor along with highly personalized service. You will find unusual antiques, fabulous and funky purses, European soaps, statuary, decorations for your home and much more. Since its establishment in 1989, Common Folk continues to hold seasonal holiday events featuring festive décor and regional folk artists to brighten your holiday enjoyment. 125 East High Street, Centralia WA (360) 736-8066

## Up the Creek Antiques

When Dan and Sue Horwath moved to Centralia from Maryland's Eastern Shore in 1975, they needed a way to furnish their first house. Those efforts blossomed into a wholesale business called Up The Creek Antiques, a fitting name for a business that began 15 miles from the nearest town near Lincoln Creek. They dealt in American antique furniture purchased from their old hunting grounds on the East Coast. Over time their business gathered a retail following, so they opened the American Antique Furniture Market in 1990. Yet a name like Up The Creek Antiques was so popular that they decided to bring it back into their business name, so they are now officially Up The Creek Antiques – American Antique Furnishings. In 2004, Up The Creek Antiques purchased their own building, restored its original tin ceilings and walls, wooden floors and period appointments. The projected 7,000 square foot showroom displays antique furniture in a variety of periods, styles and woods along with vintage appointments appropriate to the furnishings. There are also Classic Creations custom-built pieces. Their restoration shop is staffed by experienced craftsmen committed to restoring pieces authentically. Whether you need a chair re-glued or wish to explore their expertly restored building and showroom, a visit to Up The Creek Antiques is a chance to step back in time. 209 North Tower, Centralia WA (360) 330-0427 or (800) 246-0868
www.upthecreek-antiques.com

**Gifts**  I-5 Corridor

# Sauk River Trading Post

At the Sauk River Trading Post, you can find fishing supplies and a terrific selection of outdoor clothing, but most of all you can find the knowledge you need to select exactly what you need for river rafting, hunting and especially for fishing. You will also find a wonderful rustic building with old growth timber beams and, among the unique features, a spectacular two-story river rock fireplace and a stairway with naturally curved yew wood railings. The Sauk River Trading Post fishing department offers all the gear you could wish for including bait, lures and a fly fishing section. The sporting goods department has recreational equipment for hiking, camping, and backpacking, as well as survival gear. They also feature local artists, such as carvings and canes by Webb Border, paintings by Sharon London Mercantel, and work by master carver Gene Boyd. See their website for a gallery of his work. You can also see all the clothing brands and styles they carry, everything from cozy socks to bib overalls, and a list of the local events in the area. To really appreciate the Sauk River Trading Post, you should really come in to see it all for yourself. 1015 Seeman Street, Darrington WA (360) 436-1500 or (800) 488-4618  www.saukrivertradingpost.com

**Gifts**  South Puget Sound

# Olympic Cards & Comics

Gabrielle Shephard ("Gabi" to long-time patrons) started working for Olympic Cards and Comics in 1990 and bought it in 1993. Since then, thanks to her family and the support of the community ("They made it happen," Gabi explains), the store continues to thrive. At Olympic Cards and Comics, there's something for all ages. They carry a great selection of comic books and graphic novels, card and board games, collectible toys and statues, and sport cards and memorabilia. Gabi has created a positive, safe environment where the whole community can gather and hang out. The shop is open during the day for comic books and collectibles, and at night for game playing. On a typical night, there may be 25-50 people playing games or reading. They love kids and everyone is welcome as long as you respect your fellow players – no swearing, please. In the words of one customer, "it's a great place to hang out, meet new people and learn new games." 4129 Pacific Avenue, Lacey WA (360) 459-7721 www.olympiccardsandcomics.com

# BonTon Fashion

Located on the waterfront boardwalk at Percival Landing in Olympia, BonTon Fashion is a specialty boutique featuring an exciting mix of clothing and gifts. BonTon was started in 1989 by Bonnie O'Reilly and Toni Weaver (the store moniker is a combination of the partners' first names). Bonnie retired in 1997. Since then, Toni has put her own personal stamp on the business, taking special care to cater to the identity and style of her customers in Olympia. Featuring the Blue Willi's line of clothing imported from Denmark and made of all natural fabrics, BonTon also sells one-of-a-kind clothing, accessories, wearable art by local artists and unique gifts. With sizes ranging from 6 to 16, they offer the latest in women's apparel and specialize in contemporary soft-wear. BonTon participates in the Olympia Downtown Association and in Arts Walk. Next time you're in Olympia, visit BonTon for a satisfying shopping experience. You will receive personalized attention from the very competent staff, along with complimentary gift wrapping and plenty of free parking.  501 Columbia Street, Olympia WA  (360) 754-6556

# Pacific Northwest Shop

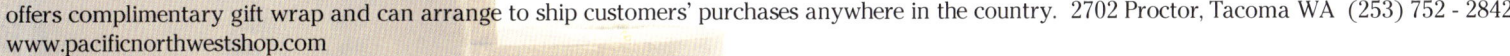

The Pacific Northwest Shop, open seven days a week, is located in Tacoma's historic Proctor district. The shop is where you'll find special gifts "Made In Our Corner Of America." Since 1978, the Pacific Northwest Shop has offered specialty foods, Pacific Northwest wines, regional books, paper goods, candles, clothing, wall décor, pottery, North Coast Indian merchandise and toys. In addition, you will find one of the largest selections of Mt. St. Helens volcanic ash art glass in the region. The store also stocks an exclusive "Mt. Rainier Box" filled with an assortment of "Taste of the Pacific Northwest" specialty foods. Delicious alder smoked salmon, chocolate truffles, huckleberry jam, specialty teas and coffees, Walla Walla sweet onion mustards, cashew roca and dozens of regional wines are just a few of the hundreds of gourmet food choices at the Pacific Northwest Shop. Located in Proctor, one of Tacoma's twelve "urban villages," the shop is near the University of Puget Sound in the city's beautiful North End and is easily accessible from I - 5. The Pacific Northwest Shop offers complimentary gift wrap and can arrange to ship customers' purchases anywhere in the country.  2702 Proctor, Tacoma WA  (253) 752 - 2842  www.pacificnorthwestshop.com

# Barker Road Collection

Opened in August of 2000, Barker Road Collection in the Old Town section of Tacoma is truly a unique and remarkable find. Started by siblings William and Linda McElroy and Ginger Shorey, the store honors both their parents and their extensive travels. From an early age the three siblings, along with their other sibling and parents, traveled the world extensively, living in the Middle East, Europe, Africa, Asia, Hawaii and several cities in the United States. Through their travels, they developed an avid passion for collecting various world treasures. After returning from separate careers, William, Linda and Ginger decided to open Barker Road Collection. They select the items for their store based upon these criteria: from a country they lived in or traveled through extensively, it reminds them of their wonderful childhood or is an item they personally use in their daily lives. They carry everything from furniture and home accessories to soaps, jewelry, stationary, limited edition merchandise and a women's apparel line by New York-based designer Yansi Fugel. A 2001 and 2003 finalist in the Best in the Northwest Washington State Family Business Awards, Barker Road Collection is the perfect place to visit for those looking for an extraordinary and enchanting experience.  2225 N 30th Street, Tacoma WA  (253) 572 - 9686

# Home Decor, Gardens, Flowers & Markets

# Home Decor, Gardens, Flowers & Markets     Olympic Peninsula

## Wild Sage
### World Teas, Tonics, & Herbs

When it's tea time in Port Townsend, seek out Wild Sage, where Susan Walker and her staff engage people with premium teas and herbs for good health and enjoyment. Susan believes teas are simple pleasures that can connect us to ourselves, or even to each other. "Tea is the world's most popular beverage, and it promotes good health, too," says Susan. Rich in antioxidants, relaxing and rejuvenating, tea is truly beneficial to the body, mind and spirit. To bring you the best and widest selection, Wild Sage offers all types of teas in bulk, loose-leaf tins and teabags from many superior-quality world distributors. Wild Sage also carries teapots, tea wares, herbal tonics, flower essences and natural body care products for holistic health. Susan has an extensive background in natural health sciences. She invites you into Wild Sage, where she provides a "sanctuary of earthly delights" in which to discover and experience the vast world of teas, tonics and herbs. 227 Adams Street, Port Townsend WA (360) 379-1222  www.wildsageteas.com

## Angel Farm & All Things Lavender

Color, aroma and old-world charm abound at Angel Farm, a 20-acre lavender farm purchased by Cathy and Leeon Angel in 1999. Nestled in the heart of Sequim-Dungeness Valley, Angel Farm, complete with its 1920's farmhouse, is known for its deliciously fragrant varieties of lavender. Open to the public the second and third weeks of July, you can pick your own as you stroll through their sun-drenched lavender fields surrounded by the majestic Olympic Mountains. The vintage barn is used to dry and process thousands of fragrant lavender bouquets, and their Garden Shed Boutique abounds with glorious lavender gifts and products. In addition to selling wholesale both in the United States and abroad, the Angels are partners in All Things Lavender, a year-round retail outlet with stores at Seattle's world-famous Pike Place Market and at 230 Taylor Street in Port Townsend, Washington. There they carry a vast selection of premium natural lavender products including handcrafted soaps, body care products and aromatherapy candles. Angel Farm is open to the public only the second and third weeks in July during the height of the lavender blooming season, and participates in the highly acclaimed Sequim Lavender Festival during the third weekend in July. 5883 Old Olympic Highway, Sequim WA (360) 681-0348, (360) 379-2573 (Port Townsend) or (206) 652 - 5951 (Pikes Place Market) www.allthingslavender.net; www.lavenderfestival.com

## Country Aire Natural Food

Born in Port Angeles and raised on a 40-acre berry farm, Robyn Miletich's dream was to bring the country to downtown in a retail environment. With Country Aire Natural Foods, she has amply brought this dream to reality. This is a store where wood barrels are still used and all goods are displayed on wood shelving. The décor of antiques give the store a nostalgic "aire" of an "Ole General Store." Robyn's exuberance, optimism and work ethic show in every aspect of the store and have helped make it a success with devoted customers and delighted newcomers. Her staff is more like family. Dan and Linda are general/personnel managers and have been at the store for more than a decade. Robyn's mother, Eloise, has been working with Robyn since the store opened in 1975 (30 years). At 86, she is still helping in the office daily. In addition to the huge selection of natural foods, Country Aire is also known for bulk herbs, spices and grains (organic when possible), vitamin and herbal supplements, unique gifts and cruelty-free cosmetics. If you need something you can't find, be sure to let them know. The staff makes a great effort to ensure everyone's needs are met and satisfied.

117 E First Street, Port Angeles WA  (360) 452 - 7175

## Oliver's Lavender Farm

Do you like lavender? If so, you won't want to miss Oliver's, the biggest and best "Little Lavender Farm" in Sequim. It's a true treasure of Western Washington in the heart of the lavender capital of the U.S. Oliver's is a family operation run by Don and Claudine Oliver, raising over 2,100 lavender plants on 1¾ acres. It includes a drying barn and a gift shop. Don and Claudine designed the property to allow them to build a comfortable house surrounded by lavender fields, and the beauty of the setting in Washington's scenic Dungeness Valley leaves a lasting impression on visitors. The Olivers raise three main types of lavender: Grosso, Provence, and Royal Velvet. Other types featured in the U-pick operations and live plant sales may be seen in the demonstration garden. During the U-pick season, from June to September, visitors can go into the fields and cut their own bouquets. The shop, Claudine's "play house," features a mix of general and unique gift items, from lavender sachets to soaps, lotions, aprons, towels and coffee mugs. The ladies' lavender t-shirt designed by local artist Iris Ebey makes an especially appealing souvenir of your visit. The Olivers also welcome visitors or groups who wish to see how lavender grows, and they offer demonstrations of lavender propagation and processing.

82 Cameron Acres Lane, Sequim, WA  (360) 681 - 3789  www.oliverslavender.com

# Home Decor, Gardens, Flowers & Markets    Olympic Peninsula

## Holly's Fine Flowers

Prior to the onset of large corporations, there was the tradition of family-run businesses built from scratch. At Holly's Fine Flowers in Port Townsend, you'll find that tradition still exists. Owner Holly Mayshark started her business by borrowing five hundred dollars and making payments on a cooler. With time, she nurtured her company the same way

she arranges flowers: with care and great attention to detail. Successful since it's opening in 1981, Holly offers everything from traditional, garden-style and contemporary arrangements to fine gifts, arts and crafts, and much more. Located in the heart of the Historic District of Port Townsend in a building over a century old, Holly's Fine Flowers has evolved into the most prominent flower and gift shop in the area. Allow Holly and her skillfully trained staff to bring their creative energy to whatever occasion you may be acknowledging. Experience the refined difference that Holly's staff of helpful individuals bring to your floral expression.   825 Water Street, Port Townsend WA   (360) 385 - 5428 or (888) 385-5428   www.hollysfineflowers.com

## Holland Haven

Holland Haven is a rare, happy find in the Pacific Northwest, a European grocery store and delicatessen. It was created by David and Rebecca Pilling to meet a need. Having been raised Dutch, Rebecca had grown frustrated with the difficulty of obtaining real European ingredients for family recipes, and the result is a store that provides the many Port Angeles-area residents of European extraction with the foods they love. Initially focused on the deli, Holland Haven was also created to enhance the American appreciation for the diversity of European meats and cheeses. Holland Haven is a family-oriented business: Rebecca's mother, Grieta Sieg, and the Pillings' children, Matthew, Benjamin and Michelle, are all involved in running the store. The store provides not only European products but also a cozy, comforting family atmosphere. With an emphasis on Dutch, German, and British products, Holland Haven offers fresh sausages, including eleven different types of bratwurst, made with all natural ingredients and no fillers.  The imported chocolate and licorice are perennial favorites for many faithful customers in the grocery section.  Holland Haven imports whole wheel cheeses from over seven countries.  The deli features indoor seating and some of the best sandwiches you'll ever eat! Holland Haven also offers European housewares and gifts. The Delft blue pottery is especially popular.   103 West 1st Street, Port Angeles WA   (360) 417-9132

# Home Decor, Gardens, Flowers & Markets — Washington Coast

## Blooms, Baskets & Beyond

Blooms, Baskets and Beyond LLC, is a creative combination that offers you the best of several worlds. This blend is the result of combining the talents of owners Vena and Jerry Ross. The "blooms" are to be found in the colorful gardens where you are invited to come and relax among the lovely flowers (the result of Jerry's horticultural expertise). The "baskets" come from Vena's talent for life's niceties. And the "beyond" part is an eclectic mix of indoor and outdoor accessories. As Vena describes it, "Beyond is anything we want to put in the shop!" Some of the things you will find are antiques and art, like the underwater photography and driftwood creations by local artists. One of Jerry's specialties in landscape design is water gardens. They are busy reshaping and refining the public gardens that they took over not long ago. But not to forget Vena's baskets: you can choose from pre-made or create your own. They range from picnic baskets, to candy or wine and cheese. Vena has a wealth of special touches and items to include. So for a stroll in the gardens, shopping in a friendly store with loads of unusual things, buying a potted plant or shrub for your garden, or maybe stepping stones, or asking Jerry to design a water feature to go with them: Blooms, Baskets and Beyond has it all. Vena and Jerry would love to welcome you.

584 Point Brown Avenue NE, Ocean Shores WA  (360) 289-2034

# Home Decor, Gardens, Flowers & Markets — Kitsap Peninsula

## Hearts & Homespun

Opened in January of 1987, Hearts & Homespun is Kitsap County's oldest country gift shop. It was born out of a love for country decorating and collecting instilled by the owner's mother. Hearts & Homespun is a destination for those who love the warmth of country style decorating. The shop carries a line of classic wooden chandeliers handmade in Ohio, a North Carolina furniture line, delightful lace curtains and runners from Iowa and so much more. From collectible wooden houses to candles and garden decor, Hearts & Homespun offers both the decorative and the functional. No visit to historic downtown Poulsbo is complete without a visit to Hearts & Homespun. It is truly a feast to the eyes and the soul. 18937 Front Street, Poulsbo WA (360) 697-6699

# Home Decor, Gardens, Flowers & Markets

## Seattle Metro

## Ambience at Milltown

The Ambience at Milltown in Edmonds provides a truly unique line of home accessories and decorating options. Owner Sharon Shannon's products marry artistic creation with recycled furniture and functional design. Her shop, located in a remodeled car repair station in Old Milltown, was originally built in the early 1900's. The area has a great deal of character and Ambience at Milltown in Edmonds captures the essence of the area. Taking an unappreciated ordinary older piece and creating an extraordinary piece that will be a treasure for you is their hallmark. Home furnishings include durable stools with classic appeal made from rear automobile axles, exquisitely designed lamps in fine arts styles and cabinets made from recycled wood windows. Home accessories include cigar boxes transformed into vignettes, antique silverware crafted into pens and frames, and special one-of-a-kind paperweights using common river rock and accessories to create "Pet Rockettes." Custom made items are available as well. Just let them know what you are looking for. With a fabulous variety of styles and designs to choose from, take some time to peruse this entertaining shop. Ambience at Milltown is one of the must stops for your trip to Edmonds. 201 Fifth Avenue, Suite 8, Edmonds WA (425) 771-1881 www.ambienceinedmonds.com

## Don Willis Furniture

Do you remember, as a child, walking through the handmade furniture stores with your parents and inhaling the deep fragrance of real wood? These days that scent is hard to come by, but it can be found again at the Don Willis Furniture stores in the Lake City and Ballard neighborhoods of Seattle. Founded in 1948, the original Lake City store contains three floors of genuine wood furniture. Allow yourself to relive the days when things were made to last. They guarantee not to use particle board, and provide finished, ready to finish and the option to customize the finish you need. With several options of wood to choose from, you can find just the right look for your needs. Paul Willis, president of the company and son of the late founder Don Willis, presents a modern store that honors its past. Although the store originally made all its pieces by hand, local furniture manufacturers are now supplying the store with an extensive inventory to fit the customers' needs. Come and see for yourself the full selection of shapes, sizes, colors and styles to provide your home or work space with affordable and distinctive furnishings. 10516 Lake City Way NE, Seattle WA (206) 524-9944 1712 NW Market Street, Seattle WA (206) 782-3333 www.donwillisfurniture.com

# Home Decor, Gardens, Flowers & Markets — Seattle Metro

## Olsen's Scandinavian Foods

Olsen's Scandinavian Foods is located in the heart of Ballard, the Scandinavian community in Seattle. Many authentic foods are prepared from traditional Norwegian recipes passed down through several generations. Most of Olsen's other products are imported directly from Scandinavia. Olsen's Foods was founded in 1960. In 1997, it was bought by the Endresen sisters, Anita and Reidun, from Sandeid, Norway. Olsen's offers a wide variety of Scandinavian food and gift products including many types of fish, cheese, breads, condiments, kitchenwares, cookbooks and more. Along with operating an authentic foods store, the Endresen sisters keep tradition alive, creating a cornerstone of culture within the thriving Ballard neighborhood that has a warm, familiar place within Seattle. 2248 NW Market Street, Seattle WA (206) 783-8288 www.scandinavianfoods.net

# Uli's Famous Sausage

In the heart of Seattle's famous Pike Place Public Market, master butcher Uli Lengenberg's shop offers a tantalizing array of handmade authentic German and international sausages. Using no coloring agents and restricting his use of preservatives strictly to those needed for safety, Uli uses his culinary skills and extensive experience to create sausage masterpieces. With all-natural cuts of pork, lamb, chicken, beef and turkey, Uli honors his German background with specialties like Nurnberger rostbratwurst, but he knows his way around a Polish kielbassa and a Cajun andouille, too. Try the English bangers, Spanish chorizo, a French merguez or perhaps the pork apple bratwurst, made with locally-grown apples. There's more to choose from, including chicken dishes and fresh turkey sage sausage for the calorie-conscious. Born and raised in Siegerland, Germany, Uli learned the art of master butchery in Germany. He then moved to Taipei, Taiwan, where he practiced his craft for twelve years. There Uli met his wife Jean, who was teaching at the Taipei-American School. Jean convinced him to bring his sausage-making skills back to her home town of Seattle. In addition to the delighted customers of his shop, Uli also supplies fresh sausage to many area restaurants. Recently Uli's Famous Sausage earned the praise of Master Chef Emeril Lagasse, who featured the shop on a recent television appearance. 1511 Pike Place, Seattle WA (206) 839-1000  www.ulisfamoussausage.com

# Larry's Markets

It's not often that one can inhale the aromas of several varieties of foods, taste wine or sample freshly prepared products while doing everyday chores. At Larry's Markets, located throughout Northwest Washington, what would normally be a mundane task of grocery shopping can be likened to dining out at a four-star restaurant. Locally owned since 1945, Larry's Markets offers only the most qualified staff along with their healthy, clean and engaging atmosphere. While you select from their outstanding variety of meats, seafood and produce from the freshest and safest of products obtained from local farmers and fishermen, the experienced staff at Larry's will entertain your taste buds and your mind. Larry's Markets not only provides recipes and tips to help improve your cooking experience, they also offer a vast selection of excellent wines, as well as boasting over three hundred and fifty different varieties of cheeses. Great atmosphere, excellent products and sipping wine while grocery shopping is what brings customers back again and again to Larry's Markets.  12321 NE 120th Place, Kirkland WA - (425) 820-2300 • 699 120th Avenue NE, Bellevue WA • 7320 170th Avenue NE, Redmond WA • 100 Mercer Street N, Seattle WA • 10008 Aurora Avenue N, Seattle WA • 3725 S 144th Street, Tukwila WA   www.larrysmarkets.com

# Home Decor, Gardens, Flowers & Markets       Seattle Metro

## Laguna Vintage Pottery

You have some fine pottery dinnerware from the 1920s through 1950s, and you're trying to find a replacement for the salad plate your child used as a frisbee, right? Then you're looking for Laguna Vintage Pottery in Seattle, one of the largest vintage pottery shops in America. Concentrating on exceptional quality, perfect condition, rare colors and unusual shapes, Laguna specializes in discontinued and collectible American dinnerware and art pottery. Collectors/owners Michael Lindsey and Bif Brigman scour the country for the finest examples of American pottery. They have been curators for local exhibitions and have lectured for the Seattle Art Museum, Historic Seattle and the National Antique Appraisers Association. Laguna has an inventory that includes all major American design styles of the 20th Century: Mission/Arts and Crafts, Art Deco, Art Nouveau, California Modern, Mid-Century Modern and others. The store has thousands of patterns of discontinued American-made dinnerware in stock to replace your lost or broken pieces. Recently, Elle Decor magazine featured Laguna as "one of the nation's most comprehensive sources for 20th Century tableware and art pottery." Country Home magazine called Laguna, "one of the 20 must see shops in the nation." Says Harry L. Rinker, a national antiques and collectibles expert, "Laguna is a Seattle landmark, equal to the Space Needle. Thank God I live on the East Coast; otherwise I would be in debtor's prison."   116 S Washington Street, Seattle WA  (206) 682 - 6162  www.lagunapottery.com

# Home Decor, Gardens, Flowers & Markets

## Skagit Valley

## Skagit Valley Gardens

Located on 25 acres in the beautiful Skagit Valley of Washington, Skagit Valley Gardens offers a wonderful experience, whether you are in the market for serious gardening advice and plants, or are on a

light-hearted search for the perfect gift. In spring and summer, the 16,000 square foot retail area is filled to the brim with an abundance of colorful annuals perennials, harvest baskets and much more. When fall comes, the Gardens

are transformed into a Christmas wonderland with theme trees, ornaments and unique gifts. For the past 22 years, the welcoming staff at Skagit Valley Gardens has been providing customers with distinctive plants and top-notch service. Just take a walk through the display gardens and you will find a wealth of inspiration created by Skagit Valley Gardens' owner, trained horticulturalist Gary Lorenz. In the center of Skagit Valley Gardens, you'll find the Garden Café, serving coffee, soups, salads, sandwiches, desserts and many other delightful treats. The Rooster Coop features great outdoor furniture and accessories, while in the Gift Barn you'll find specialty items for that hard-to-shop-for person. These are among the many amenities that make a visit to Skagit Valley Gardens fun as well as fruitful. 18923 Johnson Road, Mount Vernon WA (360) 424-6760
www.skagitvalleygardens.com

# Home Decor, Gardens, Flowers & Markets                Skagit Valley

## Cascadian Farm

Three miles east of Rockport, you can find the very best of 100 percent organic produce at Cascadian Farm, birth place of Cascadian Farm brand organic foods now sold worldwide. The roadside stand is open daily from May through October and features homemade ice cream, shakes, shortcakes, fresh organic berries, espresso, snacks, jams, pickles, salsas, u-pick berries and a pumpkin patch. All fruit and vegetables are picked fully ripe for peak flavor and nutrition. Managers Jim

and Harlyn Meyer state their philosophy this way: "Organic farming is farming in harmony with nature. At Cascadian, we take our role as stewards of the land seriously. We use crop rotation, composting and cover crops to build the soil, which in turn feeds the crops. We encourage Mother Nature's pest management program by creating habitat for beneficial insects that help us control the harmful ones. Our entire operation, from planting through harvest and packing, is scrutinized by the Washington State Department of Agriculture, which certifies that strict organic standards are followed." Enjoy fresh strawberries in June, raspberries in July, blueberries in July and August, a pumpkin patch in October and frozen berries all year. Be sure to stop by the first week in October for the Harvest Festival. Come to Cascadian Farm and see for yourself what great organic farming produces for your eating enjoyment.
55749 S.R. 20, Rockport WA
(360) 853-8173   www.cfarm.com

# Antique Rose Farm

What is an antique rose? The owners of the Antique Rose Farm will be happy to explain that to qualify as a horticultural antique, a rose must have origins that date from at least from 1863. However, they have some antique roses that may date back thousands of years. This is one of the many surprises that awaits you at this Snohomish attraction. Antique Rose Farm was originally a dairy farm that now has a breathtaking array of colors, shapes and fragrances of roses. The flowers they specialize in grow well in the Northwest and are very fragrant, as well as beautiful. Surprisingly, they are also very disease resistant and hardy. Some of the varieties they carry are hybrid teas, floribundas, bourbons, gallicas, mosses, damasks and English. Their rugosa roses, as an example, are very resilient and easy to grow, with an abundance of blooms. They can advise you on the best varieties for your particular growing circumstances. They also have a large selection of perennials and 5,000 square feet of furniture and other antiques in a charming barn, featuring folk art, gifts, rose books and more. The Antique Rose Farm gives classes in the care of roses as well. This is a wonderful day trip, just three quarters of an hour from Seattle. Plan to visit the first two weeks in June to enjoy the Farm's annual Rose Festival. 12220 Springhetti Road, Snohomish WA (360) 568-1919

# Home Decor, Gardens, Flowers & Markets — The Valley

## Feather Your Nest

Feather Your Nest is a home décor store that inspires people to look at their homes in a different light. This family-oriented business, owned by Kurstyn Schober and run with help from her mother, sister, husband and five children, features two different kinds of country décor, cottage and classic American, and specializes in items that will help homeowners create a welcoming space where friends and family can gather. Kurstyn started out as a home crafter and the shop came about almost accidentally to provide an outlet for her creativity. With an emphasis on home furnishings, she chose a name based on her mother's favorite saying, "I need a little something to feather my nest." The store features antiques and gifts as well as decorating items, with the emphasis shifting according to the seasons. In winter, items such as the Winterland Friends Collection of snowman-themed decorations are highlighted, and gardening items are brought to the fore during the spring and summer. You can find something delightful for any time or season here and in a wide range of prices, ensuring that everyone can take something home regardless of their budget.
1103 Main Street, Sumner WA   (253) 891-2149   www.featheryournestofsumner.com

## VanLierop Garden Market

At the VanLierop Garden Market in Sumner, you will find an extensive collection of unusual annual and perennial flowers. Since starting the year-round market for garden-style living in 1998, Anne VanLierop-Johnson and April and Bonnie VanLierop have successfully created a service-oriented business. Using both local floral deliveries and Teleflora, VanLierop Garden Market is able to cater to individual needs for the freshest flowers available. They carry beautifully artistic holiday décor for every season, as well as the exclusive candle line by "Illume" and pottery line "Aw." In addition to the market, there is a large outdoor garden featuring numerous Northwest artists and plantings of the newest annuals. The garden also houses a unique collection of water features and "Rocknoggins" rock carvings, taking "yard art" to the next level. In January of 2005, Sorci's Delicatessen di Roma opened in the same location, with chef/owner Patrick Amato offering a full-service Italian deli specializing in imported and domestic meats, cheeses, breads and pasta. Whether or not you wish to take the time to work on your own yard, check out the VanLierop Garden Market and marvel at what they've done with theirs.
1020 Ryan Avenue, Sumner WA   (253) 862 - 8510   www.vanlieropgardenmarket.com

# Home Decor, Gardens, Flowers & Markets                    East Side

## Front Street Market Red Apple

Do you like fresh Northwest Chioppino? Do you like it served by warm, friendly people who love their work and love taking care of you? Then you belong at the Front Street Market Red Apple in Issaquah. For over three decades, Front Street Market Red Apple has served this community, earning an outstanding reputation for customer service as well as for its vast selection of quality products.

Those products range from floral arrangements, cut flowers and plants, to USDA Choice Angus beef, fresh-daily seafood, fruits and vegetables from local farms and distant lands. They also carry a large selection of gourmet, natural, organic and \environmentally-friendly products. The Deli Department prepares party trays, hot and cold food, sandwiches and more. Bill and Rebecca Knowles are the owners here; Lori Steendahl has been the store director for 27 years. Bills' parents started the business in 1974 and have kept it in the family. Rebecca's family has lived in Issaquah for many generations. So if you're looking for convenience, freshness, quality and a warm, friendly atmosphere, you have found it. The employees love their jobs here and you'll love the way they take care of you. Seniors, note that Tuesday is Senior Discount day.
80 Front Street S, Issaquah WA  (425) 392 - 5371  www.redapplemarkets.com

## Yakima Fruit Market

Yakima Fruit Market and Nursery has been celebrating the seasons and the feeling of Bothell since 1938! The history of the Market reaches back to Prohibition when the location housed a roadhouse called the Blue Swallow Inn and, judging from the old timers' accounts, it was quite a rowdy place. In the 1940's, a local family bought the old roadhouse and used it as a residence. As a sideline, they began selling Eastern Washington fruits and vegetables from the front porch and soon had a thriving business literally on their doorstep. Over time the business evolved into a seasonal fruit market selling locally grown produce, cut flowers, groceries, blooming annuals, perennials and gorgeous hanging baskets for the garden. In December, the Market transforms into a Christmas tree forest, with fresh-cut, locally grown Christmas trees and greenery. Owners Stuart and Karin Poage have worked at the market for over 30 years and are proud to carry on this heritage business with the help of their two sons and daughter-in-law, and a dedicated staff. The Market is open from March through October with a short closure before and after the December Christmas tree season.  The owners and their crew enjoy educating customers about healthy eating and how to choose ripe, delicious fruits and vegetables. They pride themselves on providing quality produce at reasonable prices. The "Grapevine" is a free monthly newsletter that tells customers what's in season and what's coming next and also provides recipes and community news.
17321 Bothell Way NE,  Bothell, WA  (425) 486-6888  www.yakimafruitmarket.com

# Home Decor, Gardens, Flowers & Markets

## East Side

# Country Village

Bothell's Country Village Shops offer a full menu of seasonal fun for local shoppers and out-of-town visitors alike. The pleasant cluster of farm-style buildings is a perfect place to spend the day enjoying the specialty shops, day spa and restaurants that share the 13-acre grounds with the resident ducks, chickens and rabbits. Country Village is open seven days a week. You can stop in any time or you might want to schedule your visit to enjoy a special event. The Country Village Farmers Market is open every Friday from mid-May through September. Over 30 vendors gather here to sell their freshly picked produce and handcrafted items. With live music midday, it's the fun place to be on summer Fridays! Or maybe you'd enjoy a car show? Bring your own vintage car or just come and enjoy everyone else's. The PT Cruiser Show and the Father's Day Car Show are in June. The Fall Car Show takes place in early September. Gardeners might prefer to visit the Fuchsia Show in August; the Dahlia Show and the Koi Show are in September. A Latino festival, La Fiesta Viva! is also in September and features plenty of lively music, craft booths and delicious food. Country Village is a wonderful place to gather friends and family, either in a casual setting at the company picnic field with its horseshoes, badminton, bocce court and putting course, or in the more elegant Courtyard Hall, a perfect spot for weddings, meetings and parties.  23718 Bothell-Everett Highway, Bothell WA  (425) 483-2250  www.countryvillagebothell.com

# Heartland Interiors

Heartland Interiors in Bothell has a straight forward philosophy about furnishing your home: "Buy what you love." That, according to owners Diane Wainhouse and Val Scalzo, is the first step in creating interiors you will enjoy for years. It is Heartland's goal to help client design rooms that are inviting, comfortable and reflect the essence of their personality and lifestyle. There is so much more to interior design than just putting furniture in a room. The elements of scale, color, balance, light and style must all come together for a project to be successful. Most people know what they like, they just need help pulling it all together. Also, being an owner-operated business gives Heartland Interiors a hands-on approach to merchandising with a unique and charming mix of colors, fabrics, furniture and accessories. One of the things people love most about the store is that everything is constantly changing and there is always something new! Heartland Interiors, established in 1985, has participated in the Seattle Street of Dreams for over 16 years and has won many awards for design excellence including Best Kitchen Design, Best Master Suite, Best Interior Design and Best of Show. Heartland Interiors offers both in-store and in-home design services.
23716 8th Avenue SE, Suite G, Bothell WA (425) 485-1877

# Creighton Edward

Recognizing a need to open up a home lifestyle store, owner Creighton Hilstad decided to make it fun yet tasteful, by combining modern and traditional products in order to fit into the ever-changing generation. Located in Issaquah, Creighton Edward Home Lifestyle is a store that provides home care lines, accessories and gourmet foods. Also carrying natural items such as soaps, detergents, teas and more, the store is perfect for finishing touches or just-getting-started materials for your home. Beautifully packaged and colorfully decorated with a slight European flair, all the products in Creighton Edward are designed to augment current and past traditions. Affirming that products are best tasted from the source, the store imports a majority of its items from all over the world, such as Greek olives and oils. At Creighton Edward, the accent is on high quality products in a sophisticated Northwest style with personal customer service.

317 NW Gilman Boulevard #18, Issaquah WA (425) 427 - 5222   www.creightonedward.com

# Home Decor, Gardens, Flowers & Markets — South Puget Sound

## Artistry In Flowers

Trusted in the community since 1908, Artistry In Flowers is Olympia's legendary florist, where you can find floral arrangements from the traditional to the little bit wacky. Owners Jeff, Becky and Alan Hortin and Rod Sanches run a highly-regarded community enterprise. Artistry In Flowers has a wonderful reputation for having the most generous, beautiful and freshest, long-lasting arrangements of the highest quality. They are also the home of Flora, The Flower Lady, a spectacular topiary in front of the store, adorned with holiday and seasonal attire. You have to see Flora to believe her! In addition to the large selection of fresh flowers and plants, you will find gourmet and gift baskets, plush animals, balloons, greeting cards and the very latest in unique gifts.

300 Cleveland Avenue SE, Olympia WA  (360) 357 - 3557 or (800) 223-3559
www.artistrynflowers.com

# Home Decor, Gardens, Flowers & Markets — Whidbey Island

## SeaBear Smokehouse

You've seen the SeaBear catalogs for wild salmon fillets and smoked salmon, right? Now you're close to Anacortes and you're in luck – you're at the home of the SeaBear outlet store. Follow your nose for salmon to 30th Street and you're there! SeaBear started in 1957 as Specialty Seafoods, a backyard smokehouse built by Anacortes fisherman Tom Savidge and his wife Marie. Tom smoked salmon for the local taverns. When tavern owners asked him how to preserve the salmon longer, Tom (ever the tinkerer) blended canning technology with flexible packaging material to create the Gold Seal pouch, which preserved the salmon naturally, without refrigeration. Specialty Seafoods was awarded a patent on this new idea and a direct mail smoked salmon business was born. Today SeaBear remains a small custom-built smokehouse dedicated to the same principles upon which the company was founded. SeaBear uses only 100% wild salmon, caught from the abundant runs of Alaska. It is the best of the best. Less than 1% of wild Alaskan salmon meet SeaBear's strict standards. Every SeaBear salmon is hand filleted for quality and taste. SeaBear salmon is smoked consistent with centuries-old traditions of the Northwest, over slow burning native alder wood. So make it a point to visit the outlet store. While there, take a tour to view the whole process of smoking salmon. You can even have your picture taken with a huge King salmon.  605 30th Street, Anacortes WA  (360) 230-1082 or
(360) 293-4661
or (800) 645-FISH (3474)
www.seabear.com

# Health & Beauty

# Health and Beauty

# Seattle Metro

## Habitude Salon, Day Spa & Gallery

At Habitude Salon, Day Spa and Gallery in Seattle, owner Inez Gray and her staff have no intention of impressing you with fancy technology. The idea is to make a simple, honest connection with you. They treat you like family and make sure you feel welcomed and cared for each time you visit. In short, what you can expect at Habitude is a loving, nurturing atmosphere that provides inspiration and leaves their guests fulfilled. Inez feels that their goal is "to love and amaze our clients with memorable connections and positive experiences." The result is a substantial core of devoted return customers who value more depth and meaning in their daily experiences. Come visit them and you will see why the customers appreciate the attitude at Habitude. 2801 NW Market Street, Seattle WA (206) 782 - 2898  513 N 36th Street, Seattle WA (206) 633-1339  www.habitude.com

## Head to Toe Day Spa

Since 2001, Head to Toe Day Spa in Seattle has been providing clients with a wide variety of top-quality spa treatments. The exceptionally trained and qualified staff provides personal and individualized care to each client. The comfortably intimate atmosphere promises a retreat where you will be pampered and rejuvenated. Head to Toe Day Spa was an Allure Magazine top pick for facials and an AOL City Search top pick for brow waxing. In 2004, it was voted best for facials, massages and pedicures in West Seattle. They are located in the Admiral District of West Seattle, just minutes from downtown. Escape to Head to Toe Day Spa where you will float on a sea of calm, free from life's stresses. 2328 California Avenue SW, Seattle WA (206) 938-9300  www.head2toedayspa.com

# Health and Beauty          I-5 Corridor

## Princeton Athletic Club

Princeton Athletic Club is one of the Northwest's leading Fitness Centers and the only upscale adult health club in Vancouver. It has become an important part of Vancouver, having served Southwest Washington and Northwest Portland, Oregon, for 19 years. At Princeton, you won't be lost among thousands of members. In fact, don't be surprised if you're greeted by name each time you work out. This is a place that can be your sanctuary. You can be assured that here you won't have to worry about long lines, pushy sales staff or high noise levels. What you will get is a great workout in a non-intimidating atmosphere. The specific opportunities and amenities offered for physical training are outstanding, including aerobics, Pilates, yoga, spinning, physical therapy, basketball, racquetball, wallyball, an Olympic weight room, treadmills, ellipticals, bikes, spas, saunas and tanning. There is the finest selection of exercise equipment and fitness programming to enhance your overall health and wellness. To do all this, Princeton Athletic Club has recruited a staff that is committed to the members' needs. You can be guaranteed that at Princeton, you come first. Energy, vitality, tranquility and balance are benefits you can find here. Check their website for their fullschedule, then come in and take look. It could change your life for the better.
805 Broadway, Vancouver, WA
(360) 696-0231
www.princetonathletic.com

# Museums

## Museums — Olympic Peninsula

# The Port Townsend Aero Museum

The Port Townsend Aero Museum needs a new home! Currently housed at the Jefferson County International Airport, the Museum's collection began with the gift of six antique aircraft from Museum founders Jerry and Peggy Thuotte. In just a few years, the collection has outgrown its space. There are now 21 aircraft and, happily, plans are underway to construct a new 12,000 square foot state-of-the-art facility where these irreplaceable treasures of aviation history can be fully restored and displayed to the public. Groundbreaking on the construction site began on April 14, 2005. To raise money for this not-for-profit institution, Jerry and Peggy have organized a variety of enjoyable, fun community events ranging from dinner dances patterned after the USO dances of World War II to Christmas bazaars. Restoring privately-owned antique aircraft on contract also provides support for the enterprise, as well as hands-on experience for the children and teens who participate in the Museum's youth programs. They learn how to repair, restore and even fly these wonderful antique aircraft. Whether young or old, all of the workers at the Museum are volunteers, and this is a true community institution. Your visit will be welcomed, as well as any help you can give to support the Port Townsend Aero Museum through tax-deductible contributions or by volunteering. For more information, visit their website. Hanger G, Jefferson Airport, Port Townsend WA  PO Box 101, Chimacum, WA  (360) 531-0252  www.ptaeromuseum.com

## Museums — Washington Coast

# Ilwaco Heritage Museum

Since October 1983, the Ilwaco Heritage Museum has expanded from a single storefront into an array of galleries and a research library. It now fills Ilwaco's former Telephone Utilities building, and has more exhibits on display in the former Ilwaco Railway & Navigation (IR&N) depot and courtyard (including a restored 1890s Pullman Palace car from the line). The Ilwaco Heritage Museum provides a fascinating look at the Long Beach Peninsula's history, from the Chinook Indians to the present. The site was on the Lewis and Clark National Historical Trail (William Clark walked across the Museum's future location in November 1805), and the Museum also has an exhibit for the bicentennial of the expedition. It's called "Don't Bother Me with the Facts: Uses and Abuses of the Lewis and Clark Theme in Popular Culture." Scheduled to run through 2006, the exhibition invites you to marvel at the variety of two hundred years' of honoring the great explorers, and to gasp at the commercialism of efforts to cash in on their reputation. Lewis and Clark will also be honored in the Memorial Park and Historic Garden being developed by the Museum, which will also be a tribute to community members who have lost their lives at sea. Visit their website for information on becoming a member of the Ilwaco Heritage Museum.
115 SE Lake Street, Ilwaco WA  (360) 642 - 3446

# Museums

## Seattle Metro

# Museum of Flight

The Museum of Flight is known worldwide as a must-see destination in Seattle. Serving more than 400,000 visitors a year, its twelve-acre campus consists of a 361,000-square-foot main building and a 35,000-square-foot Library & Archives annex. It is one of the largest air and space museums in the world. The Great Gallery is a 3-million-cubie-foot, six-story glass and steel exhibit hall containing 39 full-size historic aircraft, 23 of which, including the nine-ton Douglas DC - 3, hang from the space-frame ceiling in flight attitude. The Red Barn features displays on the birth of the aviation industry in the Northwest, as well as other aspects of pre-World War II aviation history. The Personal Courage Wing displays 28 World War I and II fighter aircraft. There is a 268-seat auditorium and extensive rental facilities for hosting private meetings, receptions, banquets and other special events. A full-service on-premises catering kitchen is available. In addition to these facilities, the Airpark is the Museum's outdoor, large-aircraft display area. The Museum offers an extensive array of educational programs for youth and adults. The Museum's new Aviation Learning Center experiential learning environment uses interactive workstations, including a full-size functional aircraft, to teach concepts such as aerodynamics, flight planning, navigation, aircraft design, aircraft identification, air traffic control, aviation weather and aviation careers.

9404 East Marginal Way S, Seattle WA   (206) 764-5720   www.museumofflight.org

# Museums

## Seattle Metro

## Nordic Heritage Museum

The people of Scandinavia have played a significant role in the history of the Pacific Northwest, so it is only fitting that Seattle should be home to a museum that honors them and their achievements. The Nordic Heritage Museum is a fascinating place where history comes alive. Enter the museum through the "Dream of America" exhibition and discover why so many Scandinavians left their homelands and how they made the arduous journey across America to the Northwest. Beautifully designed displays let you

see what they saw on their travels. As you make your way through the museum, a remarkable selection of artifacts, such as Bibles, clothing, household china, folk art, tools and much more, provides an intimate look at the cherished treasures they brought with them and the lives they made for themselves in a new land. The second floor houses the Heritage Rooms with special exhibits on fishing and logging, and galleries for exhibitions of historic and contemporary Scandinavian-American art, including seasonal displays of traditional Christmas villages. On the third floor, five galleries focus on immigrants from each of the five Scandinavian nations. The museum also houses a library of print material and the Gordon Ekvall Tracie Music Library, which includes rare field recordings of Nordic music and dances. For a wonderful look at this unique page of history, visit the Nordic Heritage Museum.
3014 NW 67th Street, Seattle WA  (206) 789 - 5707  www.nordicmuseum.com

# Museums

## Skagit Valley

## Museum of Northwest Art

Welcome to MoNA! The Museum of Northwest Art in La Conner opened in 1981 as a small regional museum devoted to major Pacific Northwest artists. After outgrowing its original home, the second floor of the historical Gaches Mansion, a major fundraising drive enabled the acquisition of a new 12,000-foot space in downtown La Conner. The new space, open in 1995, allowed MoNA to redefine their original vision to include a permanent collection and provide exhibition opportunities for up-and-coming artists as well as established names. The only museum in the world devoted exclusively to art from the Pacific Northwest, MoNA adheres to the same high standards that distinguish the great regional museums of Europe. The museum celebrates the work of artists who founded the Northwest school, such as Guy Anderson, Kenneth Callahan, Morris Graves and Mark Tobey. Many others, from the celebrated glass artist Dale Chihuly to the unjustly neglected Sherrill Van Cott, are also shown. MoNa features work by Northwest women artists like Helmi Juvonen, whose work was inspired by her ardent interest in the Northwest Coastal Indians. One of their exhibits paid tribute to 12 women artists who pioneered modernism in the Northwest. The admission fee is waived on the first Tuesday of every month.
121 S, First Street, La Conner WA  (360) 466-4446
www.museumofnwart.org

# Museums  Skagit Valley

# Museum of Snohomish County

The Museum of Snohomish County History has been treasuring the past for more than fifty years. Exhibits at the museum provide a fascinating look at the rich history of Snohomish County and Everett. The exhibit, "Industry on Parade: Early Enterprise in Snohomish County," features a wealth of material related to logging, mining, fishing, and the many other business endeavors that built the county. Other exhibits have highlighted the fight for women's suffrage, the experience of students at the Tulalip Indian Boarding School, Asian immigrants in Snohomish County, and many other events of historical interest. The museum maintains a growing reference library of local and family history including county, community and company profiles, biographies, city directories and yearbooks. In addition to providing research assistance, the museum actively collects material relevant to Snohomish County history, including artifacts and historic photographs. The museum Store carries numerous book titles by local historians, as well as works generated by the museum through cooperative community projects. Two popular museum-produced items are "Voices from Everett's First Century," an illustrated compilation of oral histories, and "Life in Everett - 1946," a videotape reproduction of a feature-length film provided by the Everett Public Library. Local history books and other related merchandise may be purchased at the museum or through mail order. Admission is by voluntary donation.  1913 Hewitt Avenue, Everett WA  (425) 259-2022  www.snocomuseum.org

# Museums — East Side

## Museum of Doll Art

Like most girls, Rosalie Whyel collected dolls but, unlike most, she preserved her collection and added to it in a big way. All of her friends said she should have a museum to properly display her dolls. After she moved to Washington from Fairbanks, Alaska in 1989, she decided to do something about it. Three years later, the Museum of Doll Art opened its doors. One of the unique attractions of the Seattle area, the Museum has become a Mecca for doll enthusiasts and collectors. With a collection of over 4,000 dolls ranging from antique to modern, over 2,000 of which are on permanent display, plus dollhouses, miniatures, teddy bears and many other delights of childhood, the Museum was awarded the Jumeau Trophy in Paris in 1994, recognizing it as the finest private doll museum in the world! The Museum has also been recognized as an outstanding attraction by AAA and the Bellevue Chamber of Commerce, which gave it the "Emerging Business" and "Most Innovative Business" awards. The treasures range from rare Carton Moule dolls from the 1850's to such loveable 20th Century classics as Scootles.
1116 108th Avenue NE, Bellevue WA  (425) 455-1116  www.dollart.com

# Museums  I-5 Corridor

## Veterans Memorial Museum

Dedicated to the men and women who honorably served the United States in the Armed Forces during times of both peace and war, the Veterans Memorial Museum in Chehalis is an extraordinary place to visit. Co-founders Lee and Barbara Grimes and Loren and Patti Estep opened the doors of the museum on Veterans Day 1997, releasing the floodgates of painful yet incredibly important memories of our nation's history. They wanted to provide a place for veterans to congregate, release emotions and revisit their past heroic efforts. Museum director Lee Grimes is often overwhelmed with personal reflections and stories of combat, sacrifice and honor. Entering the museum, visitors are greeted by a USO canteen and World War II era music. The main gallery is host to eighty-five glass enclosed display cases housing a variety of military effects, arranged in chronological order from the Revolutionary War through Iraq. A government-issued baseball bat and glove representing fun contrast sharply with the sobering reality of war that accompanies a body bag and nurse's uniform. The Oral History Room, named after Stanton Price, a local veteran who survived more than three years in Japanese POW camps, provides video footage of battles, interviews and other military history. The Veterans Memorial Museum is a truly unforgettable experience. It is a place to pay homage to those who made this country what it is today and to ensure that "they shall not be forgotten."   100 SW Veterans Way, Chehalis WA  (360) 740-8875  www.veteransmuseum.org

# Museums

## South Puget Sound

## Washington State History Museum

The Washington State History Museum is where fascination and FUN come together! People of all ages can explore and be entertained in an environment where characters from Washington's past speak about their lives. Through interactive exhibits, theatrical storytelling, high-tech displays and dramatic artifacts, learn about our state's unique people and places, as well as their impact on the country and the world. Begin your journey through Washington with an architectural masterpiece: designed by Charles Moore and Arthur Andersson, the 106,000 square foot museum building stands proudly on Pacific Avenue in Tacoma. The museum boasts soaring spaces and dramatic archways that invite you into a history experience full of colors, textures, sights, and sounds.  1911 Pacific Avenue,  Tacoma WA   (888) BE-THERE (238-4373)  www.wshs.org/

# Museums                                    South Puget Sound

# Tacoma Art Museum

Situated in Tacoma's dynamic cultural district, Tacoma Art Museum shimmers in its sleek architecture, designed by Antoine Predock. The Museum features framed views of Mt. Rainier and a series of elegant galleries that wrap around an open-air interior stone garden. Tacoma Art Museum showcases traveling national and international exhibitions, and is dedicated to collecting and presenting Northwest art. The Museum's rich collection contains more than 3,200 significant works and key holdings in modern and contemporary Northwest, nineteenth-century European, twentieth-century American and Asian works. The Museum also features a stunning permanent installation of Dale Chihuly glass, dating 1977 to the present. In addition to several varieties of art, Tacoma Art Museum offers a studio for art-making and resource center for art study open to visitors of all ages. Visitors can also enjoy lunch or coffee in the indoor/outdoor café, and shop for distinctive items such as jewelry, books and regionally hand-crafted items in the museum store.  1701 Pacific Avenue, Tacoma WA  (253) 272 - 4258   www.TacomaArtMuseum.org

*Photo by Dana Meyer*

# Hands on Children's Museum

The Hands On Children's Museum is the most visited family attraction in the South Puget Sound, offering award-winning programs and exciting exhibits. The museum, located on the State Capitol's campus, features over 50 interactive exhibits in six main galleries. The Good for You! Gallery features a child-size farmer's market where young children can buy and sell fresh fruits, vegetables, bakery goods and cheeses. In the "family kitchen," they can prepare a "home cooked meal" and then visit the neighborhood climbing space. The museum also features a Build It! Gallery, where young children can build their own house, complete with windows, doors and roof, and also operate a dump truck. In the Working Waterfront, they can board a 3-story cargo ship to be the captain, cook meals in the galley, and load logs into the cargo hold. The museum's young at art studio features more than 50 different bins of new and recycled materials where visitors can make their own creations. The TotSpot Early Learning Center is designed for very young children and offers sensory experiences including a lentils table, play-dough table, dress up nook and several activity stations. The Hands On Children's Museum is a non-profit organization dedicated to stimulating curiosity, creativity and learning. The Museum offers an experiential preschool, camps, field trips, and its signature event, Sand In The City, held the 4th weekend in August on Olympia's quaint boat-lined waterfront.  106 11th Avenue SW, Olympia WA  (360) 956-0818   www.hocm.org

# Museum of Glass

The Museum of Glass is an international center for contemporary art with a sustained focus on glass. It's both a unique museum and the cultural cornerstone of Tacoma's $150 million redevelopment along the Thea Foss Waterway. The Museum's most distinctive architectural feature, a tilted 90-foot tall cone wrapped in stainless steel, houses the Hot Shop Amphitheater. In this dynamic glass blowing studio, visitors watch artists engaged in the creative experimentation and exploration that makes glass one of the most exhilarating mediums in the art world today. In addition to the Hot Shop Amphitheater, the

museum features three galleries with intriguing exhibitions, a 180-seat theater, a hands-on art studio, a museum store and café. The museum's exhibition schedule

introduces works by internationally known artists who illuminate trends in contemporary art, highlighting glass within a full range of media. Clear, expert commentary in the form of interpretive text panels, guided tours and other programs ensure a museum experience that is meaningful and engaging to visitors. The museum's outdoor plazas are also noteworthy. Three large reflecting pools hold a variety of large art installations. The Chihuly Bridge of Glass, a 500-foot pedestrian bridge with art by Tacoma native Dale Chihuly, leads from the museum's rooftop plaza to downtown Tacoma. 1801 E Dock Street, Tacoma WA (253) 284-4750 or (866) 4-MUSEUM (468-7386) www.museumofglass.org

# Restaurants

# Restaurants

## Olympic Peninsula

## Gordy's Pizza & Pasta

For more than 40 years, three generations of the Sexton family have served great Italian food at Gordy's Pizza and Pasta in Port Angeles. An "old fashioned" pizza place where everything is made from fresh ingredients to ensure that each dish tastes great! Gordy's Pizza and Pasta has often been voted the "Best Place" for pizza and Italian food by the citizens of the North Olympic Peninsula. It also has the distinction of being the first pizza restaurant on the Peninsula. Gordy and Pat Sexton opened the restaurant in 1961 and now their children Randy Sexton and Cynthia Dawson run the restaurant, with their grandchildren working there, too. "We cannot thank the community enough for their support throughout the years," Randy says. "We grew up in the restaurant and look forward to serving future generations great food." Gordy's offers a wide variety of pizzas including the restaurant's signature pizza, which is a delicious combination of ingredients named "The Works." If it's pasta you're looking for tonight, the restaurant offers a wide selection of pasta and also prepares calzones, specialty sandwiches, salads, soups and mouth-watering desserts. Customers can dine-in, pick-up food, including take-and-bake pizzas, or take advantage of the restaurant's friendly local delivery service. Gordy's Pizza and Pasta can also accommodate a group of up to 50 in a private dining room. Reservations are not required, but are appreciated for large groups.  1123 E First Street, Port Angeles WA  (360) 457 - 5056   www.gordyspizza.com

## Old Mill Cafe

In 1922, Carlsborg was a thriving mill town and the building that now houses the Old Mill Café was the local tavern. The area is now part of Sequim and the new café is less rowdy than the old lumbermen's haunt, but it's still a perfect place to enjoy a wonderful meal. As the new owners Larry and Valdena Culp put it, even if you're not happy when you arrive, you'll be happy when you leave. With the help of chef Timothy Disney, the Culps have created a restaurant where first-time customers become lifelong regulars "Country Style Cooking at its Best" is the motto of the Old Mill Café. Everything is made from scratch, using locally-produced ingredients whenever possible, including organic vegetables from Nash Huber's farm and hormone-free beef. Larry and Val are longtime residents of the Carlsborg district. The Old Mill Café commemorates the area's past in many ways, from the sawmill blades set in the path outside to the murals and 1/8-inch scale model of the old mill inside. The original bar and bar stools have been preserved and customers can enjoy hit tunes of times past played on the old-fashioned jukebox. The Old Mill Café is a community-supported enterprise; all of the plants used for landscaping were donated by the Sunny Farms Country Store. The Culps share their own artistic sensibilities as well. The beautiful stained glass pieces in the windows were made by Val herself.  121 Carlsborg Road, Carlsborg WA  (360) 582 - 1583

# Ajax Cafe

"It's a little out of the way, but way out of the ordinary! Come for the food and stay for the party." The Ajax Cafe is fun, friendly, casual dining spot for dinner. The major emphasis is on fresh seafood, choice steaks, delicious pasta concoctions, soul satisfying soups, addicting ribs and a selection of fine wines. The food is spectacular. It's fine dining in an unpretentious environment. Ajax Cafe is located in the old Galster House, where the founder of Hadlock lived in the late 1800s. Present owners Eileen Steimle, Laura Ferguson and Kristan McCary were waitresses for the previous owner. When he was going to sell the restaurant, no one wanted the place to change. With community support and one incredible investor, they were able to buy the restaurant and preserve its quirky ways. The atmosphere and décor of Ajax Cafe shout "FUN." It is stimulating, warm, intimate, lively, friendly, colorful and, somehow, peaceful. It is painted in bright, cheerful colors and a crazy array of hats and ties hang everywhere for guests to wear during their meals. The party continues with live music every weekend. Also enjoy the beautiful saltwater view from the deck seating. The Ajax Cafe hosts an annual "Dinghy Festival" in late September for boats measuring less than 17 feet. 21 N Water Street, Port Hadlock WA (360) 385 - 3450 www.ajaxcafe.com

# Bella Italia

For traditional Italian food in Port Angeles, visit Bella Italia. This establishment, recently picked as her first choice in Port Angeles by First Lady Laura Bush, offers patrons the freshest and best local ingredients and produce. It has established itself as one of the premier dining destinations for travelers from around the globe, as well as a favorite with the locals. Newly remodeled, abundantly textured and laden with rich colors, Bella Italia exemplifies authentic Italian hospitality and surpasses your expectations for service and friendliness. Bella Italia offers a wide range of cuisine, plus an extensive wine list that recently won an Award of Excellence by Wine Spectator. Here is a sample of the fare prepared by proprietor Neil Conklin and chef Dave Senters. Start with an antipasti such as Bruschetta, grilled Tuscan bread with garlic, olive oil, fresh basil and Roma tomatoes. Follow with a Romaine wedge, including pears, toasted walnuts and creamy Gorgonzola dressing. For the main course, perhaps Espresso Smoked Duck Breast, pan seared with a port demi glase sauce, and served with roasted garlic whipped potatoes. Or Pesci Limone, fresh local fish prepared in a classic Sicilian style featuring fresh lemons, served with pasta. If you prefer steak, try the Filetto di Manzo, char grilled beef tenderloin, served with roasted red potatoes. Several exquisite pasta and pizza dishes complete the menu. No matter your choice, you will surely enjoy a memorable evening at Bella Italia. 118 East First Street, Port Angeles WA (360) 457-5442 www.bellaitaliapa.com

# Restaurants — Olympic Peninsula

## Bushwhacker Seafood Restaurant

In 1976, Robert Grattan came to Port Angeles from Montana to manage The Bushwhacker Restaurant. He didn't realize that he'd find love as well as a vocation. When he hired a vivacious woman named Julie as a waitress, he never guessed that they'd get married and run the business together. Now Robert and Julie's daughter, Sadie Rose, is in training to eventually take over the family business. They know she'll do a fine job when the time comes. The Bushwhacker is known for its fresh local seafood and prime rib, served in a friendly manner in a relaxed atmosphere. Their homemade bread and clam chowder as well as their huge salad bar keep bringing satisfied customers back for more. The Peninsula Daily News voted The Bushwhacker "First Place" among restaurants in Clallam County for Best Seafood, Best Steak, Best Clam Chowder, Best Salad Bar, Best Happy Hour and Best Dessert! Robert truly appreciates his long term staff. He hopes that they feel like this is their restaurant, too, so they feel good about what they're doing for others. To judge by the low turnover rate, they really do. Robert and Julie also go out of their way to support the community, contributing generously to local causes. 1527 E First Street, Port Angeles WA (360) 457-4113

## Café Garden Restaurant

Dave and Laura Reynolds offer a unique dining experience to customers of the Café Garden Restaurant. The food is superb, with specialties from the in-house bakery, and everything on the menu is fresh, even the salad dressings. From the Belgian waffles and specialty egg dishes at breakfast to the stir-fries and deli sandwiches at lunch, everything

is made to meet the highest standards of quality and consistency. Short cuts are never taken here. At dinner, Café Garden Restaurant also features an extensive wine list, including wines that have been maturing in their wine cellar since the early 1990's to compliment their diverse menu of braised steaks, pastas and fresh seafood. Dave and Laura's mission is to provide the most professional and excellent service possible. They fulfill that promise with the help of their outstanding staff, many of whom have been with the restaurant for at least a decade. For them, the Café Garden Restaurant is as much a home as it is a business. The cooks are incredible and they will fix anything that you specially request, even if it's not on the menu: if it's possible, they'll do it! With such great food and service, it's no wonder that the Café Garden Restaurant is consistently ranked among the best places to eat in Washington. 1506 E First Street, Port Angeles WA (360) 457-4611

## Otter Crossing Cafe

When you own a restaurant in Port Townsend and you get repeat business from customers from Connecticut, you know you're doing something right. Heather Polizzi's grandfather was a chef. She and her father David Hoppe had a dream of starting a restaurant together. Their desire was to open a family-friendly, homestyle place that served creative food. The Otter Crossing, with "creative family style dining," is the result. Among the house specialties is smoked salmon hash with toast. It includes sautéed garlic, shallots, tomato, spinach, red potatoes, capers, lemon zest, and dill: all smothered in smoked mozzarella and topped with two poached eggs. See what they mean by creative? Enjoy all of it with locally baked European style breads and locally roasted coffee. The food comes with a scenic view as well. The Otter Crossing sits on the point of Hudson Marina with a view of Port Townsend Bay, the Olympic Mountains, and Mount Rainier.
130 Hudson, Port Townsend WA   (360) 379-0592

## Sirens

Welcome to Sirens, an irresistible pub of distinction, located upstairs in the historic Bartlett Building. A breathtaking view of the Hudson Bay delights you the moment you enter the Pub. Owned by Kristen Nelson, Sirens is a charming, old-fashioned pub, which is truly one of a kind. They feature an extensive wine list, eleven beers on tap, a progressive martini menu, and a diverse menu of appetizers, seafood, burgers and pastas. Their customers' favorite food choices are the Wild Coho Salmon, Gorgonzola Burger, Crab Cakes, and their Puget Sound Cioppino. As for drinks, they are known for their muddled then shaken margaritas and mojitos. Open for lunch and dinner, Sirens' great staff will invite you to enjoy their gigantic waterfront deck and, often, their live music. It's a friendly place to go that appeals to all ages, though only twenty-one and older are allowed.  823 Water Street, Port Townsend WA  (360) 379-1100  www.sirenspt.com

# Restaurants  Olympic Peninsula

## Silverwater Cafe

The Silverwater Café in Port Townsend is all too familiar with the term "Home is Where the Kitchen is," and has taken it to a new level. In fact, the Café can be considered almost like "therapy" for what ails you. Since 1989, owners and business partners Alison Hero and David Hero have created a restaurant that understands the relationship between food and thought. Using homemade, much-deliberated spices as their "antidote" and a growing, thoroughly trained, magnanimous staff as their "physicians," the diverse menu at Silverwater Café is designed to enhance their customers' taste buds, as well as their memories or current thoughts. Others have agreed, as the Café has been featured in reviews and articles from New York to Colorado, as well as receiving much local recognition. The Café has also been spotted in a cookbook that was published in France, one of the most recognized culinary headquarters of the world. Due to popular demand, the Silverwater Café now features their secret, enchanted spices for purchase.
237 Taylor Street, Port Townsend WA (360) 385-6448

## Port Townsend Brewing Co.

In Port Townsend, you can't keep a good brewery down. Oh, you can put it out for say 81 years, but when the demand is there, back it comes. At least that's the way it worked at the Port Townsend Brewing Company. Established in 1905, it was one of the largest breweries of its time until Prohibition forced its closure in 1916. But 81 years later, along came Guy and Kim Sands to reopen the business and start locals' mouths watering again. Today you can enjoy beers like these: Chet's Golden Ale, Reel Amber, Port Townsend Winter Ale, Brown Porter, Pale Ale, Strait Stout, Boatyard Bitter, Hop Diggidy, Peeping Peater Scottish Ale and Bitter End India Pale Ale. In addition, there's a barley wine. Flavors range from light and refreshing (the Chet's Gold) to intense-but-smooth (the Strait Stout). Guy and Kim run what they call a "European-style pub and beer garden." They have won a silver medal for their Boatyard Bitter, which is sold throughout Western Washington. As a microbrewery, the establishment can sell draft beer to go. Bring your own container or purchase one in the Tasting Room. 330 C 10th Street, Port Townsend, WA (360) 385-9967
www.porttownsendbrewing.com

# Water Street Brewing

There's energy flowing in Port Townsend and you can soak it up at Water Street Brewing. Owners Mark Burr, Nina Law and Skip Madsen think of their establishment as an extended living room for local residents, with a wide open door for visitors as well. "Vibrant," "artsy," pick your description of the atmosphere and find it at this eclectic and comfortable brewery and ale house. They are known for many things, including handcrafted ales and lagers made on premises by Brewmaster Skip. He's been brewing since 1992 and has won numerous medals at the Great American Beer Festival and other prestigious competitions.

Photos by Thomas Boggan

If fantastic brews aren't your game, fresh squeezed juice cocktails are the talk of the town. As you might imagine, the cuisine caters to the seafood lover's palate. They support local fishermen and farmers, and buy baked goods from a local bakery, Pane D'Amore, which uses the brewery's spent grain to make their own house bread. Wild, line-caught salmon and fresh halibut are among the varieties of seafood that accent the upscale pub fare. With live music and variety shows in the evening, a family dining room where kids are always welcome, and a deck on the water with bay and mountain views, you are sure to enjoy yourself in this historic building in beautiful Port Townsend.

639 Water Street,
Port Townsend WA
(360) 379-6438
www.waterstreetbrewing.com

# Restaurants

# Olympic Peninsula

## FINS Coastal Cuisine

East meets West at FINS Coastal Cuisine in Port Townsend. That's because Douglas Seaver, co-owner and chef, brings New England style food preparation to Northwest ingredients. The result? Says one recent customer, "The best chowder I have had. Excellent!" Says another, "The cod special was outstanding! The pork medallions were simply delicious. Whenever we're in town, we'll be back!" It's enough to make Doug and his co-owner Joann Saul blush. Both Doug and Joann have been in the restaurant business since the age of 15. Doug has over two decades of experience as a chef. Recently the *Peninsula Daily News* and People's Choice both awarded FINS the honor of Best Seafood in Jefferson County. *The Daily News* also called FINS the *Best Romantic Dinner* in the county. FINS provides a warm and comfortable atmosphere, looking over Port Townsend Bay with a great view of the Olympic Mountains. An outdoor dining deck has steps leading down to the beach, should you want to wiggle your toes in the water after dessert. The food and ocean await you.
1019 Water Street, Port Townsend WA  (360) 379 - 3474
www.finscoastalcuisine.com

## Macadoo's Barbeque

Jeff Crumpton, chef and manager of Macadoo's Barbecue in Port Townsend, wants you to know that his barbecue cooking has specific roots. "Tennessee Southern with some Georgia," to be exact. The menu features pulled-pork sandwiches, smoked beef brisket, ribs, salmon and chicken, slow cooked and smoked with 100% pesticide-free Eastern Washington apple wood.

Macadoo's is a fun, high-energy, hopping kind of place with a theme of "Good food for good people." There's a dog in the story, too. The name "Macadoo" belongs to Jeff's dog. The pooch started out as "Max," after being adopted at the Jefferson County Animal Shelter. Max evolved into Macadoo. One day, Jeff and his friends were sitting on the porch eating ribs and occasionally throwing Macadoo a bone. Says Jeff, "We thought, what a great idea for [the dog] to have his own restaurant. The rest, as they say, is history." So Jeff and Macadoo invite you to try their beef, pork and poultry after it's been brined for 24 hours, then slow-smoked for up to 32 hours. "It's a long process, but you'll find that kind of love in everything we do here." You have Macadoo's word, err, woof on it.
600 W Sims Way, Port Townsend WA  (360) 379-1619

## Fountain Café

It's the flavors. It's the amazing, high quality flavors of the food that sets this restaurant apart. A vegetarian dish, the roasted walnut and gorgonzola penne, is probably the Fountain Café's most popular dish, but Paella, Cioppino, and Zuppa de Pesce are close behind, highlighting the fresh local shellfish which the Café is known for. The Fountain Café also prides itself on supporting the Port Townsend growers by using locally grown vegetables. The Café has been a local hot spot for 23 years. Kristen Nelson has owned it for the past 6 years. Of her restaurant she says, "It is a cozy, fun and enchanting place where you can come and get an amazing meal, and a great glass of wine from a charismatic and friendly staff." Even the atmosphere at the Fountain Café is lively with world beat, and blues music playing, an open kitchen where you can watch the chefs toss flames (and your dinner) on the stove, and a room filled with displays, each with a story behind them. All of this is packed into a cute little Victorian building right in the heart of downtown. Open for lunch and dinner daily.
920 Washington Street, Port Townsend WA
(360) 385 - 1364

# Restaurants

# Olympic Peninsula

## Dupuis' Restaurant

The North Olympic Peninsula's oldest restaurant, Dupuis' Restaurant in Port Angeles, has quite the pedigree. Opened as a bar in 1920, it became Dupuis' Sea Food Inn in 1935. Though it has expanded its offerings over the years, the neon crab sign still stands outside and you can still get the cold cracked Dungeness crab that has drawn flocks of customers for decades. Now managed by Clallam County native Maureen McDonald, Dupuis' Restaurant is proud of its history. The original bar is now the Tavern Dining Room where, among other treats, diners can enjoy whole crabs and garlic bread, cedar planked salmon and Steak Dupuis, which is a filet mignon robed in bacon, topped with fresh Dungeness crab, a burgundy wine sauce and shiitake mushrooms. The Fireplace Dining Room offers cozy seating around a brick fireplace. All rooms are decorated with historical memorabilia and charming collectibles. A real treat at Dupuis' is the Sunday Brunch, featuring such delights as "Crabby Bill's Frittata," made with fresh crab, chanterelles and sun-dried tomatoes. Enjoy discovering Dupuis' award winning menu for yourself!  256861 Highway 101, Port Angeles WA
(360) 457 - 8033
www.dupuisrestaurant.com

# Toga's

For the finest in Northwest and International cuisine, come to Toga's in Port Angeles. Toga's uses only the finest available ingredients in superb dishes ranging from Dungeness crab cakes and sautéed prawns Provençal to sauerbraten with Bavarian potato dumplings. Specialties include "Jagersteins," stones heated to 500° F on which guests can cook their own choice of meats, and Toga's fondues including original Swiss cheese, Northwest seafood, and the meat lover's fondue. These require a 24-hour advance reservation, and they're more than a delicious meal, they're a social event! Don't miss out on the desserts, either. Who could resist Toga's signature dessert, the chocolate macadamia mousse torte? Executive Chef and co-owner Toga Hertzog apprenticed as a chef in Germany after he graduated from Port Angeles High School. After his apprenticeship, he honed his considerable skills in resort hotels in Hawaii, as well as aboard the Royal Viking Sun cruise ship. Returning to his hometown with his wife Lisa, he opened Toga's in 1995, and has received numerous local and national accolades. In addition to fine food, Toga's features a wine list with selections from the Northwest and around the world, German beer on tap, and local microbrews as well. Service is overseen by co-owner Lisa, and adds another dimension to the exceptional dining experience. Reservations are recommended.   122 W Lauridson Boulevard, Port Angeles WA  (360) 452 - 1952

# Thai Peppers Restaurant

Guests at the Thai Peppers Restaurant in Port Angeles will be enticed by the aromas wafting through the air even before setting foot in the door. With its water view dining, customers realize immediately that this is truly a Washington treasure. Owner Sonthaya Itti has always had a love of cooking. As a young boy, he dreamed of opening his own authentic Thai restaurant to bring a taste of Thailand to the people of the Northwest. His dream came true when Thai Peppers opened eight years ago. Thai Peppers offers an amazing array of mouth-watering dishes. High quality ingredients are used in every selection. While many of the dishes are prepared with the traditionalness, Thai Peppers aims to please all customers and dishes can be prepared on the mild side if requested.  Thai Peppers Restaurant was voted the #1 Best Asian Restaurant in Clallam County in 2003, was a recipient of the AAA Diamond Rates Awards in 2003, and was included in Best Places Northwest in 2002 and 2003. The restaurant also had the great honor of serving First Lady Laura Bush and her closest friends in July of 2003. Visit Thai Peppers Restaurant for a delicious lunch or dinner.
222 N Lincoln Street, Port Angeles WA   (360) 452-4995

# Restaurants — Washington Coast

## Ocean Crest Resort Restaurant

Breathtaking views, award-winning regional cuisine, and renowned hospitality: those are just a few of the features that make the Ocean Crest Resort Restaurant a destination in and of itself. Perhaps that is why the restaurant at Ocean Crest Resort is recognized by Frommer's as having the best food in the region. The Curtright family started the resort in 1953 with three cabins and "lots of enthusiasm." The restaurant followed in 1963, with founder Barbara Curtright Topete doing the cooking. The chef today turns out a full menu with an emphasis on local, fresh, seasonal ingredients. While the restaurant has been written about in *Gourmet* and *Bon Appetit* magazines, it is quickly gaining recognition for its extensive wine cellar too. More than half the wines are produced in Washington, and the others are almost exclusively from boutique wineries in the Pacific Northwest. The quality is attested to by awards like

Wine Spectator's "Award of Excellence in 2004", and the Wine Press Northwest "Outstanding NW Wine List." As the restaurant's wine steward puts it, "The purpose of our wine program is to complement and enhance our native Northwest-flavored menu." For fine dining in a peerless setting, visit Ocean Crest Resort Restaurant. 4651 SR 109, Moclips WA (360) 276-4465 or (800) 684-8439
www.oceancrestresort.com

# The Depot Restaurant

Built a hundred years ago, the historic Clamshell Railroad Station in Seaview is now home to The Depot Restaurant. The restaurant houses the only display kitchen on the Long Beach Peninsula. Owners Michael Lalewicz and Nancy Gorshe invite you to make a reservation for the special Chef's Table event, where you can watch Michael (also the chef) and sous-chef Cleveland Graham as they whip up the amazing theme dinners that bring people back to The Depot time after time. Michael has traveled and cooked around the world. After coming to the Pacific Northwest, he developed the Greek kitchen at Portland's premier jazz club, Jimmy Mak's, and served as sous Chef of Portland's Tolouse Restaurant before pulling in to The Depot. Cleveland Graham is a Northeast native who honed his cooking skills at such venues as Earth and Ocean at Seattle's famous W Hotel. Together they've created a menu that merges international cooking styles with the finest local ingredients, with signature dishes such as Willapa Bay Clam Chowder and Northwest Crab Bucatini. The food alone is more than enough reason to book your table at The Depot, but bear in mind that the restaurant also offers casual elegance with a superb selection of wines from around the world, microbrew beer on tap, and a heated outdoor deck.

1208 38th Place & L, Seaview WA  (360) 642 - 7880  www.depotrestaurantdining.com

# Ark Restaurant & Bakery

The Ark has been a favorite Willapa Bay area institution since 1950. It is firmly dedicated to the fine food and casual elegance that have been bringing people back for over half a century. As you might expect from a bayfront restaurant originally founded by a fisherman, the sea's bounty is a feature attraction here. People come from far and wide to enjoy specialties such as pan-fried oysters fresh from Willapa Bay and pan-seared halibut in a shiitake mushroom crust served with dungeness crab. The bakery at the Ark provides the homemade rolls that accompany every entrée and the delicious and decadent desserts that have been singled out for praise by many reviewers. A special seasonal favorite is the blackberry cobbler, using fresh wild berries grown in the nearby hills. Don't miss it! Rated Excellent! by 2005 Zagat Survey. 3310 273rd Street, Nahcotta, WA  (360) 665-4133 www.arkrestaurant.com

# Restaurants

# Washington Coast

## The Shoalwater Restaurant and The Heron & Beaver Pub

The Shoalwater Restaurant is located in Long Beach Peninsula's historic Shelburne Inn, along with its sister establishment, The Heron & Beaver Pub/Café. Both eateries have been owned and operated since 1981 by Tony and Ann Kischner, who moved to the Washington coast from the Seattle area. East Coast-trained Chef Lynne Pelletier has been in charge of the kitchen since 1998, and has continued The Shoalwater's long tradition of awards and rave reviews. The excellent menu changes seasonally and utilizes all manner of local products in strikingly imaginative ways, from an abundance of fresh seafood such as oysters, crab, clams and salmon to Peninsula cranberries and a wide variety of wild mushrooms, berries and greens. Many delicious condiments are also made in-house from local products. They are used in The Shoalwater's cooking and are also available for sale. Ann bakes wonderful home-style fresh breads and desserts on the premises. Superb lunches and dinners are served daily from the same kitchen in the The Shoalwater's elegant dining room and in the more informal Heron & Beaver Pub. The Pub is named after the ubiquitous local bird and Charles Beaver, who built The Shelburne Inn in 1896. Tony manages the dining room, as well as a stellar cellar of 450+ mostly-regional wines. He stocks the Pub with a full complement of fine liquors including 18 single-malt Scotches and 40+ domestic and imported beers, featuring many local craft brews.

4415 Pacific Way, Seaview WA
(360) 642-4142
www.shoalwater.com

# Restaurants — Kitsap Peninsula

## Café Beso

Café Beso, in historic downtown Puyallup, is a deliciously quaint spot to sit down and enjoy breakfast or lunch. Since 2004, owners Kenneth and Moani Brumet have offered patrons freshly roasted coffee from Batdorf and Bronson, and specialty sandwiches, soups, salads and desserts created by chef Troy Guilao. On Friday evenings, they host their wine tasting event, featuring a new region every Friday to visit vineyards around the world and savor their award-winning wines. In addition, they offer a nice selection of microbrews. When in downtown Puyallup, you'll find that Café Beso is the perfect place to relax and enjoy a bite to eat.
109 South Meridian, Puyallup WA  (253) 770-0150

## Casa Mia of Puyallup

Casa Mia had its start back in the 1950s. Phil Bellafato grew up in an apartment above one of the first Italian pizzerias in New York. When he later moved to the Pacific Northwest and realized that pizza was virtually unknown out here, he decided to change that. Casa Mia was an absolute hit. In 1974, Roger Jump acquired Phil's restaurant and his recipes and carried on his tradition. In 1982, the restaurant began to branch out to other locations in Washington. James Jump, the current owner of Casa Mia of Puyallup, has been in the restaurant business since he was thirteen. Since his father Roger owned the original restaurant in Hoquiam, James worked with him and was a hard-working prep cook by the time he was fifteen. Just as in Phil's day, Casa Mia's pizza

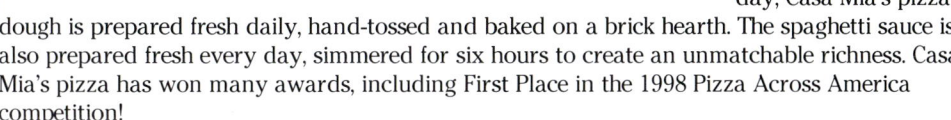

dough is prepared fresh daily, hand-tossed and baked on a brick hearth. The spaghetti sauce is also prepared fresh every day, simmered for six hours to create an unmatchable richness. Casa Mia's pizza has won many awards, including First Place in the 1998 Pizza Across America competition!
505 N Meridian, Puyallup WA  (253) 770-0400  www.casamiarestaurants.com

# Restaurants  Kitsap Peninsula

## IsaMira Gourmet Cheese & Café

Walk into IsaMira Gourmet Cheese & Café and the first thing you'll notice is the European flair that is enhanced by the imported cheeses. Many of the cheeses come directly from farmers all over the world. You can at any time sample Mango-Ginger Stilton from England or perhaps a Guiness Cheddar from Ireland. There are beautiful blues and pungent Gorgonzolas from Italy and Spain. Or homemade ricotta by Chef Debra Petitclerc, which goes into handmade pasta dishes such as Lasagna, baked Ziti or even cheesecake. While you're enjoying your delightful meal, your dining pleasure will be enhanced by the beautiful Gig Harbor waterfront location. Imagine watching all the activity that happens around the water, such as sailboats, the fishing boats passing by or the seagulls hanging around waiting under the deck for a morsel or two of crumbs to be dropped. Owner and Chef Debra Petitclerc has had a passion for cooking since the 6th grade and shares this passion with her four daughters, who also are a big part of her business, and how the name came to be. You'll also find all her daughter's names on the menu such as Petite Alena, or Olivia's Tapenade, and even Brianne's Baguette. IsaMira has been called "The Best Kept Secret in Town." Stop by and check out all the wonderful things that make IsaMira and Chef Debra's passion so flavorful!
3313 Harborview Drive, Gig Harbor WA

## Sheila's Bay Café

"Velkommen til Poulsbo" says the sign as you enter this lovely Kitsap Peninsula town, founded by Scandinavian immigrant Jorgen Eliason in the 1880s and now affectionately known as "Little Norway." Head down to the wharf at the head of the Poulsbo marina and you'll find

Sheila's Bay Café, featuring "New American Cuisine and Norwegian Entrees." Sheila's Bay Café is especially known for its beautiful view of Liberty Bay and its sumptuous breakfasts. Owner Steven Urand gives credit for the Café's success to his great staff, especially head waitress Dorothy, who's been around forever and really

keeps the place running like a top. For gourmet omelets, homemade soups and home-baked bread at old-fashioned prices, Sheila's is definitely the place to go. If you're feeling adventurous, try a Norwegian seafood platter or sausage wrapped in *lefsa* (potato bread). The atmosphere at Sheila's is warm and cozy, a friendly place where regulars hang out and people come from out of town to enjoy breakfast on the pier.
18779 Front Street, Poulsbo WA  (360) 779-2997

# Bayside Broiler

Michael Buholz wants nothing to do with mediocrity. He owns the Bayside Broiler in Poulsbo and runs it on the pillars of quality, structure, service, and fun. That means as you savor one of their chef's dishes and admire the incredible view overlooking Poulsbo Marina on Liberty Bay, Michael and his staff want to touch all your senses. The view, the ambiance, the smells, and delicious food: it's all meant to leave you feeling every penny you spend is well worth it. Local fresh seafood, steaks, and specialty cocktails call to you there. You can sit inside or outside in covered or uncovered spaces, depending on your mood and the weather. Inside you will find comfortable, ornate furnishings and more artwork than is featured at many galleries. The decor and furnishings themselves are worth a visit; interior designer Connie LaMott recently refurbished the restaurant from top to bottom. For Michael, it's part and part and parcel of running an establishment where his employees take ownership, share in his vision and love coming to work to create great dining experiences for you. 18779 Front Street, Poulsbo WA (360) 779-9076 www.baysidebroiler.com

# Hungry Goose Bistro

Visitors to the south Sound area will not want to miss the Hungry Goose Bistro. Hailed as the "downtown restaurant with the uptown flair," Hungry Goose Bistro is one of Puyallup's finest dining experiences, offering international entrees with a Northwest accent and live jazz in the lounge on selected weekends. Originally opened in 1980 as the Hungry Goose Eatery and established as a popular lunch, afternoon tearoom and gift boutique, it was owned and operated by Carolyn Hall and her sister Sandee Burrell. Current owner Tim Hall worked alongside his mother for five years before mounting an extensive renovation and remodel of the building in 2002. The former lunch and tearoom were transformed into a well-appointed dining room, and the boutique was replaced by a warm and inviting lounge with comfortable leather seating. The lounge features specialty drinks like martinis and Spanish coffee, as well as top shelf spirits, imported beer, an extensive wine list and a "tapas-style" dinner-appetizer menu. The friendly waitstaff and excellent service (it's not unusual to see the owner visiting tables and making conversation with guests) contribute to the enjoyable dining experience. Open seven days a week, Hungry Goose Bistro is a smoke-free establishment. Reservations are recommended for dinner. 1618 E Main Street, Puyallup WA (253) 845 - 5747 www.hgbistro.com

# Boat Shed Restaurant

For a delightful waterfront view and a tempting menu, you'll want to visit the Boat Shed Restaurant in Bremerton. Well-known for its fresh seafood and homemade desserts, the Boat Shed Restaurant is the perfect place to relax and enjoy a meal, rain or shine. The restaurant was converted from an old boat house marina and the historic building features warm wood tones throughout. Inside, it is spacious and cozy with windows all around affording great views of Sinclair Inlet and Port Washington Narrows. Menu items include fresh staples like steamed clams, scallops, fish & chips, chowder, steaks and pasta, as well as burgers and a variety of sandwiches. The Boat Shed Restaurant also features a full bar and is known for its prompt and attentive service. It even has a small private dock that enables you to arrive by boat if you like. 101 Shore Drive, Bremerton WA (360) 377-2600

# Restaurants

# Kitsap Peninsula

## The Harbour Public House

Jim Evans, Englishman and retired professor dreamed of an English-style pub where islanders could congregate on the waterfront. And that's just what he has done, with the help of his wife Judy and daughter and son-in-law Jocelyn and Jeff Waite. Remodeled from a historic farm house, the warm, welcoming place they have created at the Harbour Public House has no television or video games. It's a great place to talk, to build relationships, to have a wonderful time with your friends and loved ones. It's also a great place to visit if you are passing through Bainbridge Island. They are famous for their authentic Fish and Chips, as well as serving up delectable burgers

and large green salads. The Harbour Public House serves mostly Washington State Micro Brews, and supports local vendors. They hand make most of their menu items using free-range and organic products. They even squeeze to order fruit juice that they use in their cocktails and drinks. The pub overlooks the Harbour Marina, which enables you to arrive by boat as well as land. You can enjoy phenomenal views of the Seattle skyline and Puget sound while you have your Fish and Chips. The Bainbridge Island Review has dubbed the Harbour Public House as the best in seven different categories, including best beer selection and best wait staff. 231 Parfitt Way SW, Bainbridge Island WA (206) 842-0969  www.harbourpub.com

# Silver City Restaurant & Brewery

The Silver City Restaurant & Brewery, located in Silverdale, is just the right size for any occasion. Operating for almost a decade with excellent service and a long list of happy customers authenticating their guarantee, Silver City is jammed full every workday and weekend. Proudly boasting a variety of food with Asian, Southern and Italian influences, their menu doesn't hinder their popularity. Accompanying the fine service and memorable food is their own line of beers prepared by award-winning brewmaster Don Spencer, friend of owners and brothers Steve and Scott Houmes. With over two decades of experience, Don has created several different types of beer without migrating too far from traditional brews. With their story in the Home and Garden Spring 2005 edition, the Silverdale community strongly supports the hard-working, thoroughly experienced brothers in their quest to provide excellent service, mouth-watering food and beer, and an incredible

experience. You might need to wait to be seated during their busy times, but the atmosphere and dining are definitely worth it.

2799 NW Myhre Road, Silverdale WA  (360) 698-5879
www.silvercitybrewery.com

# Restaurants  Kitsap Peninsula

## Molly Ward Gardens

At the Molly Ward Gardens restaurant in Poulsbo, Washington, owners Lynn and Sam Ward buy and grow many of the organic vegetables and herbs they serve. They love the gardens and land surrounding their establishment and like to give back and leave it all healthy. The result is "fine dining in the country." That's not to say you can't find something "decadent" there – for example the homemade desserts. But first of course there's a meal to eat. Relish the thought of dinner choices like these. For starters, baked fig, gorgonzola and pancetta with toast points, or herb-rubbed, pan-seared sea scallops with mango sauce. Entrees include spaghetti squash, port tenderloin, Alaskan king salmon filet, Dungeness crab cake, New Zealand rack of lamb, and prime filet mignon. If you visit for a Sunday brunch, you'll find an Italian Joe's special with sausage, eggs, spinach, shallots, mushroom and parmesan, a frittata, pan-fried potatoes, stuffed French toast, pan-seared flank steak with mushroom and pepper medley, roasted potatoes, and Dungeness crab and asparagus omelet with Hollandaise sauce. The restaurant is in a converted barn, and the dining room has been described as "homey ... warm and cozy ... European." Lynn and Sam simply think of it as "artful."  27462 Big Valley Road NE, Poulsbo WA   (360) 779-4471   www.mollywardgardens.com

## Le Bistro

When in the mood for delicious food and a warm, inviting atmosphere, visit Le Bistro in Gig Harbor. This family restaurant is sure to please. Le Bistro is owned by Ken and Debi McAlpine and is truly a family business. Daughter Danielle manages the restaurant while daughter Stephani and granddaughters Kirah and Aimee, the chef, are also part of the attentive staff. The restaurant is the perfect place to meet family and friends for lunch and dinner. People often come from the surrounding towns to enjoy the wonderful food and excellent service. The cozy setting is enhanced by an old-fashioned café bar where regulars can sit and visit.   Le Bistro is well-known for its specialty breakfasts and eggs benedict. Lunch favorites include homemade quiche, vegetarian specialties, crab melts, fish and chips, and enormous specialty sandwiches. Only the freshest ingredients are used. The fresh bakery breads and desserts are simply delicious. On occasion, Ken entertains the guests by playing his bagpipes.
4120 Harbor View Drive, Gig Harbor WA   (253) 851-1033

# Restaurants

# Seattle Metro

## Pacific Rim Brewery

Take one sip of the beer offered at Pacific Rim Brewing in Seattle and you will want to come back for more. The flavorful selections are sure to please. Pacific Rim Brewing is owned by Scott Swansen and Erik Barber. After purchasing the brewery in 2002, they have dramatically increased production and sales of their delicious ales. Head brewer Scott Lord worked with the former owner for 13 years and is now clearly a master brewer. The Brewery Tasting Room is open seven days a week and is the perfect spot to meet friends and relax. This popular hangout offers a wide assortment of seasonal ales, as well as beers available year-round. During the autumn season, be sure to try the Pumpkin Patch Ale. This unique ale contains pumpkin pie seasoning and fresh pumpkin and is sure to please on a cold day. One of the popular summer ales is the delicious "Ring of Fire." Every ale offered by the brewery is well-balanced and smooth, with an amazing flavor. While some ales are full-bodied and stronger, others offer delicate malt flavors. There is clearly something for everyone. Pacific Rim Brewing is known in Seattle as one of the finest micro breweries and one of the last true micro breweries to brew beer. Because of its popularity, the owners will soon be offering a menu featuring local cuisine. 9832 14th Avenue SW, Seattle WA (206) 764 - 3844  www.pacificrimbrewing.com

## Elliott Bay Brewery Pub

Rumors have it that the best burgers in Seattle are at the Elliott Bay Brewery Pub. Perhaps it's because their gourmet beef burgers are made with all-natural Black Angus beef raised locally on Vashon Island and served on buns baked with spent grain, a high fiber by-product of their brewing process. Or maybe it's because the beer you wash the burger down with makes you smack your lips. In any case, owners Todd Carden and Brent Norton and head brewer Doug Hindman invite you to discover for yourself some of the region's highest quality pub food. You will probably want to order one of their hand-crafted beers first. You might choose Alembic Pale, a gold medal winning amber ale; Elliott Bay IPA, a bold and hoppy golden brew; Luna Weizen, light and refreshing with a hint of citrus; or No Doubt Stout, dark, robust and smooth. They use only certified organic pale malt as the base malt in the regular house beer. Elliott Bay Brewery Pub is a 100% smoke-free establishment.
4720 California Avenue SW, Seattle WA   (206) 932-8695   www.ElliottBayBrewing.com

# Restaurants

## Seattle Metro

## Brindisi Osteria

There are many areas within every big city that are full of good Italian restaurants. Places claiming Italian authenticity of their domains, while boasting signs that they serve good American food. Brindisi Osteria is strictly Italian and proud of it. Owner Luigi DeNunzio brought another dream alive in 2003 with the Osteria, following the success of his other three restaurants. Luigi emigrated from Italy in the seventies determined to honor the traditions that raised him, and opened his first restaurant in 1989. Living up to that honor, Brindisi Osteria offers truly authentic Italian cuisines, from venison carpaccio to roasted resteiceria vineria, complete with select brands of wine to accompany your meal. A true Italian, Luigi believes that a real Italian restaurant needs to have the right environment, starting a custom and creating a true "Little Italy" within Seattle. Dedicated to keeping the history alive, Luigi offers cooking lessons twice a month. Not only does he demonstrate how to cook complicated main dishes and desserts, but also discusses how to hand select just the right wine for every dish.
106 James Street, Seattle WA  (206) 223-0042

## Webster's Charlestown St. Cafe

When you have customers who eat with you daily, you're probably doing something right. When you've won a wall full of awards, including chowder cook offs from every corner of the country; you know you're doing it right. That's the story at Webster's Charlestown St. Cafe where Larry Mellum and Ron Hanlon make everything they serve from scratch. They say, "We provide our guests with great food and value. Although many restaurants say it, we live it." To maintain high quality, they hand-cut the fruits and vegetables and bake and slice the meats. "We feel our emphasis on freshness and quality sets us apart from our competition." You can also walk into the cafe confident that you'll be served and back to work within 45 minutes. Experience Webster's Charlestown St. Café for yourself and see why it was designated "West Seattle's Best Restaurant and Best Breakfast" eight times.  3800 California Avenue SW, Seattle WA (206) 937-3800

# The Madison Park Cafe

The Madison Park Café opened in 1979 as a tea and coffee house serving breakfast and lunch and boasting one of Seattle's first espresso machines. More than 26 years later it has blossomed into the quintessential neighborhood dinner restaurant offering French bistro specialties and an award-winning weekend brunch. It all started because owner Karen Binder couldn't find croissants or espresso in her neighborhood. She had recently returned from living and working in molecular biology in Geneva, Switzerland. "After returning from Europe I had reverse culture shock," Karen says. "I wanted to bring the experience of a little slice of Europe to Seattle." She left her career in science and, with an old friend, opened The Madison Park Café in a converted 1927 house in Seattle's Madison Park neighborhood. Karen worked as one of the restaurant's first cooks, but soon realized her interest and strengths lay in the front of the house. After the birth of her daughter she hired a cook and, in addition to serving breakfast and lunch, built a thriving business catering private parties on and off site. In 1999 Karen became the café's sole owner, hired a professional chef and opened for dinner five nights a week. The café, now under a classically trained chef, turns out French bistro favorites such as escargots, coq au vin and cassoulet. Meanwhile the café's weekend brunches have become a neighborhood tradition. In summer guests enjoy the private, flower-filled courtyard for outdoor dining, in winter they dine in the 30-seat restaurant warmed by an indoor fireplace.
1807 42nd Avenue E, Seattle WA  (206) 324-2826  www.madisonparkcafe.com

# Perche'No

Perche'no means "Why Not!" in Italian. That's how David and Lily Kong felt about the opportunity to open and operate a family Italian restaurant, despite their Chinese heritage. Perche'no is touted as the best Italian restaurant in Seattle. Their menu features a large selection of traditional Italian dishes including antipasti, insalate, zuppa, homemade pasta, risotto and main courses. For the final touch, remember to indulge in their Tiramisu or Chocolate Lasagna. Chef David Kong features rotating daily specials that might include market fresh seafood or exotic meats. The restaurant uses only the best quality ingredients in their cooking. All items are cooked from scratch, the Italian way. There are no shortcuts, so please allow time in your dinner plans for all entrees to be cooked to your order. Your patience will be rewarded with the freshest food. Ask the chef about the authentic special dinners, just like in Italy. Perche'no also hosts special events and wine tastings. The Italian Opera Night features a five-course dinner and wine tasting with live opera. Buon Appettio!  621-1/2 Queen Anne Avenue N, Seattle WA
(206) 298-0230  www.perchenorestaurant.com

# Restaurants          Seattle Metro

## Café de Paris

For over twenty years, Café de Paris has been providing Edmonds with a taste of traditional French cuisine at moderate prices. Swiss born chef/owner Firmin Berclaz has created a restaurant that embodies romantic ambience, provides the best in fine food and offers a pleasant view of the Edmonds Ferry Terminal. His intention to bring a taste of France to his customers has kept this café a destination spot for decades. The classic French offerings include skillfully adapted French onion soup with jack cheeses rather than gruyere, escargots de Bourgogne, pate maison, and seafood dishes of perfectly prepared scallops and scampi. Additionally, fish specials such as salmon and filet of sole meuniere are excellent representations of the anticipated traditional recipes. The Beef Bourguignon is exceptionally affordable and hearty. A variety of crepes are available including savory ones stuffed to overflowing with chicken or sweet ones, such as the global favorite crepes suzette flambé. Delectable salads come mixed with ample tender lettuces, inspired traditional dressings and expertly combined flavors. Looking for something decadent? Try the thick and succulent chateaubriand for two and the light, rich and creamy chocolate mousse.  109 Main Street, Edmonds WA   (425) 771 - 2350

## Chanterelle Restaurant

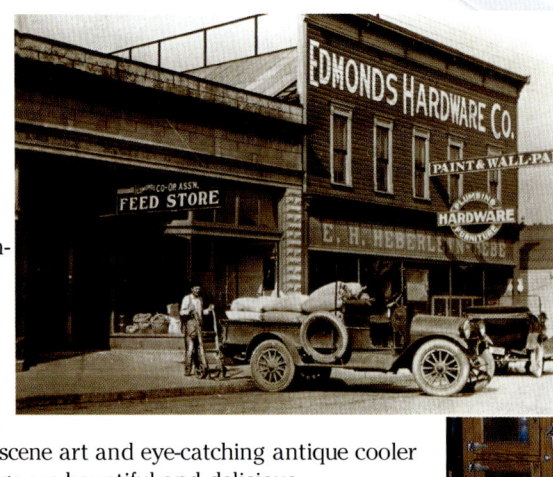

It was a treasure hunt of a very specific sort that lent this restaurant its name: the love of foraging for the coveted golden chanterelle mushrooms. Now it is the love of both well-known comfort foods and innovative International dishes that has brought praise and loyal customers to Chanterelle Restaurant for years. When in Edmonds, known as the friendliest town in Puget Sound, you will find this neighborhood gathering spot just three blocks up from the ferry. The bustling old town café housed in a delightful historic building was the original hardware store in town circa 1905. Today its warm wood floors, soft butter yellow walls, street scene art and eye-catching antique cooler will please your aesthetics as well as your palate. Breakfast offerings are bountiful and delicious. Cinnamon-raisin French toast, orange cornmeal waffles and specialty egg dishes are served along with more traditional fare. Midday brings in the lunch crowd for incredible entrée salads, hot and cold sandwiches and homemade soups. The rich and herby "famous" tomato bisque is not to be missed. The dining room transforms at night to a first class dinner house that will please the most discriminating and sophisticated of diners. An incredibly tender lamb shank, Main Street meat loaf, and pork loin with cranberries and apricots are popular choices. Fresh fish are prepared with various tasty sauces; some say the Cioppino (Italian fisherman's stew) is the best anywhere. Locals and visitors alike rave about the special four-course dinner menu that changes monthly.  316 Main Street, Edmonds WA  (425) 774-0650

# Restaurants

## Skagit Valley

# Buffalo Run

"Dine on the Wild Side" is the motto of Buffalo Run, one of the most exceptional restaurants in the Pacific Northwest. The restaurant is an offshoot of Candi and Marshall Cooper's Buffalo Run Ranch in Rockport, begun in 1986. Candi and Marshall decided in 1995 to make the bison meat raised on their ranch and other heart-healthy game meat available to the public. They bought the Mountain Song restaurant, changed the name and, to their delight, discovered that given a chance to eat buffalo, the public loved it. One of the most popular dishes is the 24-ounce charbroiled buffalo chuck steak, topped with grilled mushrooms and onions. The meat has fifty percent less cholesterol than beef, almost seventy percent more iron and the flavor is exquisite. Another favorite is the 16-ounce Tatonka burger. Amazingly there is a full vegetarian menu as well, so everyone can have a wonderful time here. Buffalo Run's ambience evokes the rustic cedar mountain cabins of the 19th Century. Among the features that bring customers back time and again is the garden patio where guests can watch the hummingbirds dart among the flowers and trees while they enjoy a meal or sip a cocktail. The success brought about by good food, persistence and skillful application of management and marketing techniques has enabled the Coopers to expand. They recently acquired the Log House Inn, a historic establishment built as a roadhouse for gold miners and mule skinners in 1885. They are currently remodeling it into a hotel to be named the Buffalo Run Inn, which is on schedule to open to the public in April 2005.  60084 State Route 20, Marblemount WA  (360) 873-2461 or (360) 873-2103   www.buffalorunrestaurant.com

# Chuck's Seafood Grotto

"Better than the Best." Nestled approximately 35 miles north of Seattle, Chuck's Seafood Grotto is an eclectic hotspot nestled on the banks of the Snohomish River in historic downtown Snohomish. The Grotto is a favorite of the town's residents and the patrons who travel for miles in order to dine on the scrumptious fare.  The family owned business offers a simple menu providing entrees and ala carte selections ranging from appetizers to seafood at its best.  Favorites are prawns and chips, fish and chips, and the freshest fish and oysters available daily.  In addition to retail seafood, seafood meals, and specials at the requests of local residents and businesses, Chucks's caters private parties and provides food for local community functions. On Friday and Saturday nights, Chuck's offers seasonal crawfish and crab cooked the old-fashioned way.  The kitchen is open and customers can see how their meals are prepared.

Since 1996, Chuck Gibbs, owner and operator of the Seafood Grotto, has successfully developed products used by the Grotto. The process of creating Chuck's Seafood tartar sauce and Chuck's Seafood cocktail sauce has been one of developing the perfect flavor and the exact measure of "quality" ingredients which satisfy the taste buds of their friends and customers. 1229 1st Street, Snohomish WA.  (360) 568-0782   www.csgp.net

# Restaurants

## Skagit Valley

## Piccadilly Circus

Whether you're specifically looking for a menu with European influence, or you are just tired of sipping coffee for breakfast and looking for something different to enjoy, try Piccadilly Circus, located in historic downtown Snohomish Washington. Serving thirty different gourmet teas to sip from in

the "best selection of China in the Pacific Northwest," and a menu that covers everything from salads and meat pies to time honored finger sandwiches, as well as scrumptious homemade desserts, you'll be delighted with delicious, British food as well as a unique atmosphere that is rarely found outside Europe. Seated in their elegant restaurant, you'll be enclosed by beautiful painted scenes of the hills of England, complete with a dome ceiling displaying a lifelike sky. Owned by Geoff Wall, a former European professional soccer star, and his wife Marion, this exceptional restaurant has been deemed by its community as "on its way to being the most popular full-service restaurant in Snohomish."
1104 First Street, Snohomish WA   (360) 568-8212

## Farmhouse Restaurant

In the heart of the Skagit Valley lies tulip country. At the heart of tulip country lies the Farmhouse Restaurant, widely known for its turkey dinners and homemade desserts that keep people coming back again. Owner Terry Brazas uses local crops and berries from farmers who deliver daily. Terry and staff deliver the hospitality and home cooking. If you're anywhere near, here's some of the reasons you should make it a point to stop in. A favorite is the Tulip Buffet, with an all-you-can-eat selection of rotisserie turkey, hand-rubbed prime rib, home-baked corned beef, pit ham, many tempting side dishes, along with the soup of the day and dessert. For breakfast, the specialty is an omelet called the "biggest and best in the valley." There's also cinnamon

French toast, heuvos quesadilla, Swedish pancakes, biscuits and gravy, and bacon, ham or sausage and eggs. Lunch favorites include Farmhouse burgers, hot turkey sandwiches, an avocado melt, turkey faccacia, and fish and chips. For dinner, in addition to the turkey, there is prime rib, local pan-fried oysters, chicken and dumplings, BBQ ribs, Farmhouse pot roast, and Swedish meatballs. Among the dessert favorites are mile-high lemon meringue pie and whiskey bread pudding.
13724 LaConner Whitney Road, Mt. Vernon WA (360) 466-4411

# Du Jour Bistro & The Vines Wine Shop

Michael and Becki Petersen invite anyone who delights in "the perfect pairing of food and wine" to visit their bistro in the heart of downtown Bellingham. Enjoy food made with fresh local and seasonal products; pick out your own accompanying wine at the wine shop, pay retail price for it and enjoy it with your meal for only a small corkage fee, or plan to be there on Tuesday night when the corkage fee is waived. The menu changes daily with availability of various ingredients, but on any given day you'll find an incomparable selection of appetizers, antipasto, cheese platters, exotic calzones, entrees and desserts. Entrees feature fresh local seafood such as Washington's world-famous Dungeness crab. For dessert, try vanilla bean crème brûlée or other fantastic confections. The food alone would make this a must, but don't miss out on the wine. The Vines offers an extensive selection of Washington State and other Pacific Northwest specialties, including limited editions not readily available elsewhere. Join the Wine of the Month

Club to keep up on special events such as wine tastings and appearances by visiting experts. Reservations are recommended at the Bistro. 1319 Cornwall Avenue, Suite 102, Bellingham WA   (360) 714-1161 or (866) 915-WINE
www.thevinesdujour.com

# The Oyster Bar

The Oyster Bar was originally built as a shack to sell fresh shellfish on Washington State's first scenic highway, Chuckanut Drive. The shack gradually expanded into a restaurant, and in 1946 Otto Amos bought it and renamed it The Oyster Bar. Otto and his wife coined the slogan "The oysters that we serve today slept last night in Samish Bay." The restaurant has changed hands several times since, but all owners, including Guy and Linda Colbert, who now run The Oyster Bar, have given the noble oyster its due. Under the guidance of the Colberts, The Oyster Bar has become a premier dining destination for people from all over the country. People come for the ambience as well as the food, enjoying romantic candlelit dinners while gazing out at the spectacular views of the San Juan Islands. Samish Bay Oysters are still on the menu, as well as other local shellfish from Washington and British Columbia. But now you can also get wild game, such as Alaskan Caribou grilled with julienne apples, or Morro Bay Abalone and other sumptuous dishes. At The Oyster Bar, even a grilled cheese sandwich for lunch is a delicacy, prepared with taleggio cheese, tomato, basil and red onions on sourdough. With its award-winning wine cellar and fabulous desserts like the Cappuccino Crème Brulee, The Oyster Bar is a treat not to be missed.

2578 Chuckanut Drive, Bow WA  (360) 766-6185   www.theoysterbaronchuckanutdrive.com

# The Maltby Cafe

Imagine sticky, warm cinnamon buns that don't fit in your hands, fresh hot coffee that is quickly brought to your table and constantly refilled, and breakfast menu that is everything you've ever wanted in a home-cooked meal. This isn't heaven, it's The Maltby Café snuggled in the hearts and stomachs of the community of Snohomish. Located in what used to be a small school cafeteria, it is still crowded with hungry diners. This café is rated as one of the top five places to enjoy breakfast in the United States, as well as receiving several other awards for their outstanding dishes. Bring your appetite as the friendly, family-oriented waitstaff serves such hearty portions that you may want to take some home to enjoy another day. If you're prepared to venture into serious breakfast food, you might try a platter of biscuits and gravy or an enormous homemade omelet or, if you're watching your waistline, you can select from their fabulous low-carbohydrate or low-fat menu. The delectable food at The Maltby Café is worth a special drive. If there is a wait, you can request a table then browse through their neighboring stores or situate yourself at their traditional counter fitted with true bar stools. This popular country-style bistro is especially packed on the weekends, so plan to arrive early.
8809 Maltby Road, Snohomish WA   (425) 483-3123

# Buck's American Cafe

Buck's American Cafe in Everett's historic Riverside district has been delighting diners for nearly twenty years. Housed in one of the city's oldest buildings, Buck's abounds in classic charm: a marble-topped bar, mahogany, and warm brick walls. Cold beer and wine are served from a vintage Frigidaire reach-in cooler, and antique hunting trophies adorn the walls. Buck's offers a wide variety of fine food every day. In addition to the Blue Plate Luncheon Special, there are homemade soups, entree-sized salads, tempura-battered fish with hand-cut chips, and sumptuous hamburgers. Mel's Burger is the gold standard for cheeseburgers. The dinner menu changes nightly and features fresh seafood, choice steaks and chops, and intriguing ethnic selections. Be sure to save room for Buck's world famous peanut butter pie or the homemade pecan pie (with a little whiskey added). Buck's has a

full bar with cocktails, microbrews, and a comprehensive wine list featuring many of Washington State's celebrated vintages. If you love live entertainment, go on Saturdays for jazz night when you'll hear music performed by some of the area's finest talent. But come before the 8:30 starting time to get a good seat: the place fills up fast! A small banquet facility is also available for private parties of up to 25.
2901 Hewitt Avenue, Everett WA   (425) 258-1351

# Restaurants
## Skagit Valley

# Calico Cupboard & Café Bakery / Seeds A Bistro & Bar

Linda Freed has two wonderful places for you to visit in La Conner. One is the original Calico Cupboard Café & Bakery, an award-winning restaurant. (It was given the title of best bakery, best lunch, best breakfast, best brunch, and best salad), and the other is something more than a little different – Seeds, a Bistro and Bar. At Seeds, the name comes from the farming community and from the historic building. From spinach and beet seed plants as decorations to the walls covered with vintage photos of seed farming and other Skagit Valley agriculture, the former seed company building is now a charming and nostalgic piece of history where you can enjoy a drink and a bite to eat. At the Calico Cupboard Café & Bakery, you can enjoy the food that Linda has made her reputation on since she started it in 1981. "Simply delicious." The atmosphere is cozy and the food is of the highest quality, with everything made from scratch. You will find an extensive and incredible breakfast and lunch menu that will please everyone. The bakery products are beyond compare, resulting in her motto, "The sweetest buns in town...Naturally!" Be sure to also visit Seeds to experience its unique ambience and exceptional food and beverages. Lunch and dinner are served daily, featuring the bounty of Skagit Valley with local produce, fresh seafood, grass fed beef, Martinis and other sips. Calico Cupboard Café & Bakery  720 S First, La Conner WA   (360) 466-4451  -  Seeds, a Bistro & Bar  623 Morris Street, La Conner WA  (360) 466 - 3280

# Chuckanut Manor Seafood and Grill with Bed & Breakfast

Pat Woolcock's award-winning restaurant is also a great bed & breakfast. Chuckanut Manor Seafood and Grill with Bed & Breakfast is located on scenic Chuckanut Drive overlooking world-renowned Samish Bay and the San Juan Islands. A fine dining destination with Bed and Breakfast has served the Northwest for over 40 years. Reserve the two-bedroom suite with Jacuzzi tub and enjoy its glorious view and revel in the luxury. "Sip a glass of wine as the sun sets over Samish Bay, enjoy a relaxing dinner in the restaurant and wake refreshed the next morning." On Sundays a wonderful Champagne Brunch is offered. Chef Margarito Brito oversees the preparation of mouth-watering meals using fresh, local ingredients. The Manor also offers a "Famous" Friday Seafood Smorgasbord featuring Dungeness crab, Blau's Samish Bay oysters, Taylor's Samish Bay clams, Penn Cove mussels, salmon, Dover sole, roasted New York ribs, scallops and prawns with wonderful salads and much more! The wine list is extensive with emphasis on Northwest wines. The home that is now the Chuckanut Manor Seafood and Grill with Bed & Breakfast was built in 1934. The property was purchased by John and Carolyn Paulson in 1963 and expanded in 1968 to its present size. 3056 Chuckanut Drive, Bow WA (360) 766-6191

# Restaurants — East Side

## Big Time Restaurant & Bar

If you're searching for a new place to enjoy a fresh and delicious meal, or just relax after work and have a cocktail, Big Time Restaurant & Bar, located in Redmond, is just the place to go. Their menu boasts a world of flavors from Italian, Latin and Asian, to Pacific Northwest specialties. Big Time has been a Redmond favorite since 1990, offering a warm and down to earth atmosphere that keeps their customers coming back. Founding owners John Priebe and Marla Araki brought on chef/partners Kris and Cindy Jones in 2002. Kris and Cindy have brought over 20 years combined restaurant experience to Big Time. Their passion and dedication shows with each and every plate that comes to the table. Big Time is proud to offer ingredients free of trans fat and hydrogenated oils, taking great care with each dish to exceed their guests' expectations. Big Time offers hand tossed pizzas, from eclectic to traditional, as well as tempting appetizers, house made soups, great salads and sandwiches, seasonal entrees, and sinfully decadent desserts. Big Time's Corner Bar boasts an ample wine list and countless varieties of beer, with seasonal rotating taps. In addition, they have a full service bar including house drinks and top shelf liquors. This diverse restaurant is housed in the Bill Brown building, a 1910 historic landmark building in downtown Redmond. The building has been home to a stage company, a brothel, a general store and an undertaker, to mention a few. Big Time is proud of the history of the building, and displays photographs courtesy of the Eastside Heritage Center. Set inside the restaurant on the original brick walls are photographs of historic Redmond buildings, as well as photographs of the people who called Redmond home. Hanging in the entryway of the restaurant is an antique "Redmond" sign that was from the old train station. As you make your way through the restaurant, you will notice the floors are the original wooden planks from the early 1900's. Big Time Restaurant & Bar certainly lives up to its name.
7824 Leary Way NE, Redmond WA   (425) 885-6425

## Crab Pot Restaurant

With locations in Seattle and Bellevue, the Crab Pot Restaurant & Bar is the best place to go for the finest in fresh seafood when you're visiting King County. The menu features nautical delights from fish and chips to cioppino, but the Crab Pot's specialty, the Seafeast, is a unique treat. They take a variety of crabs, clams, mussels, shrimp in the shell, salmon, halibut, oysters, potatoes, corn on the cob, and andouille sausage steamed with mouthwatering spices and pour it right on the table! Then, no need for silverware, all you need is the bib and mallet they give you and your own appetite. Try any of the five varieties available and you won't be able to wait till you can come back and try the others! The Crab Pot Restaurant & Bar is one of the most enjoyable places to eat in the Pacific Northwest. The Seattle restaurant is centrally located on the waterfront. Either location is perfect for family and friends to enjoy a classic seafood meal that you'll never forget. Groups of all sizes can be accommodated for lunch or dinner, and customers are welcome to walk right in. Both locations offer a homey atmosphere and friendly service. The Bay Pavilion, 1301 Alaska Way, Pier 57, Seattle WA  (206) 624-1890  Two Lake Bellevue Drive, Bellevue WA  (425) 455-2244

# Restaurants　　　　　　　　　　　　　　　　　　　East Side

## The Herbfarm Restaurant

Imagine a world where everything is as perfect as you had always hoped life would be. That's the goal of The Herbfarm Restaurant where each night the lights go down, the candles come on, and you are swept away to a nine-course dinner extravaganza that Seattle Best Places calls "the fastest five hours you'll ever experience." The Herbfarm, located 20 minutes outside of Seattle in rural Woodinville, is dedicated to showcasing the foods and wines of the Pacific Northwest. Frommer's Seattle calls The Herbfarm the Northwest's most-celebrated restaurant: "the ultimate expression of the Northwest's bounty." Each evening's dinner begins with a wine cellar open house and, weather permitting, a hosted herb garden tour. The prix fixe menu is set in the afternoon featuring foods harvested, gathered, and rushed from farm, field and sea. Six wines are included with each night's dinner. The wines are chosen by The Herbfarm's wine staff to carefully enhance the menu flavors. The cellar houses over 19,000 bottles and offers a staggering 3,275 different wines, other than the ones chosen for that evening. Nightly music flows from the strings of virtuoso guitarist Patricio Contreras. Between courses you can explore the wine cellar, take snacks to The Herbfarm's pet recycling pig in the garden, or play a game of bocce on the restaurant's grass court. Dressy casual attire is suggested for this, the only AAA 5-Diamond restaurant north of San Francisco and west of Chicago. Reservations required. 14590 NE 145th Street, Woodinville WA  (425) 485 - 5300

## Purple Café & Wine Bar

Purple Café and Wine Bar is a multifaceted food and wine concept specializing in an eclectic Northwest inspired menu coupled with an extensive global wine selection, including seventy-five wines by the glass, wine flights and hundreds more by the bottle. With Café locations in Kirkland and Woodinville, the atmosphere is often described as an urban retreat with rustic elements, including wrought iron furniture, used brick walls, concrete tabletops and a curved wine bar. Patio dining is available. Purple Café specializes in sophisticated hors d'oeuvres, appetizers, homemade spreads, crackers and flat breads to accommodate their upscale patrons. Desserts are made from scratch. Purple Café offers catering in three ways. "Purple Direct" is a quick and easy way to have fresh high quality food delivered to your home or office. You may have your selections served buffet style or boxed in individual meals. "Purple Select" features custom designed menus to your specific tastes and event style. "Purple House" is adjacent to the Woodinville location and is literally your "house" for your next business luncheon, rehearsal dinner or high tea. Purple Café also offers wine classes to educate your palate.  323 Park Place, Kirkland WA  (425) 828 - 3772
14459 Woodinville-Redmond Road, Woodinville WA  (425) 483-7129   www.thepurplecafe.com

# Restaurants — I-5 Corridor

## Sowerby's

British travelers heading up and down I-5 often do a double take around Exit 77 when they see the little house with the Union Jack prominently displayed on its roof. If they're curious enough to stop they'll find Sowerby's Restaurant where Sue Smith, who was born and raised in the British Isles, will make them feel right at home. Sowerby's name is a tribute to Sue's mother, Vera Sowerby, and its bill of fare is homage to Vera's native land with traditional United Kingdom dishes done right, such as shepherd's pie, fish and chips, and haggis. Sue does make a few concessions to traditional American tastes, most notably with her special chicken, which is made from a secret recipe that delights customers no matter where they're from. The traditional English food didn't catch on right away. Sue estimates that only about ten percent of her customers ordered anything British when the restaurant first opened. But once the word spread, locals as well as visitors from across the Atlantic started tucking into treats like the steak and Guinness pie. In August 2004 she began offering high tea as well. It's a reservation-only affair: a wonderful repast of real English tea, watercress sandwiches Scotch eggs, shortbread biscuits, and much more, served in a properly cozy manner. Whether you're accustomed to such luxuries or you've never tried them before, you don't want to miss Sowerby's.

227 SW Riverside Drive Chehalis WA
(360) 748-8060

# Restaurants  South Puget Sound

## 32 Silvers Thai Cuisine

Chef Narong has brought to America the very best gourmet Thai dishes for you to experience. While many Thai restaurants think that if they just serve American patrons something sweet with soy sauce and a little rice, they think they're eating authentic Thai cuisine, Chef Narong knows differently. "That's not what we eat in Thailand," he states. When you eat at 32 Silvers Thai Cuisine, Chef Narong prepares an authentic, delicious feast with a celebration of flavors that will make your mouth say "Wow"! He proudly says, "you will remember it for the rest of your life." He believes that when people come to America, they are given an opportunity to succeed and succeed he has. He appreciates what America has done for him and shows it by serving authentic gourmet Thai cuisine. Chef Narong knows it is all a matter of understanding the ingredients and how they react at certain temperatures. He prepares dishes like Pot of Gold, Tiger Crying and Seafood Volcano, which are among the more than 70 dishes that most Americans do not have a chance to experience. So while many Thai restaurants serve ordinary food, Chef Narong believes America deserves better. 32 Silvers is a true treasure of Thai cuisine!
440 E 25th Street # 51, Tacoma WA  (253) 272 - 2787  www.32silvers.com

## The Bair Restaurant & Catering

The Bair is famed for its superb food. Breakfast is a big meal at the Bair, which features a wonderful seafood omelet and French toast that customers say is the best around. Homemade soups and sandwiches highlight the lunch menu, including such favorites as the Muffaletta (a delightful specialty sandwich from New Orleans) and the Reuben. Vegetarians enjoy the Black Bean Burger, a delight made with Creole seasoning and sun-dried tomato mayonnaise. Afternoon tea and a complete dinner menu round out the day's offerings. Everything is made from scratch using fresh and, whenever possible, organic ingredients. Owners Edward Lintott and Martha Gray-Lintott strongly believe in supporting small local farmers. All their produce is grown in the state of Washington, with much of it from nearby farms. In addition to sit-down meals, The Bair sells old-fashioned jams and jellies, candies, specialty ice cream (featuring Olympic Mountain, "the world's greatest"), and highlighting a soda bar that children love. Edward, the former executive chef for Washington State's Senate, now serves as executive chef at The Bair, while the role of catering chef is in the capable hands of Jeff Lott. The Bair is located in the heart of downtown Steilacoom in a historic building that served as the town drugstore and hardware store in the 1800's. Afternoon tea requires reservations at least 24 hours in advance.  1617 Lafayette Street, Steilacoom WA (253) 588-9668  www.thebairrestaurant.com

# East and West Cafe

The best advertising is word-of-mouth. Just ask the regulars of East and West Cafe in Tacoma where owner Vien Floyd and her family have created a soothing atmosphere where you can get good, fresh, healthy food at an affordable price. The cafe is busy all the time. Diners enjoy sitting inside surrounded by warm wood tones and a beautiful collection of art glass, or outside on the patio surrounded by the fragrant herb and flower garden. The garden is the source of many of the vegetables and herbs used at East and West; the rest come from local Tacoma markets. No MSG is used, and fat is removed from the meats to ensure the leanest, healthiest portions. Among the savory Vietnamese and Thai offerings you are sure to find personal favorites for lunch or dinner. Menu items change often, but once an item is introduced you can always request it. 5319 Tacoma Mall Boulevard, Tacoma WA (253) 475-7755  2514 N Proctor Street, Tacoma WA (253) 756-5092  www.eastandwestcafe.co

# Trattoria Grazie Ristorante

In Old Town Tacoma, you can follow the evening floodlights to Trattoria Grazie Ristorante, where well-known chef Guiseppe "Peppe" Nappo and business partner Thomas Day have been offering authentic Italian cuisine, steaks and the freshest Northwest seafood for nine years now. Day states that Nappo makes Trattoria Grazie successful "with his incredible ability to create with food" and, were it not for him, the business would not exist.  Nappo's exceptional skills in the kitchen have earned him a reputation as an energetic and spectacular culinary artist. Each day the restaurant's sparkling menu is carefully crafted by Nappo, who marries traditional and exotic flavors to perfection.  Some of the mouth-watering items on the menu include appetizers like Insalata Caprese: slices of fresh mozzarella and ripe Roma tomatoes served with Gaeta olives and artichoke hearts, and main courses like Vitello Saltimbocca: medallions of veal topped with prosciutto and fresh mozzarella in a sage-sherry sauce served over a bed of spinach, or Misto alla Griglia: marinated lamb chop, fresh chicken breast and Italian sausage broiled to perfection and served under a light Marsala wine sauce. Enjoy it all with a selection from their extensive wine list. Reservations are highly recommended. The restaurant's two floors with multiple rooms overlooking Puget Sound that accommodate 20 to 250 people makes it a premier destination for rehearsals, receptions and other special functions.  2301 N 30th Street, Tacoma WA  (253) 627-0231  www.trattoriagrazie.com

# Restaurants

# South Puget Sound

## Traditions Café and World Folk Art

At Traditions Cafe and World Folk Art in Olympia you can eat, attend a concert or public forum, and discover folk and art from cultures around the world. Owner Dick Meyer makes all this available through fair and equitable trade relationships with low-income artisans and farmers from more than 50 countries. Events include servings of healthy foods, concerts, theater, and poetry readings.

Traditions Fair Trade started at the Antique Sandwich Company in Tacoma in 1993. Since 1974, Antique Sandwich has been a place for tasty and healthy food, as well as for classical concerts, open microphones, plays, and social benefits. Dick was a working part of the Antique partnership until 1994, when he decided to devote all his time to his new Olympia location, Traditions Café and World Folk Art. 300 5th Avenue SW, Olympia WA (360) 705 - 2819  www.TraditionsFairTrade.com

## Falls Terrace Restaurant

Imagine sipping a glass of select wine, enjoying a carefully made, mouth-watering meal, and overlooking a gorgeous view of water swirling and rich vegetation. At Falls Terrace Restaurant in Tumwater, this dream-like scene will arouse all of your senses. Boasting a full menu complete with gourmet salads and several varieties of steaks and seafood, Falls Terrace allows you to slip into a comfortable and soothing atmosphere for any occasion. Nestled next to Deschutes River and Tumwater Falls Park, Falls Terrace is perfectly located with a mild trail running through the fifteen-acre park for your walking pleasure. Anointed by The Olympian as "one of Olympia's finest restaurants," Falls Terrace staff makes sure to take care of their customers. Owned for thirty years by Michael Vavrinec, the restaurant is in the brilliant hands of general manager and executive chef Ralph Lund, with his extremely competent and meticulously experienced waitstaff. Whether you're planning an out-of-office meeting or a romantic dinner, allow yourself to be entranced at Falls Terrace Restaurant.
106 Deschutes Way SW, Tumwater WA   (360) 943-7830   www.fallsterrace.com

# Restaurants — Whidbey Island

## Toby's Tavern

On Whidbey Island in the scenic town of Coupeville, Toby's Tavern has stood since 1869. That's right, 1869! When you've been around that long, to call an establishment a "community gathering place" has got to be an understatement. Besides the beverages, Toby's is widely known for its steamed mussels, drawn from tranquil Penn Cove. Everything on the menu is homemade. So stop in and enjoy the sense of history and the relaxed atmosphere. Make a selection from a menu that includes not only seafood, but steaks, salads, sandwiches, burgers, soups and chili. Among the seafood items are broiled halibut, salmon and cod, grilled oysters, and deep-fried jumbo prawns. Steaks include a bar steak (8-ounce sirloin), New York and prime rib. The burgers include a selection of hamburgers and cheeseburgers, plus buffalo burgers, salmon, halibut, and garden burgers. Patty melts and grilled Reubens are among the favorites from the full selection of deli sandwiches that are offered. There's more, of course, so come in and taste for yourself. While there, perhaps owners John Rodriguey and Gary Sims will have time to give you a rundown of the tavern's 135+ year history!   8 NW Front Street, Coupeville WA   (360) 678-4222   www.tobysuds.com

# Restaurants — The Valley

## Berryland Café

Berryland Café is Sumner's best-kept secret! A cozy, family-oriented restaurant where customers come back so often that they're on a first-name basis with the staff, Berryland Café is a delight for young and old. Owner Lola Hansen, with help from great cooks Kristi and Dalles and waitresses Judy and Debbie, keeps families happy with wonderful food and non-stop fun. Every month there's a new theme related to the time of year. Berryland has the best burgers in Sumner, and its French fries have been honored as the Best Homemade Fries in the United States. The prices are family-friendly too; you won't find a better value anywhere in the area. You can even take a little bit of Berryland home with you in the form of their homemade jams and cookies. How do they keep Berryland a secret? No one knows, but as you sit back and enjoy yourself you'll be glad you're in on it!   1101 Main Street, Sumner WA   (253) 863-4567

# Wineries

# Wineries

## Olympic Peninsula

## FairWinds Winery

Situated on the outskirts of historic Port Townsend, FairWinds Winery draws on the maritime flavor of this Victorian seaport for its label and décor. Whether you have a sophisticated palate or you just like good wine, you will be welcomed and treated to a great experience at FairWinds Winery. It is a small winery, so you can take a tour and see the entire winemaking process with minimal walking. Owners Micheal and Judy Cavett are proud that customers have remarked that they are treated as guests rather than customers. Here are a few of the recent FairWinds vintages. Aligote: FairWinds is the only winery in Washington state to produce this white wine from the Burgundy area; tasty and fruity, it recently won a Silver Medal at the Northwest Wine Summit competition. Lemberger: a great wine with a mellow flavor, it is a consistent medal winner. Cabernet Sauvignon/Merlot: a 60/40 blend of grapes from the Yakima Valley. Port O'Call: a Bronze Medal winner in a recent Washington State wine competition, this is a mellow Port that can be served after dinner, with dessert or just to sip. Gewurztraiminer, Fireweed Mead and Blush wines were also available recently.
1984 Hastings Avenue West, Port Townsend WA (360) 385-6899
www.fairwindswinery.com

## Hoodsport Winery

It all started long ago with Dick Patterson's hobby of making wine at home. Now his expertise and years of experience have been recognized by awards from around the nation and the world. Hoodsport Winery's 1994 Cabernet Sauvignon took the gold at France's 1996 Challenge International du Vin. Other award-winners include the Gewurztraminer and Hoodsport's unique Island Belle wine, made from a Puget Sound hybrid grape that originated in the mid-1800s and is now used by no other winemaker. When Dick and his wife Peggy moved from Montana in 1978 and founded Hoodsport Winery, it was one of only sixteen wineries in Washington State (there are now more than three hundred). Hoodsport is now incorporated, with Peggy as CEO and Dick as Chairman, but it is still in many ways a family business. The Pattersons' daughter Ann now works in the Marketing/PR department. Dick did share the task of winemaking with Brent Trela, who has earned an international reputation for his knowledge of wines. Come to the winery and gift shop where you'll not only find great wine and an invigorating view of the Olympic Mountains, but also a few surprises in the form of their special chocolate wine truffles, gourmet coffees and specialty fruit wines, featuring raspberry, cranberry and loganberry. The Hoodsport Winery is open daily. North 23501 Highway 101, Hoodsport WA (360) 877 - 9894 or (800) 580-9894 www.hoodsport.com

# Camaraderie Cellars

Port Angeles on the Olympic Peninsula is not where you would necessarily expect to find an award winning winery, but you will find that and more at Camaraderie Cellars. For over a decade, Don and Vicki Corson have been crafting some of Washington State's finest wines. Dozens of major international medals have come their way from such significant competitions as held in San Francisco, Los Angeles, New York and Dallas. Additionally, wine ratings in the 90s by national publications validate the words of the Seattle Times "wine advisor" that Camaraderie Cellars "gets good fruit and does it proud." Don, as wine maker, sources grapes from well-known vineyards in Eastern Washington on Red Mountain, Champoux Vineyards and the Waluke Slope. Known for full flavored yet food friendly wines, Camaraderie's Cabernet Sauvignon, Merlot and other Bordeaux-style red and white wines are found in some of the State's finest restaurants. Visiting Camaraderie is more than a tasting experience. Known for warm hospitality, where all guests are invited to celebrate their philosophy that the best things in life are meant to be shared, tasting award winning wines is the beginning of a friendship. Views of the Olympic Mountains and an intimate garden picnic location with a giant slab of granite as your table will make your visit memorable at Camaraderie Cellars.
334 Benson Road, Port Angeles WA  (360) 417 - 3564  www.camaraderiecellars.com

## Wineries — Kitsap Peninsula

# NorthWest Vintage

If you are looking to enjoy great Washington wines, you will find the perfect location in Puyallup, the home of NorthWest Vintage, a premier Washington wine bar.  It is here in the heart of downtown that owners Nicola, Jaime, and Joyce McDonald bring you excellent Washington wines, a unique atmosphere and wonderful hors d'oeuvres chosen specifically to enhance the wine selection.  The menu also includes fantastic salads, cheese and fruit plates, and desserts that pair perfectly with the wines.  The mission of the owners of NorthWest Vintage is to increase people's appreciation for the quality of Washington wines.  "Many people don't realize that Washington is the second largest producer of wine in the United States," says Nicola.  "I want us to be a resource for people who love Washington wines."  She also promotes other local products in their shop, such as Martin Henry Coffee, roasted locally in Puyallup.  When you enter NorthWest Vintage, you will feel right at home.  The atmosphere is relaxing and enjoyable, which is the perfect setting to enjoy a great glass of wine.  "Our inventory of wines is continually expanding as we discover all the excellent wines from around Washington State.  If you have a favorite Washington wine that we do not currently carry, just let us know and we will be sure to have it for your next visit!"   208 South Meridian, Puyallup WA  (253) 864-WINE (9463) www.northwestvintage.com

# Wineries  The Valley

## Baron Manfred VonVierthaler Winery & Restaurant

Come visit our "Bavarian Style" Winery Restaurant and enjoy good food, great wine and a fantastic view of the Sumner Valley, especially at sunset. After lunch or before dinner on weekends you can also visit the Baron's Train Museum in "O" Scale. Besides a display of just about every engine that ever ran on American rails including at least 12 currently running trains, a huge 3,800 square foot operating layout is also under construction. Baron Manfred and Baroness Ingeborg von Vierthaler's restaurant features authentic German cuisine. Among the home cooked meals, you will find venison, along with several kinds of schnitzels and a good fare of traditional German dishes and desserts. Besides their own wines, you can also have a real German draft beer imported from Muenchen in Bavaria. On the American side of the menu, you will find a variety of juicy, tender prime cuts of steaks, as well as seafood and pasta dishes. They also offer samples of their own private label wines made to the Baron's own formulas in the tasting area of the restaurant. Specialties include a white and a red late harvest (Auslese) slightly sweet wines.  17136 Highway 410, 3 miles east of Sumner WA  (253) 863-1633

# Wineries

## East Side

## Facelli Winery

Nestled away in the heart of Woodinville's "Wine Country," you will find Facelli Winery. Upon entering the tasting room, you are likely to be greeted by at least one member of the Facelli family. Winemaker Lou Facelli, his wife Sandy and their three daughters, Lisa, Lori, and Kristi, take turns welcoming visitors each weekend. Celebrating over 24 years of winemaking using grapes from some of Washington's premier vineyards, the wines here should not be missed. Lou Facelli focuses on "Reds" and small lots of various varietals, including a Late Harvest Syrah, believed to be the first in the state. At Facelli Winery there is very little blending. With increasing interest in Italian varietals, new wines look promising in the future. Paying close attention to detail is a Facelli tradition. Taking tremendous pride in the bottles that bear the family name, they work hard to bring

you a great bottle of wine at a reasonable price. The winery produces approximately 3000 cases annually from grapes grown in the Yakima and Columbia Valleys. It is evident that this family loves what they do and they convey their enthusiasm from the moment you walk in. Whether receiving further education about their wine or a recipe to go with a glass of Sangiovese, you are likely to leave with a bottle in hand and a smile on your face. Autographed bottles are also a big hit.

16120 Woodinville-Redmond Rd. NE #1, Woodinville WA
(425) 488-1020
www.facelliwinery.com

# Wineries

## I-5 Corridor

## English Estate Winery

English Estate Winery specializes in Pinot Noir in all different styles. English Estate Winery recently released an elegant new innovation: a refillable wine box. The new boxes are the result of winemaker Carl English's research and development. The English Estate Winery has named these refillable wine boxes "BIBB…Bag In Beautiful Box" (trademarks of English Estate Winery). They are the world's first winery to offer premium wine in a refillable box, rather than in a throwaway cardboard box. The BIBB is designed and built to dispense wine from a bag, which reduces oxidation and maintains the quality of wine after it is opened. The eye catching boxes in wood or marble are adorned with scenes of English Estate Winery and the grounds, and holds a 3-liter wine bag which can easily be replaced. Consumers responded instantly to this novel concept and BIBB wine has become the winery's most popular product. Most customers become BIBB Club members, receiving one 3-liter bag (equal to 4 bottles) per month or quarter, discounts on the boxes, and lower prices on wines, whether in bottles or wine bags. In 2003, the fifth and sixth generations of the family celebrated the 100-year anniversary by sharing wonderful meals with their guests, accompanied by the wines that they now grow on the farm. English Estate Winery is located east of Vancouver, Washington just 10 minutes from the Portland, Oregon airport, at the mouth of the Columbia River Gorge (making it the closest vineyard to downtown Portland, only 20 minutes to the city center). They welcome visitors and have outstanding facilities for events. 17806 SE First Street, Vancouver WA (360) 772 - 5141

## Oly's Wine Cellar and Olympic Card & Gift

Ron and Carol Nelson always wanted to own a wine and gift shop. That dream came true in Centralia with Oly's Wine Cellar and Olympic Card & Gift. Featuring great Northwest wines, wine gifts and accessories, the shop also offers a large selection of cards, wine and gift baskets, and gourmet chocolates. They also have a lovely array of quality gifts and contemporary

jewelry. Their shop was voted Lewis County's best gift shop for three consecutive years. Wine tastings, open houses and other special events occur throughout the year. If you can't make it to one of the scheduled tastings, call to set up a wine tasting. 1616 South Gold Street, Suite 8, Centralia WA (360) 736-2857
www.olyswinecellar.com

# Port Gamble

# Port Gamble

## Olympic Property Group

Olympic Property Group, a division of Pope Resources, manages over 2,000 acres of residential and commercial development. They offer development services, project feasibility studies, permitting and entitlements, and infrastructure and utility construction. Among their properties is the 150-year-old Port Gamble town site, a National Historic District. Port Gamble is an authentically restored 120-acre slice of history. The quaint New England architecture, tree-lined avenues and breathtaking views of Hood Canal draw visitors from all over the world. With fine art galleries, boutiques, day spa, restaurants, historic company store, antiques shops, bed & breakfasts and many colorful annual events, there is something for everyone here. Meetings, conferences, weddings and other important gatherings can all be handsomely accommodated in Port Gamble. A wide range of facilities are available, including the Historic Museum, a circa-1916 boardroom, St. Paul's Church, the Masonic Lodge, Port Gamble Guest house and numerous alfresco venues on the expansive grounds. Once you've visited Port Gamble, you may want to move there. With beautiful homes, office and retail space available, you, too, can become a part of this delightful community. So come for a day or come to stay in beautiful Port Gamble, the jewel of the Kitsap Peninsula.

#3 Rainier Avenue, Port Gamble WA  (360) 297-8074  www.portgamble.com

## Ms. Bee Haven Antiques

Janice Robin has always had a passion for shopping, finding great deals and recycling. Annually, she had a huge outdoor sale where she "recycled" many of the treasures she gleaned throughout the year. Her husband Michel figured they needed overflow protection, so he talked her into setting up shop in beautiful Port Gamble. Ms. Bee Haven Antiques nestles charmingly into this quaint and historic town. Wrapped in the warmth of the wood burning stove, you will find wonderful early American and European furniture and an amazing array of unusual antique and collectible items. Janice and Michel look forward to seeing you in the relaxed and peaceful atmosphere of Ms. Bee Haven Antiques, where you will surely find yourself a treasure.

32180 Rainier Avenue NE, Port Gamble WA  (360) 297 - 1804

# Best Friends Antiques

Owner Sheila Walters and her sister Martha Segerman are pleased to invite you into this 100-year-old home and antiques shop. Already a dealer in antiques, Sheila participated in one of Port Gamble's summertime antique markets and she fell in love with the town. She decided to retire from her long career as a teacher and counselor in Poulsbo, pulled up stakes and took off on her "adventure in retirement." Settled into this lovely old building, Best Friends Antiques specializes in primitive furniture, as well as fine oak and mahogany. On display is a wonderful collection of the delicate and beautiful Belleeck china of Ireland. Sheila also features candlesticks and candy dishes, pottery and prints, and clocks and quilts. On your next visit to Port Gamble, stop in at Best Friends Antiques where you will find beautiful objects and a friendly welcome. During the summer they're open seven days a week.
32239 Rainier Avenue NE, Port Gamble WA  (360) 297-4848

# Port Gamble General Store & Cafe

Erected in 1916, this company store is located on the bluff overlooking the former Puget Mill site and the beauty of Gamble Bay. Originally the Pope & Talbot Office & General Store, the Port Gamble Store & Café remains true to the tradition of purveying pretty much everything a body could need, and it is still the thriving social hub of Port Gamble. If you're looking for directions or want to know anything about anything in the area, the friendly and family-oriented staff can fix you up with whatever you need. Along with everything from walking sticks and picnicking gear to vintage clothing, you will find canned goods and dry goods and dairy and deli. Be sure to belly up to the old-fashioned candy counter, too. What once was the cookhouse is now a café where visitors enjoy breakfast and lunch buffets, as well as Robbie Morshead's extra-special homemade baked goods, soups and sandwiches. Comfortably combining tradition with high technology, proprietors Pat and Susan Wright are hooked up, with wireless Internet available for your convenience. You can also catch local entertainers at the monthly open mic performance. So come on in for supplies, a meal, and signature beers or just to smash a penny in the souvenir coin press. There's no place else like the Port Gamble General Store & Cafè. 32400 Rainier Avenue #3, Port Gamble WA  (360) 297-7636  www.genstore.net

# Port Gamble

## The Spa at Port Gamble

With 15 years in the spa business, Carol Etherington was pleased to bring her company of highly trained staff to the elegantly restored, 1872 House #10 in historic Port Gamble. The spa offers a big-city range of services in a quiet and beautiful country setting. Licensed massage therapists and hairstylists, as well as nail technicians and cosmetics and skin-care specialists are there to treat you like royalty. You may decide to melt away stress in the 160-jet Champagne Hydro Tub, then have an aromatic oil massage in the spa suite. Custom packages are designed to provide a full day of personalized care for singles, couples, or groups of friends. Or you can just tuck in a back and neck massage with the Express Lunch Break. There is also a six-week Essential Bridal Package with every-two-week spa visits leading up to and including your wedding day. It provides facials, manicures and pedicures, as well as hair and makeup. The spa offers a boutique of personal care products including aro- aromatherapy bath oils, body scrubs, bath salts, and homeopathic remedies. Get away to pampering and serenity in this lovely setting.   As Carol says, "The Spa at Port Gamble isn't out of the way; it's out of this world."
32199 Rainier Avenue NE, Port Gamble WA  (360) 297-8889  www.spaatportgamble.com

## Port Gamble Historic Museum

Port Gamble is a privately owned National Historic Landmark. This mill town was built by Andrew Pope and Frederick Talbot, who modeled it on their home town in Maine, bringing down-East architecture to the Pacific Northwest. The Port Gamble Historic Museum displays objects and photographs that date from the founders' arrival in 1853 until the 1995 closure of North America's longest continuously running sawmill. Dedicated to the preservation and documentation of this important piece of Pacific Northwest history, the museum offers visitors tableaux depicting the local forest products industry from its infancy. The original Land Grant Deeds are here, with their signatures of Abraham Lincoln and Andrew Johnson. Heirlooms and photos from the 1800s and beyond portray the people whose lives and work helped write the story of this area. There are the original offices of the first mill managers and recreated staterooms of Andrew Pope and Captain William C. Talbot. There is a collection of local Native American artifacts, including a small dwelling from the 1800s. The museum also offers research and archive photography services. Open every day from May through October and by appointment the rest of the year, the Port Gamble Historic Museum is available for group tours and private parties. Step through the door and enjoy the rich tapestry of Port Gamble's history.
#3 Rainier Avenue, Port Gamble WA  (360) 297-8074  www.portgamble.com/museum

# Port Gamble Guest Homes

Established in 1853, Port Gamble is one of the original mill towns in the Puget Sound area of Washington State. Located one hour northwest of Seattle by passenger or car ferry, Port Gamble offers festivals, events and shops to make your visit enjoyable any time of year. Port Gamble Guest Homes are two historic homes situated on a low bluff overlooking Hood Canal across from the Olympic Mountains. An authentically renovated 1903 single story Craftsman home offers a family friendly vacation rental with fully-equipped kitchen, three bedrooms, two baths and gas fireplace. Up to eight adults and children (pets by prior arrangement) can be accommodated. The second home is refurbished in a "New England Nautical" style, and offers two bed and breakfast rooms with private baths and full breakfast. These rooms can also be combined with the other home for larger family gatherings. Spacious grounds and easy beach access as well as miles of hiking and biking trails make Port Gamble Guest Homes the perfect family retreat, wedding destination or romantic getaway.
32440 Puget Avenue NE, Port Gamble WA  (360) 297-5114  www.innsatportgamble.com

# Port Gamble Trading Company

Port Gamble Trading Company is an eclectic gallery of local artists and talented craftspersons. Owners John and Stacy Chugwater display John's unique Beach Bum Furniture, made from driftwood collected on the local beaches. The Beach Bum and his fanciful work have been featured on local TV shows, Northwest Backroads and Evening magazine. The Trading Company has been featured on ABC's Extreme Makeover - Home Edition and How'd They do That? Visitors will find Native American works, quilts and handcrafts, antiques, jewelry, fine art, cedar water features, landscape accessories, and custom furniture. John and Stacy attribute the success of the Trading Company to the energy, heart and soul of 40 plus artists whose work is featured in the store and the garden. For one-of-a-kind treasures, come in to the Port Gamble Trading Company.  4719 NE State Highway 104, Port Gamble WA  (360) 297-8114

# Index

**Acampo**
    Attractions .................................................. 22

**Aberdeen**
    Accommodations ........................................... 31

**Anacortes**
    Attractions ............................................. 88, 90
    Home Decor, Gardens, Flowers & Markets ............. 171

**Arlington**
    Attractions .................................................. 82

**Auburn**
    Attractions ............................................. 83, 84

**Bainbridge Island**
    Accommodations ........................................... 38
    Attractions ............................................. 62, 65
    Candy, Ice Cream, Bakeries & Coffee .................... 95
    Galleries ................................................... 113
    Gifts ....................................... 126, 127, 130
    Restaurants ............................................... 202

**Bellingham**
    Accommodations ........................................... 44
    Restaurants ............................................... 211

**Bellvue**
    Museums ................................................... 179
    Restaurants ............................................... 215

**Blaine**
    Accommodations ........................................... 43
    Attractions .................................................. 76

**Bothell**
    Home Decor, Gardens, Flowers & Markets ... 167, 168, 169
    Gifts ....................................................... 144

**Bow**
    Accommodations ........................................... 42
    Restaurants ......................................... 212, 213

**Bremerton**
    Attractions .................................................. 65
    Restaurants ............................................... 201

**Camano Island**
    Attractions .................................................. 89

**Carlsborg**
    Restaurants ............................................... 186

**Centralia**
    Accommodations ........................................... 40
    Attractions .................................................. 86
    Gifts ................................................. 144, 145
    Wine ...................................................... 228

**Chehalis**
    Museums ................................................... 180
    Restaurants ............................................... 217

**Coupeville**
    Accommodations ........................................... 52
    Restaurants ............................................... 221

**Darrington**
    Gifts ....................................................... 146

**Dungeness**
    Accommodations ........................................... 24
    Attractions .................................................. 56

**Edmonds**
    Attractions .................................................. 69
    Candy, Ice Cream, Bakeries & Coffee .................... 98
    Gifts ....................................................... 143
    Home Decor, Gardens, Flowers & Markets ............. 159
    Restaurants ............................................... 208

**Everett**
    Museums ................................................... 178
    Restaurants ............................................... 213

**Forks**
    Accommodations ........................................... 30

**Gig Harbor**
    Accommodations ........................................... 37
    Attractions .................................................. 66
    Gifts ....................................................... 128
    Restaurants ......................................... 200, 204

**Greenbank**
    Candy, Ice Cream, Bakeries & Coffee .................. 104

**Hoodsport**
    Wine ...................................................... 224

# Index

## Ilwaco
- Accommodations ...32
- Museums... 174

## Issaquah
- Candy, Ice Cream, Bakeries & Coffee ... 100, 101
- Galleries ... 119
- Gifts ... 142, 143
- Home Decor, Gardens, Flowers & Markets ... 167, 169

## Kenmore
- Accomodations ...84

## Kingston
- Accommodations ...36

## Kirkland
- Accommodations ... 38, 39
- Galleries ... 114
- Gifts ... 131, 134

## La Conner
- Accommodations ...41
- Attractions ...81
- Gifts ... 137, 138
- Museums... 177
- Restaurants ... 214

## Lacy
- Gifts ... 146

## Long Beach
- Accommodations ...32
- Attractions ...61

## Lynnwood
- Gifts ... 134

## Marblemount
- Accommodations ...41
- Restaurants ... 209

## Moclips
- Accommodations ...34
- Restaurants ... 196

## Mt. Vernon
- Attractions ...63
- Home Decor, Gardens, Flowers & Markets ... 163
- Restaurants ... 210

## Mukilteo
- Accommodations ...45

## Nahcotta
- Accomomdations ...33
- Restaurants ... 197

## Ocean Park
- Accomodations ...33

## Ocean Shores
- Accommodations ... 31, 35, 36
- Galleries ... 110
- Gifts ... 124, 125, 126
- Home Decor, Gardens, Flowers & Markets ... 157

## Olympia
- Accommodations ... 49, 51
- Attractions ...87
- Candy, Ice Cream, Bakeries & Coffee ... 103
- Galleries ... 119
- Gifts ... 147
- Home Decor, Gardens, Flowers & Markets ... 170
- Museums... 182
- Restaurants ... 220

## Port Angeles
- Accommodations ... 25, 26
- Candy, Ice Cream, Bakeries & Coffee ...94
- Gifts ... 122, 123
- Home Decor, Gardens, Flowers & Markets ... 155. 156
- Restaurants ... 186, 187, 188, 194, 195
- Wine ... 225

## Port Gamble
- All ... 232-235

## Port Hadlock
- Accomodations ...23
- Port Hadlock ... 187

## Port Ludlow
- Accomodations ...28

## Port Orchard
- Attractions ...63

# Index

## Port Townsend
- Accommodations .................................... 27, 28, 29, 30
- Attractions .................................. 56, 57, 58, 59
- Galleries ....................................... 108, 109
- Gifts .......................................... 122, 123
- Home Decor, Gardens, Flowers & Markets .............. 154, 156
- Museums ........................................ 174
- Restaurants ....................... 189, 190, 191, 192, 193
- Wine ............................................ 224

## Poulsbo
- Attractions ...................................... .64
- Candy, Ice Cream, Bakeries & Coffee ................. .95
- Galleries ..................................... 111, 112
- Gifts ............................... 127, 128, 129, 130
- Home Decor, Gardens, Flowers & Markets ............. 158
- Restaurants ............................. 200, 201, 204

## Puyallup
- Galleries ........................................ 111
- Gifts ............................................ 141
- Restaurants ................................. 199, 201
- Wine ............................................. 225

## Redmond
- Candy, Ice Cream, Bakeries & Coffee ............. 101, 103
- Restaurants ...................................... 215

## Renton
- Accommodations .................................. ..45
- Attractions ..................................... .83

## Rockport
- Accommodations .................................. .41
- Home Decor, Gardens, Flowers & Markets ............. 164

## Seattle
- Accommodations .................................. ..39
- Attractions ............ 67, 68, 69, 70, 71, 72, 73, 74. 75
- Candy, Ice Cream, Bakeries & Coffee ....... 96, 97, 98, 99
- Galleries ........................... 114, 116, 117, 118
- Gifts ...................... 131, 132, 133, 135, 136
- Health & Beauty ................................. 150
- Home Decor, Gardens, Flowers & Markets ...... 159, 160, 161, 162
- Museums ................................... 175, 176
- Restaurants ............................ 205, 206, 207

## Seaview
- Accommodations .................................. ..35
- Restaurants ................................ 197, 198

## Sedro-Woolley
- Attractions ...................................... .87
- Candy, Ice Cream, Bakeries & Coffee ............... 100

## Sequim
- Accommodations .................................. 22, 24
- Attractions ................................ 56, 59, 60
- Candy, Ice Cream, Bakeries & Coffee ............... .94
- Gifts ........................................ 122, 124
- Galleries ........................................ 110
- Home Decor, Gardens, Flowers & Markets ....... 154, 155

## Silvana
- Gifts ............................................ 137

## Silverdale
- Restaurants ...................................... 203

## Snohomish
- Attractions ................................ 76, 77, 79
- Home Decor, Gardens, Flowers & Markets ............. 165
- Restaurants ........................... 209, 210, 213

## Steilacoom
- Restaurants ...................................... 218

## Stevenson
- Accommodations .................................. ..47

## Sumner
- Gifts .............................. 138, 139, 140, 141
- Home Decor, Gardens, Flowers & Markets ............. 166
- Restaurants ...................................... 221
- Wine ............................................. 226

## Tacoma
- Accommodations .............................. 49, 51, 52
- Gifts ............................................ 147
- Museums ............................... 181, 182, 183
- Restaurants ................................ 218, 219

## Tukwila
- Home Decor, Gardens, Flowers & Markets ............. 161

## Tumwater
- Attractions ...................................... .88
- Restaurants ...................................... 220

# Index

## Ilwaco
- Accommodations ..32
- Museums. 174

## Issaquah
- Candy, Ice Cream, Bakeries & Coffee 100, 101
- Galleries 119
- Gifts 142, 143
- Home Decor, Gardens, Flowers & Markets 167, 169

## Kenmore
- Accomodations .84

## Kingston
- Accommodations ..36

## Kirkland
- Accommodations 38, 39
- Galleries 114
- Gifts 131, 134

## La Conner
- Accommodations ..41
- Attractions .81
- Gifts 137, 138
- Museums. 177
- Restaurants 214

## Lacy
- Gifts 146

## Long Beach
- Accommodations ..32
- Attractions .61

## Lynnwood
- Gifts 134

## Marblemount
- Accommodations ..41
- Restaurants 209

## Moclips
- Accommodations ..34
- Restaurants 196

## Mt. Vernon
- Attractions .63
- Home Decor, Gardens, Flowers & Markets 163
- Restaurants 210

## Mukilteo
- Accommodations ..45

## Nahcotta
- Accomomdations ..33
- Restaurants 197

## Ocean Park
- Accomodations .33

## Ocean Shores
- Accommodations 31, 35, 36
- Galleries 110
- Gifts 124, 125, 126
- Home Decor, Gardens, Flowers & Markets 157

## Olympia
- Accommodations 49, 51
- Attractions .87
- Candy, Ice Cream, Bakeries & Coffee 103
- Galleries 119
- Gifts 147
- Home Decor, Gardens, Flowers & Markets 170
- Museums. 182
- Restaurants 220

## Port Angeles
- Accommodations 25, 26
- Candy, Ice Cream, Bakeries & Coffee ..94
- Gifts 122, 123
- Home Decor, Gardens, Flowers & Markets 155. 156
- Restaurants 186, 187, 188, 194, 195
- Wine 225

## Port Gamble
- All 232-235

## Port Hadlock
- Accomodations .23
- Port Hadlock 187

## Port Ludlow
- Accomodations .28

## Port Orchard
- Attractions .63

# Index

## Port Townsend
- Accommodations .................................................. 27, 28, 29, 30
- Attractions ................................................... 56, 57, 58, 59
- Galleries ........................................................ 108, 109
- Gifts ............................................................ 122, 123
- Home Decor, Gardens, Flowers & Markets ................. 154, 156
- Museums .......................................................... 174
- Restaurants ......................................... 189, 190, 191, 192, 193
- Wine ............................................................. 224

## Poulsbo
- Attractions ....................................................... 64
- Candy, Ice Cream, Bakeries & Coffee ............................ 95
- Galleries ........................................................ 111, 112
- Gifts ............................................... 127, 128, 129, 130
- Home Decor, Gardens, Flowers & Markets ..................... 158
- Restaurants ..................................... 200, 201, 204

## Puyallup
- Galleries ......................................................... 111
- Gifts ............................................................. 141
- Restaurants ..................................................... 199, 201
- Wine ............................................................. 225

## Redmond
- Candy, Ice Cream, Bakeries & Coffee ..................... 101, 103
- Restaurants ..................................................... 215

## Renton
- Accommodations .................................................. 45
- Attractions ....................................................... 83

## Rockport
- Accomodations ................................................... 41
- Home Decor, Gardens, Flowers & Markets ..................... 164

## Seattle
- Accommodations .................................................. 39
- Attractions .................... 67, 68, 69, 70, 71, 72, 73, 74, 75
- Candy, Ice Cream, Bakeries & Coffee ............. 96, 97, 98, 99
- Galleries .......................................... 114, 116, 117, 118
- Gifts .............................................. 131, 132, 133, 135, 136
- Health & Beauty ................................................ 150
- Home Decor, Gardens, Flowers & Markets ......... 159, 160, 161, 162
- Museums ....................................................... 175, 176
- Restaurants ............................................. 205, 206, 207

## Seaview
- Accommodations .................................................. 35
- Restaurants ..................................................... 197, 198

## Sedro-Woolley
- Attractions ....................................................... 87
- Candy, Ice Cream, Bakeries & Coffee ........................ 100

## Sequim
- Accommodations .................................................. 22, 24
- Attractions ............................................... 56, 59, 60
- Candy, Ice Cream, Bakeries & Coffee ............................ 94
- Gifts ............................................................ 122, 124
- Galleries ........................................................ 110
- Home Decor, Gardens, Flowers & Markets ................. 154, 155

## Silvana
- Gifts ............................................................. 137

## Silverdale
- Restaurants ..................................................... 203

## Snohomish
- Attractions ............................................... 76, 77, 79
- Home Decor, Gardens, Flowers & Markets ..................... 165
- Restaurants ..................................... 209, 210, 213

## Steilacoom
- Restaurants ..................................................... 218

## Stevenson
- Accommodations .................................................. 47

## Sumner
- Gifts ............................................ 138, 139, 140, 141
- Home Decor, Gardens, Flowers & Markets ..................... 166
- Restaurants ..................................................... 221
- Wine ............................................................. 226

## Tacoma
- Accommodations ........................................ 49, 51, 52
- Gifts ............................................................. 147
- Museums ................................................. 181, 182, 183
- Restaurants ..................................................... 218, 219

## Tukwila
- Home Decor, Gardens, Flowers & Markets ..................... 161

## Tumwater
- Attractions ....................................................... 88
- Restaurants ..................................................... 220

# Index

**Union**
Accommodations . . . . . . . . . . . . . . . . . . . . . . . . . . . . . . . . . . . . . . . . . ..50

**University Place**
Gifts . . . . . . . . . . . . . . . . . . . . . . . . . . . . . . . . . . . . . . . . . . . . . . . . 139

**Vancouver**
Accommodations . . . . . . . . . . . . . . . . . . . . . . . . . . . . . . . . . . 47, 48
Health & Beauty . . . . . . . . . . . . . . . . . . . . . . . . . . . . . . . . . . . 151
Wine . . . . . . . . . . . . . . . . . . . . . . . . . . . . . . . . . . . . . . . . . . . . 228

**Woodinville**
Accommodations . . . . . . . . . . . . . . . . . . . . . . . . . . . . . . . . . . . ..46
Attractions . . . . . . . . . . . . . . . . . . . . . . . . . . . . . . . . . . . . . . . . .85
Gifts . . . . . . . . . . . . . . . . . . . . . . . . . . . . . . . . . . . . . . . . . . . . 143
Restaurants . . . . . . . . . . . . . . . . . . . . . . . . . . . . . . . . . . . . . . 216
Wine . . . . . . . . . . . . . . . . . . . . . . . . . . . . . . . . . . . . . . . . . . . . 227

**Woodland**
Accommodations . . . . . . . . . . . . . . . . . . . . . . . . . . . . . . . . . . . ..48